SELVES IN DISCORD AND RESOLVE

SELVES IN DISCORD AND RESOLVE

Kierkegaard's Moral-Religious Psychology From *Either/Or* to *Sickness Unto Death*

Edward F. Mooney

Routledge
New York & London

Published in 1996 by

Routledge
29 West 35 Street
New York, NY 10001

Published in Great Britain in 1996 by

Routledge
11 New Fetter Lane
London EC4P 4EE

for Kailen

Contents

Acknowledgments

MANY OF THESE CHAPTERS BEGAN AS ESSAYS READ TO THE AMERICAN KIERKEGAARD Society, whose forums have provided welcome stimulation. Chapters Four and Five continue discussions begun at an "Author Meets Critic" session of the American Philosophical Association devoted to my book on *Fear and Trembling, Knights of Faith and Resignation.* I thank my friendly critics on that occasion—Ronald Green, Alastair Hannay, John Donnelly, David Wisdo, and Andrew Cross—for providing challenging responses. A version of Chapter Two appears in *International Kierkegaard Commentary, Either/Or,* ed. Robert L. Perkins, (Macon: Mercer University Press, 1995). Bob has been a devoted instigator throughout. A precursor of Chapter Three was read at California State University, Fullerton, Spring, 1993. I thank my hosts there, especially Steven Simon and Merrill Ring. (A later version appears in *International Journal for Philosophy of Religion,* 34: December, 1993.) Chapter Six has evolved from a paper first read to the Kierkegaard Conference at St. Olaf College, 1986, convened by Steven Evans. It was updated for *The Southern Journal of Philosophy,* 27, no. 2, Spring, 1989, and has been further revised here. Chapter Seven is an altered version of "Living with Double Vision: Subjectivity, Objectivity, and Human Understanding," *Inquiry,* 31 Fall, 1988; the present account is directed far more toward Kierkegaard than the original. Chapter Eight appeared in *International Philosophical Quarterly,* October, 1992. I thank the editors of these journals and collections for permission to reproduce parts of this material.

In addition to the colleagues noted above who have graciously encouraged my work, I'd like to thank M. Jamie Ferreira, who read the entire manuscript with great insight and care, Phil Clayton, who has commented on nearly every chapter (and provoked two of them), and Phil Temko, who has likewise listened, read, and helped. Finally, I thank Ann Smith, Sterling, Dianne, Penny and Kailen for their ever present patience and support.

Preface

LONG BEFORE HIS WRITING BECAME AVAILABLE IN BRITISH AND NORTH AMERICAN intellectual circles, Søren Kierkegaard's thought surfaced unheralded in literature—in Ibsen's *Brand*, say, or in Kafka's "Abraham Parable" or *The Trial*—and flowed with silent force through the influential philosophical, political, and theological work of Heidegger, Tillich, Sartre, and even Wittgenstein.[1] He continues to provoke philosophers as diverse as Habermas and Ricoeur, Cavell and Putnam, and provides an explicit point of reference, along with Nietzsche, for literary-philosophical "postmodernists" generally.[2] Kierkegaard wrote in a minor European language, and although his works proved scandalous in his provincial Copenhagen, he was largely undiscovered in the Europe of his time (1813–1855). In the century that followed, despite his "rediscovery" by Heidegger and Sartre, Kierkegaard's work has been overshadowed by the German writers with whom he bears comparison—Hegel first, and later, Marx and Nietzsche.

As if to compound the handicap of provincialism, Kierkegaard intentionally disguised the import of his legacy by writing under pseudonyms and by adopting or inventing a surprising array of literary-philosophical formats. Time has granted no advantages in sorting out interpretations of his work. We now look back from what should be the comfortable distance of a century-and-a-half, yet the excavation and interpretation of his works remains hauntingly unfinished. The finds I gather and assemble here are but fragments of his rich and innovative moral-religious psychology.

Kierkegaard's project in his pseudonymous authorship seems to shift between an only loosely coordinated multiplicity of perspectives and an intelligible overarching progress of refinement in self-structure. He distinguishes between different "stages on life's way" and orders these in terms of adequacy or moral-spiritual depth. At the same time, transitions between stages, or even the relations among them, turn out to be tangled and diffuse, resisting simple exposition. His project of self-definition, exploratory as it must be, wavers between discord and resolve. Perhaps that is not only the fate of Kierkegaard's writing about selves, but indeed the fate of those recognizable selves he so relentlessly, humorously, urgently lays bare—selves inevitably at risk and underway.

In *Either/Or* we have discussions of the role of choice in the development of a moral personality. Much later, in *Sickness Unto Death*, selfhood is presented as a complex set of relationships, like the tensed relations of a community. There are dialectical, abstract and theoretical expositions. But Kierkegaard will as often present portraits, pictures of exemplary figures that embody concretely the complex dimensions of a self in crisis or repose. Thus we have several portraits of Abraham in *Fear and Trembling*. Socrates appears prominently throughout the pseudonymous authorship, and at length in *Concluding Unscientific Postscript*. Judge Wilhelm and his correspondent, the nameless esthete, appear as writers or speakers in *Either/Or*. Kierkegaard's short work *Repetition*, often characterized as a novella, contains letters between friends, and haunting allusions to another exemplar, the biblical Job. Concrete poetic-literary portraits are entwined with dialectical-philosophical excursions.

This characteristic shuttle between rational critique and lyrical portraiture insures that Kierkegaardian perspectives do not collapse into a single abstract theory of selves, stages, or stage-shifts. Nor do we have a theory of moral principle or public virtue. We have instead a moral-religious psychology, a way of approaching, through concrete narrative and portraiture, issues of the self in motion, its identity and its aspirations. Moral-religious reflection and advance are placed in the context of speakers and interlocutors, in a "communicative space" where shifts in articulation of self are underway against the background of dialogue with specific others.

"Communicative space" contains the tonality of a Kierkegaardian life-sphere. It is akin to the dynamic structure of musical tonality, defined as a field relating to itself and to others. Pursuing this simile is like focusing moral-psychological images one finds in Plato—his picture of humanity locked in a cave, for example, or his "divided line," or his picture of souls at the river of forgetfulness in the myth of Er. It is like pursuing Nietzsche's characterization of a person's development passing from Camel to Lion to Child in *Thus Spoke Zarathustra*. Here, not only our finesse in dialectic but also our powers of imagination are awakened and put to work.

Kierkegaard is psychologist and philosopher, poet and dialectician and, if only anachronistically, even an existentialist or "postanalytical" philosopher. I try to convey this range of theme and voice in his work. This gives access to his world, one which surely shapes our own, and thereby sharpens our critique of the present. Further, it adds momentum to contemporary discussions of self-articulation, character, and moral growth by philosophers who increasingly find the old walls between literary form and philosophic argument breaking down or shifting in locale. We come to rethink the roles of imagination, reason, and poetry, and to reaffirm the importance of particular individual selves in the largest scheme of things.

In his mobile portraits of the self, Kierkegaard continues the venerable tradition of Socratic care for the soul, of dialectical critique as bringing things to birth, a midwife's art, a ministering art. I follow these portraits through materials he provides, shoring up my reconstructions with some contemporary analytic (and "postanalytic") timbers.[3] The itinerary is as follows. I first look at the interplay between poetry and philosophy, between imagination and argument, opening with Kant's anticipation of the German Romantic tradition (Chapter One). Then I consider Kierkegaard's *Either/Or*, exploring especially Judge Wilhelm's models of self-acquisition and their implications for responsibility (Chapter Two). Taking up Kierkegaard's discourse on the *Book of Job*, and his book *Repetition* (also concerned with Job) allows us to trace his reading of this biblical story of crisis and renewal (Chapter Three). Several issues from *Fear and Trembling*, which explores Abraham's willingness to sacrifice Isaac, get disentangled next (Chapters Four and Five). I then lay out from an analytic or "postanalytic" perspective a number of claims about subjectivity and related topics articulated in *Concluding Unscientific Postscript* (Chapter Six). Placed next is an exploration of Kierkegaardian themes in Thomas Nagel's *The View from Nowhere*, including subjectivity, moral psychology, and enigmas surrounding birth and death (Chapter Seven). I complete the journey by taking up the relational view of self that "Anti-Climacus" presents in *Sickness Unto Death*, giving it a musical elaboration (Chapter Eight). In my reading, the self is akin to a musical ensemble of contrasting voices. The parts these voices play, or sing, are illustrated in the preceding discussions of Abraham, Socrates, Job, and Judge Wilhelm. Self, as self-ensemble, resolves, or wrestles to resolve, discord and despair through relating to itself and to its grounding power.

As this book neared completion, I came upon a pertinent and perhaps disturbing remark by a distinguished contemporary thinker who has established his own subtle and unexpected relationship to Kierkegaard:

> [I]nheriting, by interpreting in some way, the texts of...Kierkegaard...will not, so far as I can see, suggest one's credibility as a present philosophical voice, not for an American writer.[4]

I take these words of Stanley Cavell to mark an obstacle but not an ultimate deterrent to Kierkegaard interpretation. I have acted here in trust that one can chart a Kierkegaardian path without forfeit of one's philosophical voice or credibility.

Still later, I encountered another thought to give me pause. Although not intended with Kierkegaard as its target, I read it with his work in mind:

> The text is experienced as one whose meaning crystallizes, not in particular passages or sequences or lectures, but in the spaces between them; and this makes it almost impossible to attain real conviction that that meaning has been correctly grasped.[5]

These words could ring defeat, but I take them otherwise. Passages or constructions in Kierkegaard do not lack meaning piece by piece. Nevertheless, their meaning for the text or *oeuvre* as a whole is never definitively given. This describes a moral weight internal to interpretation, one to acknowledge and to grapple with rather than to evade or to set aside. Thus though closure is uncertain, one proceeds; and with good enough address, these texts reciprocate enlivening response.

You would not find out the boundaries of the soul, even if you should travel along every path: so deep is its account.

– Heraclitus

It is only if it remains rooted in the human and the ethical that our search can be about, and towards, the human soul—that is, about what is deepest and most essential about human living.

– Martha Nussbaum

PRELIMINARIES
Philosophy, Portraits, and Poetry

[I]n a sense, to write your own words, to write your own inner voice, is philosophy.

—Stanley Cavell[1]

[I]f will can be captivated, or conversely, if vision can be transforming,...imagination [is] at work.

—M. Jamie Ferreira[2]

MIDWAY THROUGH HIS THUS FAR LANDBOUND CRITICAL PROJECT IMMANUEL KANT allows himself a prospect on the sea:

> I have now explored the territory of...understanding, and...measured its extent, assigning to everything its rightful place. This domain is an island...surrounded by a wide and stormy ocean, the native home of illusion, where many a fog bank and many a swiftly melting iceberg give the deceptive appearance of farther shores, deluding the adventurous seafarer ever anew with empty hopes and engaging him in enterprises which he can never abandon and yet is unable to carry to completion.[3]

Kant tells us quite incautiously that he's mapped the land of understanding, but in his seaward gaze, he captures something else, a sense of risk, allure, and limits—limits paradoxically opening on the wondrous.

In this lyrical passage from his *First Critique*, Kant counsels caution, for the turbulent and alluring sea is the natural home of illusion. Yet his ambivalence shows through, as if the "adventurous seafarer" might be prized for his hazardous attempts at navigation, which he will pursue despite the dangers.[4] Philosophy at last for Kant beckons seaward—for freedom at least, and more generally for some sense of the ideals that lie beyond the landlocked realm of exclusively cognitive activity. This becomes explicit in remarks on poetry from his *Third Critique*. As he has it there, poetry "strengthens the mind by making it feel its faculty—free, spontaneous, and independent of natural determination—...as a sort of schema for the supersensible."[5] Ideals of free, creative activity inspire and make possible moral, esthetic, and religious practices, practices that, Janus-faced, look now upon the securities of the familiar, now upon the uncanny, uncertain realm beyond the breakers.[6] An esthetic image or narration focused seaward, toward "illusion," "adds to a concept the thoughts of much that is ineffable, but the feeling of which quickens our cognitive powers, and connects language, which otherwise would be mere letters, with spirit [or soul, (*Geist*)]."[7] In this attunement to his work and world, Kant could well be a sort of poet—dialectical, to be sure—who ventured out in searching tasks he could neither "abandon nor carry to completion."[8] In any case, he sets the scene for Kierkegaardian lyrical explorations of the self, a course from the familiar and secure out to the wondrous and back.

PORTRAITS AND VOICE

Kierkegaard's doctoral dissertation in theology was titled *The Concept of Irony, with Constant Reference to Socrates*. This signals Kierkegaard's interest in irony both as a literary device and as a way of life; and it also signals his abiding attachment to Socrates.[9] *Either/Or* followed, appearing in 1843 initially in two separately bound volumes. Speaking from the first is the esthete, "A," an anonymous voice known only through his productions and through the characterizations provided by a "Judge Wilhelm" in the second volume. Collected in the first volume are bits and pieces of the esthete's musings and reflections, flights of fancy and psychological reflections. And in lengthy letters addressed to the esthete from the second volume, we have the sober intonations of Judge Wilhelm. Readers are left poised within this "either/or," between the appeals of an esthetically varied but fragmented life and an ethically coherent but conventional life. The balance may be tipped toward the second view, the portrait of an ethical existence. But this justly famous double portrait is only one of many sketches hung in Kierkegaard's museum of pseudonymous works.

These figures speak inwardly and outwardly to one another. In addition to the Judge and the esthete, there are, as we have mentioned, portraits of Socrates, whose voice emerges especially in *Concluding Unscientific Postscript*, of Abraham, whose trial with God is sketched in *Fear and Trembling*, and of Job, whose voice is heard both in Kierkegaard's "Job Discourse" and in a short work titled *Repetition*, published along with *Fear and Trembling*. Each portrait and voice embody a stance toward life, towards its moral, esthetic, and religious dimensions. In the chapters that follow I map the placement and listen for the dialogue among these figures. Themes overlap and interlock as Judge Wilhelm, Socrates, Job, and Abraham appear and reappear in sketches of ordeals of emerging moral and religious self-hood.

Perhaps halls of portraiture suggest too quiet a setting. An alternative metaphor, recurrent in Kierkegaard's works, is the theater. Taking this cue, Kierkegaard's views are dispersed among pseudonyms, allocated to characters in a drama vaster than the banquet depicted in his *Stage's on Life's Way*. In the pages of *Repetition*, a young man anticipating his night at the Königstädter Theater reflects that "no young man of any imagination…has not at some time felt himself caught up by the magic of the theatre and desired himself to be transported into that fictitious reality, so that like a *Doppelgänger* he can hear and see himself, [desired] to split himself up into all manner of possible differentiations of himself from himself, so that each differentiation is in turn a single self."[10] In this light, Kierkegaard's pseudonymous works emerge as a polyphonic religious-comic-tragic theater of action and idea, as a dialectic of self-development spread out among figures on a stage, or among a sequence of stages. Our task is then to draw the multiplicity of selves and stages into meaningful pattern.

The metaphor of theater is powerful, but not the only alternative to halls of portraiture. There is another metaphor for dynamic unity-in-multiplicity among voices that we will have occasion to invoke. The interplay among voices can be rendered musically. The shifts in tone and orientation of Kierkegaardian pseudonymous selves in discord and resolve are akin to voices sounding variations on a gathering of themes. Their links resonate in concert as the movements of an orchestral suite, or as the arias, choruses, and recitatives of an extended oratorio. *Sickness Unto Death* presents just such a relational view of self. Its formula for a self, a "relation relating to itself," can be spelled out as a performing musical ensemble, an ensemble of voices that model self, a community of selves, and the stage or world that each inhabits.

POETRY AND PHILOSOPHY

While demonstrative argument holds an undisputed place in philosophy's varied traditions, the role for poetic inspiration and verse is less certain. Plato introduces Diotima, a muse appearing dream-like in the *Symposium* who lyrically recounts to Socrates the tale of love's transport of the soul toward the beautiful. But perhaps a true philosopher would excise the poetry from this tale.

In the *Republic*, Plato refers to an "ancient quarrel" between philosophy and poetry, and seems to cast the poets beyond the pale, exiling them from a city ruled by wisdom.[11] But Plato, like Kierkegaard, was a dramatist by inclination, and whatever his protest against poetry, at crucial points he cannot resist the appeal of lyric myth and imagery. In the *Republic*, the image of the cave or the closing myth of Er are prominent examples. His deep ambivalence is starkly framed in the death scene where Socrates converses with friends about life and immortality and then takes hemlock. In that most existential and lyrical of his creations, Plato has him confess: "[A] vision has often come to me...[It] always says the same thing: 'Socrates, make music and compose.'"[12]

If Plato leaves the quarrel between poetry and philosophy less than settled, later writers—say Heidegger, Nietzsche, or Kierkegaard—have philosophy embracing poetry, the "ancient quarrel" now a companionable affair.

In contrast, 17th- and 18th-century philosophers, with some exceptions, model their work on the newly emerging physics; the insights and style of drama or poetry become correspondingly submerged.[13] Poets are granted as little standing before the bar of intellect as rustic village priests. But 19th-century German Romanticism and Idealism bring poetry back to center stage.[14] And between an Enlightenment veneration of science and the philosophical upheavals that followed, we have Kant, who aimed to give Newtonian physics a sure and honorable footing, and as important, also aimed to secure a vision of human freedom and creative imagination. The scope of "pure reason" is sharply curtailed in Kant's *First Critique*. But this tethering of reason seems to have invited poet-philosophers to imaginative exploration of what lay beyond the scope of what could now be called "mere reason." Kant's *First* and *Second Critiques* established laws that physical objects and human actions must obey. His *Third Critique* allows nature to infuse poetic or artistic Genius with power to freely give law to art.[15] Imagination links commanding freedom to poetic creativity. Poetry, as we have seen, "strengthens the mind" reinforcing it as "free, spontaneous, and independent of natural determination."[16] Imagination "quickens the cognitive powers, and thus [also gives material to] the cognitions."[17] In his notes on religion, Kant discusses archetypes of wisdom or faith, exemplary figures whose "essence" is conveyed through imaginative narrative and symbol rather than rational doctrine or principle.[18] Thus the champion of enlightened, rational critique simultaneously inspires writers in the tradition of Romanticism and Idealism whose bent is lyrical and literary.[19]

Kierkegaard exploits this mixed Kantian heritage, combining skeptical critique with poetic "languages of the heart."[20] Verse can portray the tangled webs of freedom and contingency, the fluid stances that become the characters or selves through which we meet the world. No longer focused solely through the lens of physics, nature may be a place of respite or consolation and storms may emanate a terror. Poetic sensibility conveys the relevant "existential" reality missed by a more scientific stance. Personal quests for meaning or fulfillment can compete with or overshadow the wider search for impartial, objective knowledge.

Possibilities for poetic-imaginative depictions of self and world blossom fully in Kierkegaard's comic array of pseudonyms. The first volume of *Either/Or* collects discourses and fragments with such literary nonphilosophical titles as "Shadowgraphs," "Diapsalmata," and "The Unhappiest Man." The nameless esthete who composes these also writes "The Seducer's Diary." The second volume contains rambling letters from a Judge Wilhelm. *Repetition* is composed by Constantine Constantius; it too contains a sheaf of letters from a nameless esthete. *Concluding Unscientific Postscript to Philosophical Fragments*, a mammoth work, is subtitled "A Mimic-Pathetic-Dialectic composition: An Existential Contribution," authored by Johannes Climacus, full of satire, humor, and irony.

Kierkegaard anticipates the polyphony of Nietzsche's wanderer poet-prophet Zarathustra and his cast of circus characters and wilderness companions, figures who argue, preach, scold, and sing. This is the polyphony Bakhtin finds in *The Brothers Karamazov*, each character voicing an independent stance, none belonging uniquely or unambiguously to Dostoyevsky.[21] As the novelist himself writes, with regard to Father Zossima's "reply" to Ivan Karamazov's nihilism and despair,

[T]he answer here…is not a point-by-point response to any previously expressed positions…but only an oblique response…so to speak in an artistic picture.[22]

Later in this lyrical-dialectical tradition, we have Heidegger assigning to the poet—say, Hölderin or Rilke—the role of "shepherd of Being," and "guardian of language." These philosophers, poets, and *littérateurs* take on topics well beyond the scope of Enlightenment philosophy. They unveil human risks and insecurities in God-abandoned worlds, measure the nearness of death, track penumbras of dread and hope, and trace disconcerting plasticities of self and chasms dropping sharply between self and others.

VARIETIES OF "THE POETIC"

We can distinguish several lines of complexity in Kierkegaard's philosophical or dialectical use of "poetry" or "the poetic": 1) Lyrical, aphoristic or "edifying" styles are often at play in competition with more familiar Aristotelian expositions, Kantian deductions, or Cartesian meditations. 2) Poetry, music or dance are models and metaphors for creative production, displacing an exclusive reliance on models from geometry or physics. 3) Poetic or literary work becomes an explicit topic of analysis and discussion, as in *Either/Or's* lengthy critique of Mozart's *Don Giovanni*, and its comparison of ancient and modern tragedy. 4) The figure of "the Poet" often appears, a voice as integral to the philosophical exposition as (say) the voice of a scientific, academic, or lawyerly intellectual. 5) An entire way of life, an existential "life-sphere" or stage in human development, is charted as poetic or esthetic, contrasting with familiar philosophical sketches of the religious, scholarly, or civic life. And to complicate matters, (6) there may be a way of "living poetically" that is part and parcel of the religious life—not in opposition to it.[23]

These multiple layers of poetic infusion are illustrated vividly in Kierkegaard's *Fear and Trembling*. The pseudonym in charge, Johannes de Silentio, opens with a section called "Attunement," a notion Heidegger later adopts in *Being and Time*.[24] Variations on the biblical story of Abraham and Isaac are imagined by the poet, each sketch meant to "tune" the reader's mood. The narrator then sets out in verse to snare his hero, Abraham. Bathed in self-importance, he wonders if the true hero is Abraham—or perhaps rather himself, "The Poet" who preserves Abraham in Art. In any case, we know the writer is not a bookworm, absent-minded scientist, or pious priest.

A subsequent section of *Fear and Trembling*, the "Preamble from the Heart," spins out sufferings of unrequited love.[25] To offer solace for the lovesick of this world, knights of faith and knights of resignation, transformed Don Quixotes, enter stage left and right. Tales of suffering and relief offer momentary consolation. "The esthetic" constitutes an existential "life-sphere," a mode of relating (or mis-relating) to the world that, as Kierkegaard has it, is incomplete, its melancholy sheen covering deep indifference of despair.

Nietzsche and Heidegger depict the esthetic or poetic way of life as potentially satisfactory and complete, not just a way station to higher modes of life.[26] Perhaps Kierkegaard's placement of an ethico-religious sphere *above* the esthetic seems to them untenable for moderns who fearlessly acknowledge the death of God. In any case, they share Kierkegaard's sense of the power of poetic depiction. Poetry retards an easy (and disastrous) assimilation of a thinker's work to a particular system or set of objective doctrines, ready-made for popular consumption. If independence of mind and spirit are dulled by doctrine, they are quickened by poetic image and metaphor. Nietzsche's Zarathustra ecstatically proclaims "Sing!—Speak no more!"[27] Kierkegaard's knight of faith forgoes discursive explanations, instead shouldering silence and its burdens. Heidegger also is explicit about the weight of what cannot be said in traditional philosophic prose. He wonders if in an otherwise dark and rootless time it will be the thinker-poet alone who is capable of composing true modes of human dwelling.

Does Heidegger thereby collapse Kierkegaard's contrast between the esthetic-poetic and the ethico-religious life-worlds? Perhaps, but matters are not simple.

From Heidegger's side, the poet is not a decadent bourgeois entertainer or dropout. He performs the essential human task: he names the holy—apparently a religious function. And the poet's way of thinking, dwelling, and composing involves an open stance toward Earth and Sky, Mortals and Immortals. This is

Heidegger's mythic Fourfold, the "Gods" or "sacred powers" through which worlds are assembled and unveiled as human habitats.[28] Of course, from Kierkegaard's side, this seems too pagan. Nevertheless, it might qualify as a pre-Christian religious stance, perhaps akin to the *Postscript's* "religiousness A."[29] Furthermore, not every sort of poetic stance is equally culpable for Kierkegaard.[30] In *Sickness Unto Death*, he speaks of a "poetic existence in the direction of the religious" and in *Repetition* he has an esthete's soul gain "a religious resonance."[31] But ultimately Kierkegaard and Heidegger will part ways. Heidegger will take Hölderin, not Socrates or Jesus, as his teacher.[32] He treads the silent "forest path" alert for that opening where earth and sky may mingle in a dawning light.

The route from Kant and Kierkegaard through Nietzsche and Heidegger establishes a tradition in which the Enlightenment's presumably clear and distinct boundaries between poetic, philosophical, literary, and ideological or cultural critiques become blurred and problematic.[33] In this new setting, traditions of discourse that had become insular and removed from acknowledged common ground begin to intermingle and cooperate as much as compete within the cultural landscape.

THE QUESTION OF IRRATIONALISM

Given the ample license in this post-Kantian tradition for poetic metaphor and image and for poetic ways of life, it should come as no surprise that some have refused to grant Kierkegaard a place among the "true Philosophers." This buries Kierkegaard's brilliant satire of Hegelianism, *Concluding Unscientific Postscript*, which is dialectical throughout; it dismisses the "dialectical lyric" of *Fear and Trembling*; it shrouds Judge Wilhelm's dialogue with Kant in *Either/Or*, and forgets the presence of Socrates throughout the pseudonymous authorship.

Rational critique is everywhere apparent in these texts, however artfully framed or delivered. Of course, Kierkegaard can appear to endorse unreason in rhetoric that makes the wider culture wary. The passions are exalted. He (or Johannes Climacus) writes that "Truth is subjectivity." We hear in *Fear and Trembling* that belief is held "on the strength of the absurd."[34] But the import of these banners is not transparent. Beneath the surface, there is almost always some specific *view* of reason that is discounted or deflated.

A detached and abstract intellectualism is roundly scorned in Kierkegaard's works. An omnivorous theoretic-explanatory reason is mocked as arrogant. A quantitative or prudential mask of reason as the final arbiter of all that is worthy or vital in life may be the target of ridicule. Poetic or literary evocation may unmask each of these distortions of reason. If the overflowing sweep of life's strivings, forebodings, and triumphs is not easily captured in the nets of juridical or explanatory reason, then poetry may be better suited to track these shifting currents; if so, a dialectical lyric seems worth the effort. If a *pose* of reason is undermined along the way, so much the worse for that disguise.

Some attunements to the world, webs of mood, emotion and desire, are best articulated by poetic voice, dialogue, aphorism, rhapsody, or complex polyphony. But this does not amount to a whimsical free-for-all for irrationalists. Lyrical dialectic can be Socratic. Image, thought, and argument can conspire mutually in care for souls at risk. As poetic articulation *shapes* a value, mood, or life, we're led to *see* this mood or life in all its rich particularity.

Familiar modes of philosophical delivery that work to minimize ambiguity present a format resembling a lawyer's brief, a scientific report, or a logician's demonstration. Yet the pursuit of demonstrable and finished doctrine is, as Kierkegaard has it, bound to calcify a self in process. Esthetic works force us to cope reflectively and on our own. At the last, this is a *necessary* human task: there is no alternative to ongoing interpretation of our place and destination. Moreover, it exemplifies what is best in liberating human labor. A poetic-literary philosopher will embrace the risks and promote the responsibilities that befall a reader who on her own must decipher an often clouded and conflicted world.

We have here an implicit rationale for Kierkegaard's use of pseudonyms, related not just to a desire to explore a point of view free from personal commitment to that view. Rather, we have here a picture of moral reasoning as dialogue between figures aiming to clarify, resolve, amplify, or even justify their points of view or judgments, not against some easily accessible absolute standard, but in openness to one another, in openness to the other's situation and placement, and in critical openness to opposing points of view.

In *Sources of the Self*, Charles Taylor pictures practical reasoning as dialogue between interlocutors attempting to understand transitions in moral sensibility—their own and others. This is not so much measuring one's sensibility against some absolute standard—say, the requirements of a Christian or Stoic way of life—as a comparison between one's present position, as clearly as one can grasp it, and some proffered alternative.[35] Stephen Mulhall puts the connection with Kierkegaard this way:

> The emphasis this [view of practical reason] places upon comparative rather than absolute judgements, combined with its reliance upon the model of biographical narrative, implies that the proper locus of moral argumentation is the confrontation of one person and another. A party to moral dispute speaks from a perspective defined by the moral intuitions that her best reading of her own experience has delivered, and speaks to the perspective of her interlocutor, attempting to engage with the detailed texture of that other's experience and life story; it is a confrontation between two resolutely first-person viewpoints. The competing notion that there might be a once-and-for-all, perspective-free, absolutely impersonal moral truth of any given matter is rejected in favor of something profoundly resonant of a Kierkegaardian perspective on the nature of human intercourse about morality.[36]

Thus reading Kierkegaard through this lens, the Judge does not so much refute the esthete as offer an alternative, drawn from within his own experience, yet tuned also to the esthete's world. It is an alternative he hopes the esthete may be ready to hear of something resonant of his, the Judge's life, and resonant also of a life that he, the esthete, could embrace, whose embryo, as it were, he may already find within himself. Likewise, the Socratic view of inwardness does not so much refute the Judge as offer a transition to a richer view geared to the ears of that municipal official—who in turn may have *his* response to Socrates. All the while, Kierkegaard's imperial authority to settle the matter from *outside* these dialogues—say, from the perspective of a true Christian—is emphatically *not* asserted. In fact, the device of pseudonymity insures that this imperial authority is explicitly erased. Moral-religious discourse is in the service of freedom. As Johannes Climacus puts it in *Concluding Unscientific Postscript*,

> The highest degree of resignation [or respect] that a human being can reach is to acknowledge the given independence in every man, and after the measure of his ability, do all that can in truth be done to help someone preserve it.[37]

At the close of the *Postscript*, Kierkegaard underscores this fact, claiming to revoke any claim to the views pseudonymously expressed in favor of granting to his figures authority to speak as independent figures, to speak their own heart or mind—and in favor of having us, the readers, in a position to enter the dialogue freely, without the cards stacked against us.[38]

So far from an irrationalism, or a suspension of reason, we are offered in Kierkegaard's lyrical-dialectics a nontheoretical, noninstrumental reason engaged in comparative judgment meant to lend intelligibility to moral growth, to moral change, transition, and conversion. And such reason may itself be grounded in a faith, in a trusting acknowledgment of our independent self-worth, of the worth of independent others (whose value we are committed to respect and nourish even in critique), and the worth of exploring the communicative space between—a forum or community of engaged interlocutors. Lyrical narrative, as well as dialectical analysis, exhortation, and evocation of a self's placement in a life then become natural partners in this exercise of reason.

PARTICULARITY, VISION AND TRUTH

Whatever its simplifications, a generic portrait of the Kierkegaardian outlook can orient discussions in succeeding chapters. Say we begin in a biblical vein with the thought that where there is no vision the people perish, and that vision flourishes in the light of a truth indigenous not just to science but to ethics, art and the holy. Attentive, committed selves find amplitude to flourish amid the lights and shadows vision can cast. We might say, too, that power to receive identity through vision is essential for a life true to itself. My *particular* outlook or vision—and *yours*—is of irreplaceable importance. Adopting a "view from nowhere," the standpoint where any self is replaceable by any other, is both illusory and morally corrupting. What matters is not some kind of disembodied general consciousness, or aggregate of interchangeable selves, but my self—and your self.

Let me make preliminary notes, to be filled in later, on three of the issues focused by this sketch. First, the sort of thought we find in Kierkegaard (or Nietzsche, for that matter) is not anarchic individualism. If I am a unique and irreplaceable center of significance I discover this fact largely through encounters with others who also take each of *themselves* to be unique and irreplaceable. Recognition is reciprocal and presupposes community.[39] Its structure can be laid out in a roughly Hegelian way.

If I seek recognition from another, I thereby confer significance on that other as a bearer, because she is a potential *bestower*, of significance. Or reversing the picture, if another seeks recognition from me, I am myself thereby acknowledged as someone who can confer significance and recognition and hence become a bearer of significance.

Furthermore, nearly any identity I could truthfully admire and embrace will include projects joining me to others in shared endeavors or commitments. Yet my irreplaceability and self-responsibility need not diminish through such reciprocal participation and connection in community. In family, sports, or musical activities, it may as easily become enhanced.

A second point is this, that an "existentialist" or Kierkegaardian vision has a place for subjective truth, and this idea need not be shallow or corrupt. If truth were construed along certain narrow lines—say, as necessarily universal and impersonal—then the idea of subjective truth might quickly collapse upon itself. But both existentialists and modern analytical (or postanalytical) writers like Thomas Nagel have come to doubt that truth must be at odds with every sort of subjectivity.[40] We pay too large a price when truth is disengaged from our particularities, from our self-conceptions and most inward promptings and allegiances. Quite simply, we pawn the very *possibility* of being true or false to ourselves or to our condition. This unnecessarily contracts the scope of truth and leaves life hopelessly bereft. Martha Nussbaum puts it this way. "Much though at certain times we may long to be told from outside what to do and to be, it is only from ourselves that we can find (or rather, go on searching for) the answer to the question that we have actually asked."[41]

A third and final note. A Kierkegaardian emphasis on individual freedom does not exclude recognition of authoritative, "external" sources of inspiration and regard. If I grant authority to something other than myself, that act does not automatically put my freedom or responsibility in debt. Embedded "external factors"—whether social, natural, traditional, or religious—cannot all be suspect simultaneously, to the same degree. *Some* dimensions of importance, or "horizons of significance," are necessary to the fabric of a viable self.[42] Individual appropriation or embodiment of social or religious values is central to the project of our becoming selves. And such objects of commitment or appropriation have standing independent of particular wish or desire. Neither they, nor the self confronted by them, are created *ex nihilo* by a choosing self.

Evaluative commitment inevitably advances one tradition or value and retards another. The tradition or value in question is inextricably part of the world the self confronts. But equally it can be part of the self confronting the world. One might lobby for human rights or cultivate a reverence for the "otherness" of wild things or devote oneself to familial cares. Or these might be discounted, each seen as sentimental or otherwise illusory. Such options are neither closed to nor required of a self *in general*. Through imaginative vision they appeal to a receptive self on the verge of commitment, to a self on the verge of becoming itself.[43] Imagination can show the free creativity of the dialectical poet (spinning out a particular tale), or it can show the richness of the tale or world (spun out by a particular poet). Emphasis can fall on singer or on song. In any case, self and world are articulated jointly and with gains that are reciprocal. A freedom-seeking self embraces things of independent status (*this* value, *this* hero, *this* mood) without thereby diminishing itself.

This motif of mutual imaginative elaboration of self and world is developed in the following chapters on *Either/Or* and on Kierkegaard's view of the biblical Job. Judge Wilhelm offers traditions and values for the esthete to choose or receive. And with regard to the *Book of Job*, selfhood emerges in this active reciprocity. Job's praise of the Lord is *his, Job's* existentially authentic praise. Confronting a whirlwind, an abundant wildness independent and beyond the orbit of the self, mitigates Job's pain. He is significant in his acknowledgment of insignificance. The selves offered or embodied by Judge Wilhelm or presented in *Job* are not lonely surds stripped of world and bearings. At least as Kierkegaard has it, the esthetic and the rational, poetry and philosophy, need not forever quarrel. They can join in truthful articulation of bearings, roots and world.[44]

SELF-CHOICE OR SELF-RECEPTION
Judge Wilhelm's Admonition

The I chooses itself, or more correctly, it accepts itself.

What is crucial is not so much deliberation as the baptism of choice by which it is assumed into the ethical.

– Judge Wilhelm, *Either/Or II*[1]

"CHOOSE YOURSELF!" IS THE ADMONITION DELIVERED BY JUDGE WILHELM TO HIS friend, identified only as "A," in an avuncular, terribly wordy letter. The editor of *Either/Or*, one Victor Eremitor, provides an imposing title for this second letter from the Judge: "The Balance Between the Esthetic and the Ethical in the Development of the Personality."[2] Although Judge Wilhelm disclaims any standing as a trained or knowledgeable philosopher, he nevertheless presents an important contribution to moral and religious psychology. There are reflections on freedom, responsibility, choice, and despair; thoughts on the contrast between moral action and choosing to be ethical; persuasive depictions of the nature of the self and its grounding in community; and homilies on the secular and religious vocations of the self, and on the role and limits of moral exhortation, advice, and judgment. Wilhelm couches his advice informally, conversationally, though as a municipal judge, he naturally speaks with some moral authority. And he is not afraid to invoke the deeper authority of Greek philosophy. "Choose thyself" is Judge Wilhelm's self-conscious amendment to the Socratic formula "Know thyself."[3]

The idea of self-choice branches out toward autonomy, rights, and responsibilities. Self-choice is an exercise and confirmation of autonomy, a value protected by rights. And autonomous agents will be responsible for what they do and who they are. This cluster of moral concepts has permeated and even come to dominate Western thought and institutions, from politics to law, from literature to psychology. Yet the specifically Kierkegaardian version of self-choice, and its links to responsibility, has been left in relative obscurity. In fact, the Kierkegaardian concept turns out to be at odds with what have become tacit assumptions of this tradition.

Exploring the ins and outs of the Judge's formula "Choose yourself!" will carry us through a range of issues central to *Either/Or*, and should expand our understanding of specifically Kierkegaardian choice, receptivity, and self-responsibility, as well as widen our understanding of moral and religious psychology more generally.

CHOOSE THYSELF

The admonition "Choose thyself" is addressed to a somewhat obsessive yet clever and poetic observer of others, the world, and himself. From the perspective of the Judge, the young esthete shows a dangerous indifference to deep moral realities. What the Judge finds unpalatable in his friend is not any breach of etiquette, or legal impropriety, or the violation of some simple moral injunction. The youth is well-mannered, in many ways charming and attractive, not in any obvious way a liar or a cheat. Unlike the Abraham of *Fear and Trembling*, who seems ready at a moment's notice to sacrifice his son, the esthete does not appear to pose a threat of moral scandal. He is, we may assume, a fairly well-assimilated member of Danish society. Nevertheless, Judge Wilhelm fears for the man's soul.

As the Judge has it, this nameless esthete is empty, his existence devoid of any inward moral worth. As Kant might put it, whatever outward behavior he may display, whatever acts may lie in *accord* with a moral code, if the esthete does not act *from* a moral stance or source, his actions will lack specifically *moral* worth—specifically *human* worth.[4] The esthete has no moral self and hence can form no moral intentions. He can at most conform to public codes. At issue is the esthete's disengaged spectatorship. He tests the waters of a true "inward morality" (as opposed to a civic or role morality) only gingerly, if at all. But to acquire a proper self, he must take the plunge and *choose* the ethical, choose himself. One hundred years later, the injunction "Choose yourself" will be reiterated by Sartre—but the meaning of that phrase will by then have lost most of its Kierkegaardian complexity.

Why is it necessary to amend self-knowledge to bring self-choice to center stage? For the Judge, this is a strategy to combat the shallowness inherent in a merely esthetic existence. The esthete is brilliantly versed in human psychology, a master of subtle self-observation and description. He possesses a refined awareness of the intricate variety of motives, pains, and pleasures, that course through human consciousness. If he can converse perceptively about himself and others, then in what sense does he lack a self?

As the Judge sees it, "A" faces a problem of will and of the structures of perception and conception rather than a simple problem of self-knowledge. The esthete feigns moral indifference to all he sees. He is like a revolving door through which all manner of perception or opinion will effortlessly pass. This hollow form of intuition permits exquisite articulation of experience. But the esthete's reflections flow from a morally vacant channel, unstructured by any qualitative measures of good and evil. Insofar as one acquires selfhood, the channels of reception and expression must show moral modulation, must cast good and evil, love, marriage, work, and community, in their proper moral light. If he heeds the Judge, the esthete must strip from these channels their sheen of sophisticated indifference. It is not this or that opinion, not this or that specific policy or public action, that must be changed or altered. Instead, he must choose—that is, acquire—the moral framework or self that will modulate all his reception and expression of experience, giving a moral cast to everything within that frame or channel.

There is a clear analogy here with Kant, whose "forms of intuition" and "categories of understanding" shape any possible experience of the physical world. Of course Kierkegaard—or at this point, the Judge—is dealing with moral experience. And in this domain, as Kierkegaard has it, forms of ethical reception and judgment are not built-in as biological or psychological inevitabilities. Rather, they are acquired through moral or spiritual labor as the personality develops from premoral to ethical existence. Although the esthete retains a somewhat passable "moral" *persona* he nevertheless remains essentially premoral. What he lacks is inward "spirit" or "selfhood." The Judge declares that, in choosing the ethical, "It is less a matter of choosing between willing good or evil than of choosing to will, but, with this latter, good and evil are posited once again."[5] And he continues, noting that in making the choice that restructures the self, the esthete cannot but choose the good. "My either/or does not denote the choice whereby one chooses good and evil or excludes them. The question here is, under what categories one wants to contemplate the entire world and would oneself live. That someone who chooses good-and-evil chooses the good is indeed true, but this becomes evident only afterwards, for the esthetic is not evil but indifference...."[6] According to the Judge, it cannot but be good to take in the world and act upon it through moral or ethical sensibilities and categories.

The esthete seems half to believe that becoming a solid nondespairing self requires no more than continuing the detached self-observation and thoughtful reflections on life at which he is so adept. Or perhaps he does not care to become a self with moral depth or does not grasp the fact that moral depth or moral despair are concrete realities, that they are more than bourgeois illusions. In any case, the Judge, as a friend of "A," knows that the time for idle observation is past. If "personality is to develop," then "A" must be disabused of the thought that it is sufficient to "know thyself"—in the shallow way that the esthete is presumed to take this formula. The Judge confronts the esthete with an urgent, commitment-requiring "either/or," and makes it clear that the demanding, non-spectatorial "Choose thyself"—not the potentially passive and disengaged "Know thyself"—is the only real option.

Note that the admonition or plea is context-sensitive. It is practical advice offered to a young man in particular straits that others may avoid. That is, although a full-time philosopher of moral development might take a hint from the Judge and erect a general theory around the idea that moral selfhood is acquired mainly by self-choice, the Judge is not in the business of offering general theories and is not a full-time philosopher. Perhaps he would advise another friend to attend more to the requirements of civic duty, or to become more self-aware. Perhaps self-choice is not a viable option for a person unversed to some degree in self-reflection, and so could not be recommended in all cases. But, no doubt, the Judge has assessed his friend correctly. We can trust that his counsel that "A" choose himself, rather than know more about himself, is appropriate.

We should note, too, that the advice to choose oneself does not in fact countermand the Socratic advice to know oneself. "The ethical individual knows himself, but this knowledge is not mere contemplation...it is a reflection on himself, which is itself an action."[7] Self-choice, actively reflecting on oneself, *complements* the Socratic admonition. It calls attention to a neglected issue: What does one *make of* or *do with*, the products of self-reflection or self-examination? "When the individual knows himself *and* has chosen himself, he is on the way to realizing himself, but since he must realize himself freely he must know what it is he would realize."[8] A narrow construal of the Socratic "Know yourself" can diminish a rich self-knowledge to mere self-observation or self-commentary. The broader goal of moral self-actualization requires something more.

Finally, it is important to see that the plea or admonition is meant to work as a corrective to an inflated Hegelian drive toward absolute knowledge—or knowledge of the absolute. Assume that some of the Danish readers of *Either/Or* were acquainted with the Hegelian project of tracing the historical journey of Spirit toward ever-richer conceptions of Freedom and Reason. One might naturally expect that this Hegelian project would also lead to greater wisdom, fuller selfhood. But the Judge's challenge to the esthete applies as well to the Hegelian: What does one *make* of, or *do* with, this story? It may be essential to individual growth to have some reflective, narrative grasp of one's history, autobiography, and culture. But such a grasp of developing historical structures, in the Judge's view, remains vastly insufficient to save a soul. "Choose yourself" remains pertinent advice

So the motivation for stressing self-choice should now be clear. To power moral development we must be more than reflective, perceptive, or even creative renderers of experience, whether that experience is personal, social, or world-historical. If one is to become a self with moral tasks, there must be regulative standards, values, or ideals in place *prior* to the rendering of experience or the production of knowledge. One then confronts a world infused with moral value. To acquire a self is to acquire standards, ideals, or values which then operate in a Kant-like fashion as *a priori* categories of moral understanding or presuppositions of (moral) activity.[9] To choose the ethical, in the Judge's view, is to acquire a self-structure that henceforth frames all relevant experiential material, casting experience in its proper moral and aspirational shape.

THE AMBIANCE OF SELF-CHOICE

Let me provide a preliminary sketch of some of the terrain through which the concept of self-choice travels. This will help place the explorations that follow.

Self-choice is one element within an array of moral concepts at work within the Judge's project of tracing the "development of the personality." It is clearly allied with freedom, autonomy, and the will. With moral freedom comes the burden of responsibility. Standards constituting the moral self operate reflexively: the self takes responsibility for itself. In addition, the Judge alludes to "the eternal validity" of the self.[10] When work, marriage, and civic duty are morally unstructured, the would-be self engaged in these practices lacks validity or truth—the validity or truth of moral selfhood. This validity does not vary with time and place and so is deemed "eternal." The moral values animating everyday practices, and the moral self that they underwrite, will have a depth and duration greater than the transitoriness or whimsy of "merely" immediate, esthetic experience.

The Judge links self-choice to "choosing despair." "A"'s existence has so far been permeated by moral indifference, a perdition that he has refused to fully face. Confronting this despair or moral perdition will trigger repentance. In this regard, Judge Wilhelm speaks of "repentance back into the family, back into history, back into the [human] race."[11] The esthete *needs* to reassess his past in the light of ethical standards. As we will elaborate below, accepting these standards against which the self will be measured and found wanting is, in the Judge's terms, choosing oneself and choosing despair. Recognition (and repentance) of such fault will unite the esthete with his past, with his family and with an historical community of fellow sufferers—or so the Judge believes. Identification with this *moral* community will be central to the esthete's self-development. Thus he must drop the pose of "alienated outsider." His life as a detached intellectual or poet, a rootless voyeur gazing indifferently upon the human scene, will be finished.

The Judge presents himself as living in the light of "inner" values related to self-choice, which color the more public virtues related to marriage, friendship, and the arts. "The self...is not just a personal self but a social, a civic self."[12] This ethical personality points forward toward a life of *religious* depth. A properly ethical self will "...develop the personal, the civic, the religious virtues, and his life proceeds through his constantly translating himself from one stage to the next."[13]

The Judge models a moral-religious confidence that may "rub off" on the esthete. Taken in its proper light—the light the Judge provides—the esthete's despair foretells "a metamorphosis": "Everything returns, but transfigured. So only when life is regarded ethically does it acquire beauty, truth, meaning, substance."[14] This is an early formulation of Kierkegaard's concept of "repetition," the central theme of Kierkegaard's subsequent book of that title, and of his discourse on the *Book of Job*, which we explore in the following chapter. What is lost in despair or inattention may be subsequently regained, wondrously transformed.[15] The sphere of esthetic life is returned, now reframed in moral-religious terms.

Although the Judge is an exemplar for the esthete, this rather stuffy and conventional bureaucrat falls short of Kierkegaard's later articulations of a fully moral-religious self. His failure as a religious prototype is suggested even within the covers of *Either/Or*. This collection of various letters and appeals concludes with a sermon by a Jutland Priest who castigates self-satisfied complacency. The Judge claims he has read and pondered this sermon which he appends to his letters to "A." Perhaps he has applied it to himself. Or perhaps he appends it without grasping the possibility that this sermon is (at this moment) more relevant to *his* life than to the esthete's. Could Kierkegaard intend this sermon as a device to take the Judge, whose own "sermons" have filled far too many pages, down a peg or two?[16]

The moral-religious framework embodied by the Judge will come under withering scrutiny in later works, notably in *Fear and Trembling*, published soon after *Either/Or*. Although the Judge is meant to embody an ethical orientation in need of revision, it's clear his stance is already ethico-religious. So the outcome of this later critique will be complex. The Judge does not represent an ethical position free from religious grounding—as if the simple introduction of a religious basis would correct the defects of his stance. There is an inkling of a proper ethical stance in the esthete's dominantly nonethical stance, and it is to this that the Judge appeals. Similarly, there is an inkling of a more adequate religious stance in the Judge's dominantly ethical stance.[17] There is a latent religious core that can be addressed by the Jutland Priest and by the author of *Fear and Trembling*, Johannes de Silentio, even if the Judge does not fully grasp the implications of this core nor the extent to which he is himself a target of the admonitory sermon which closes out *Either/Or*.

WHAT SELF-CHOICE IS NOT

In 1843, when *Either/Or* was published, the notion of self-choice would have seemed stranger than it does today. In the wake of Sartre and liberal-libertarian views of selfhood, the notion of self-choice has become a cultural icon. Philosophers as diverse as Hare, Sartre, and MacIntyre present a picture—really, a caricature—of continually renewable (and arbitrary) choice of self or principle, sometimes in lonely existential anguish, sometimes in the calm of rational equilibrium.[18] But Kierkegaard (or his Judge Wilhelm) would not endorse this descendant version of self-choice. The differences are several and severe.

Self-choice is *not* radical Sartrean choice. The Judge denies that self-choice is "identical with creating myself."[19] The ethical individual ". . . does not become someone other than he was before, he becomes himself; consciousness unites."[20]

Thus we are neither the collected string of our free choices nor always placed at the brink, ready by our next choice either to continue on our path or to become a new person. By choosing himself (or herself), the individual "is not the product of whim, making it look as though he has absolute power to make himself into whatever he wanted."[21] At most, one ethically "edits" the self one is, improving its particular expression.[22]

Neither is self-choice picking a social role or career. Judge Wilhelm imagines the esthete fancifully musing along these lines: "I have it in me to be a Don Juan, a Faust, a robber chief; I shall now cultivate this trait…[to] let the seedling planted in me develop fully."[23] But ethically speaking, as the Judge avers, this would be folly: "…even the richest personality is nothing before he has chosen himself, and on the other hand even what might be called the poorest personality is everything when he has chosen himself; for the great thing is not to be this or that, but to be oneself; and every person can be that if he wants."[24] So choosing oneself is not plotting a career or pursuing a Rawlsian rational "life-plan."

Self-choice is not separating oneself off from others or becoming a solitary recluse or mystic. Civic duties can be embraced in self-choice. In this, Kierkegaard undermines the sharp distinction between public and private life promoted, for example, by Richard Rorty. As Rorty has it "…the vocabulary of self creation is necessarily private…[and] the vocabulary of justice is necessarily public and shared."[25] But self-development can include embracing public values and roles, and be no less a matter of *self*-choice. Kierkegaard's Judge insists that self-choice is "repenting oneself back into the race."[26] This means accepting a concrete historical and communal continuity with others. "[R]eligion," claims the Judge, "has a tendency to isolate the individual."[27] But "every withdrawal, every ascetic self-torment" is a mistake.[28] When a person chooses the ethical "he would say something that reconciled him absolutely with every human being, with the whole of humankind."[29] Finally, self-choice is *not* a heroic or extraordinary feat which elevates the individual pridefully above his fellows. It embodies "the self-love that has the interest of its own self at heart in just the same way as it has that of any other."[30]

The view of self and of self-choice that the Judge unveils in *Either/Or* and the view of self-choice in the Sartrean or liberal-libertarian traditions are only distantly related. Perhaps Rorty comes closer than Sartre or MacIntyre to the Judge's view when he avers that our lives are essentially a never-ending weaving and reweaving of "a web of relationships." Yet Rorty sees this activity as responding to "the need [of each individual] to come to terms with the blind impress which chance has given him, to make a self for himself by redescribing that impress in terms which are, if only marginally, his own."[31]

In contrast to Rorty, the Judge sees self-choice as a matter of *moral* action or responsiveness rather than "redescription"—a linguistic activity which Rorty keeps largely at the esthetic level. Rorty's paradigm of the "self creator" is "the strong poet."[32] The Judge would find no need to strip the riches of family and civic life, not to mention the riches of human history and tradition, down to a "blind impress" we are forced to animate by our creative "redescriptions." Finally, the outcome of self-choice for the Judge is the achievement of full and *self-responsible* personhood—not a self whittled down to terms that are, as Rorty has it, "only *marginally* his own."[33]

But questions remain for the Judge's account. How can self-choice be squared with the intuition that ethical duties are *given* or *imposed* rather than chosen? Selves also appear (at least initially) largely given—whether construed as strands of memory, an accumulation of experience and action, a cluster of root convictions or cares, or a web of relationships. Finally, how can something not-yet-a-self muster resources to *choose* a self? From whence does the esthete—not-yet-a-self—derive cares, projects, and powers of integration sufficient to bring himself into existence?

THE IDEA OF SELF-RECEPTION

In an unguarded moment the Judge allows a competing image into play. Reminding us that human will does not have a single structure, he introduces the idiom of self-reception. Volition can be modeled as a relatively active process—say, as selective or assertive choice. But volition can also be modeled in a less active mode as something responsive—say, as willing receptivity. Perhaps the questions left unanswered by self-choice can be answered by the alternative idiom that now suddenly appears in the Judge's ruminations. In the following rhapsodic passage, he lapses into the idiom of receptive will:

> When around me all has become still, solemn as a starlit night, when the soul is all alone in the world, there appears before it not a distinguished person, but the eternal power itself. It is as though the heavens parted, and the I chooses itself—or more correctly, it accepts itself. The soul has then seen the highest, which no mortal eye can see and which never can be forgotten. The personality receives the accolade of knighthood which ennobles it for an eternity.[34]

Judge Wilhelm often exhorts the esthete in stern and scolding schoolmaster's terms. But in this passage, the tone softens. The Judge is less concerned to penetrate the esthete's consciousness than to share a moment of reverie. Dropping his role as friendly adversary, the Judge sketches a picture that the esthete can contemplate with him as an equal. He is captured by a vision that quiets his otherwise insistent preaching. The Judge seems to have shed the robes of masterly authority over his moral life. He yields center-stage—to a vision. His will recedes to a receptive mode.

Starlit heavens, grand or modest visions, can silence mundane discussion and mundane selves. This occasion of self-submission or rebirth is something "no mortal eye can see." A dogmatic pedagogy becomes instead a poetic context that sweeps consciousness itself into new modes. As volition assumes its second mode, it becomes an organ of responsive sensibility, of imagination, of "openness-to-otherness."[35] The Judge switches idioms, shifting almost imperceptibly from "the heavens part and the I chooses itself" to "the heavens part and the I chooses itself, or *more correctly*, accepts itself."[36] Something other than the productive, choosing or assertive will is now engaged.

That the Judge changes idioms, adopts the phrase "the I accepts [or perhaps 'receives'] itself," is just one piece of evidence that a reception model of self-acquisition now competes with the more familiar choice model.[37] Here are three other indications of a change from choice to reception.

The Judge, in the passage at hand, has the soul *see* "the highest." An immediate perception, a seeing, is more a receiving than a choice or an assertion. Second, the beneficiary of this self-bestowal *receives* therein an ennobling "accolade of knighthood." Accolades are *given*, not chosen. Finally, the Judge will write of "the baptism of choice" that occurs when one attains the ethical. Baptism too is something that is not chosen but given or received.[38]

The formula "Choose thyself" works to deprive the esthete of his spectatorial stance. It depends on a contrast between volition and knowledge. But if we take the idiom of receptivity and vision seriously, the Judge's earlier "knowing/choosing" contrast will now seem distorting and simplistic. Each term in the "knowing/choosing," "cognition/will" contrast is complicated by the reception model. In addition to the detached intellectual process of observation that Kierkegaard ridicules, there is cognition that is poetic, cognition that displays how the world is *seen*, known by *this* self, and moved by *these* emotions, sentiments, and commitments. The Judge's epiphany "that no mortal eye can see" is not a species of simple esthetic or theoretical spectatorship. So perception shifts from mere onlooking to rich and overarching vision.

Will is likewise complicated. It now can be receptive as well as selective, assertive, or productive. Volition becomes a deep, willing responsiveness. The receptivity model of self presupposes something received, and a Power that confers.

TWO SIDES OF WILL

In the milieu of industrial-bureaucratic society, the domain of free activities is modeled on selective choice. In politics, one chooses (or votes) for one policy or candidate over another; in the marketplace, one chooses (or buys) one brand over another; in relationships, one "shops" for the right partner.

Everything from recreational vehicles to lifestyles to religions can be presented as choice-options for autonomous agents. Even moods and emotions are characterized as outcomes of choice.[39] In this vein, we picture ourselves, in Iris Murdoch's phrase, as "pinpoints of will" confronting an array of items to select, try out, purchase, or consume, guided by our preferences (and perhaps by some rational principles).[40]

Yet clearly my self is not one among several *items on display* awaiting my appropriation. As Hume observed, a self is not an item I come upon in consciousness. However much I am assured of its existence, its contours are elusive, lacking distinct definition. Although I may speak easily enough of "taking charge of" or "choosing" myself, this activity has none of the relative simplicity of consumer or political choice. "Taking charge of," or "taking responsibility for oneself," is linked to "self-choice." But the relevant volition seems more akin to willingness or readiness for embrace than to selective choice. We accept demands or requirements, values or ideals, "absolutes," esthetic or religious visions. Each of these varying "objects" of receptivity becomes our own—through that embrace. Moments of love, creativity, moral sensitivity, or reverence illustrate this process.[41]

LOVE, CREATIVITY, REVERENCE

Falling in love is not selection from a field of candidates. If it is "love-at-first-sight," love *gives way* to another rather than appropriating its target. A single face or flower can crystallize my consciousness in willing acclamation. Volition is engaged, enchanted. Giving way to an enchanting smile excludes weighing alternatives. Deliberation or comparison would break the spell. Responding to *this face* or *this flower*, does not devalue or discount other choice-options because I face no option-array. If there are no competing objects for my embrace, then my response is noncomparative and in this sense absolute. Will is present, alert, and energized but in a mode of responsive receptivity rather than deliberate choice.

What is true of falling in love can also be true of creativity. I can exert my will trying to capture in poetic line a mood now striking me. Perhaps I'll line up an array of phrases, consider each, and finally decide deliberately on one that fits. But as often, it seems that at a crucial unwilled moment of recognition, one phrase strikes with brute necessity, allowing for no competitors. I embrace a given line that fits. The words arrive already tagged with my endorsement. Or take an unchosen moment of awe before some natural or moral grandeur—say Job's encounter with the Whirlwind's Voice. Here the focus of good calls on my receptive willingness to acknowledge the single value that addresses me. In these moments of willing receptivity, an encounter molds or informs the self I am. As the Judge has it, "the heavens part," and the self receives itself.

A sense of what is *morally* good or fitting can also jell apart from choice or selection from an array. The idea of choosing values may mean that I am *responsible* for them. But it cannot mean that one by one I select ideals or values that ground my identity. They are not set out like icons, products awaiting my anxious or eager purchase. Responsibility for self or for the values that ground it is not a selective affair.

This shift toward receptive will does not eliminate but rather relocates enigmas surrounding value and the will. We confront an all-important yet imponderable Source of value that resists explication in terms of anything deeper than itself. How are we to characterize this conferring Source to which the self becomes attuned?[42] Granting these disturbing issues, the idiom of self-reception nevertheless highlights features of experience otherwise left obscure—moments of love, creativity, moral demand, and self-embrace.

CAN RECEPTIVITY REPLACE SELF-CHOICE?

The choice model of volition presupposes that available options are clearly defined. The self needs only to decide and follow through. The receptivity model of volition presupposes an overarching good, a value source that may not be clearly articulable. The self is marked by a willingness to respond to this source in ways that may be subtle and hidden from public view. Responding to this overarching good is linked to accepting or answering for what we are and may become. As Kierkegaard's Judge presents the case, there is a unique telos offered for the esthete's acknowledgement: the self he is and can become. Its value is noncomparative. Becoming a self is choosing—or under our revised account, *accepting* or *receiving*—the absolute, the ethical, the "eternal validity" of the self.

How should we interpret this tension between the idioms of self-choice and self-reception? Perhaps the model of self-reception is superior. In the Judge's words, it is the "more correct" account. The tension reflects development in the Judge's view. He struggles toward an improved idiom of self-reception from an initial preference for the idiom of self-choice. In retrospect, having the benefit of the Judge's labors, we should revise the final letter to "A." We should substitute the phrase "Receive yourself" for every occurrence of the phrase "Choose yourself."

A second strategy would be to declare a simple equivalence between these idioms. Perhaps self-choice just *means* receptivity or willingness. "Choice" *translates* as "reception." When Wilhelm writes that the esthete "chooses [the self] absolutely from the hand of the eternal God,"[43] choice and reception are interlocked, and nearly indistinguishable.[44] "Choice" marks the core of an other-regarding readiness to receive what may be given.

But will the Judge be willing thus to muffle overtones of resolve, of urgency, of decision? Surely the esthete must seize, if not his self, then his *opportunity*? The choice model fits a kind of wholehearted embrace of an "object" without real competitors. We embrace—that is, "choose absolutely"—the self we are, the ethical standpoint, the *focus* of our love or commitment. But this embrace is also a kind of receptivity or responsive acceptance. These apparently conflicting idioms coexist in dialectical tension. The Judge does not, however, spell this tension out, or coordinate its elements. A picture of this relation self appears much later in Anti-Climacus's discussion of self-acquisition in *Sickness Unto Death*. But for the moment, we must settle for the rough divergence of idiom the Judge bequeaths. And perhaps there is virtue in this unresolved divergence. Discarding either of these models may well cost more than living with the discord of having both at hand.

The Judge addresses the needs (and limitations) of a friend. The informality of personal exploration and counsel may produce expressive metaphors with diverging structures. If there are deep-set conceptual and ideological tensions in the wider culture in which our self-conceptions have their ground, then we should *expect* a writer like Kierkegaard (or the Judge) to bring these into the open.[45] Idioms or ideals separately plausible but only problematically conjoined are left intact. Conflicting stories of the self receive their separate turn.

CHOICE, RECEPTIVITY, AND FREEDOM

The receptivity or responsive model of self is apt for articulating key features of love, creativity, and reverence. It also illuminates responsibility for self.[46]

The idea of receiving one's self depends for Kierkegaard on the idea of a divinity, a Source, conferring or bestowing selves and the grounds that nourish them. These grounds are independent ideals that call or bear on a self. In self-reception, value flows *to*, rather than exclusively *from*, the self. But this picture makes inhabitants of a "modern" or even a "postmodern" sensibility uneasy. We are happier with the idea of a self *projecting* or *choosing* or *inventing* values or ways of life than with the idea of a self responding *to* independent meaning-sources, to objects of love, or awe, or aspiration. A self that is dependent on an external source of meaning seems to have its freedom and responsibility restrained or occluded.[47] Modern political, bureaucratic and consuming routines make autonomy and responsibility paramount, if not absolute. But perhaps the fear that the receptive self must sacrifice autonomy or freedom is exaggerated or outright false.

Our discussions of love and creativity, of awe or reverence suggest that receptivity, autonomy, and responsibility are mutually compatible. Although love, reverence, or creativity can be articulated in terms of responsiveness to an external object of regard and inspiration, the self is nonetheless answerable for its loving regard, for its embrace of a poetically apt phrase, or for an effusion of reverence. Poets, lovers, or awestruck admirers are free in their responsiveness. The task before us then is to elaborate freedom and responsibility without relying on the idea of selective or explicit choice. For the poet gives us verse without always deliberately *choosing* the fitting line. The lover gestures lovingly without *selecting* the loving response (as opposed, say, to the envious one). The person is spellbound or awestruck without a discernible *decision* to acknowledge a reverence-invoking object. But *how* can we have self-responsibility if choice, decision, or selection play no dominant or explicit role?

SECTORS OF RESPONSIBILITY

We can distinguish three domains of responsibility. Within the realm of act-responsibility, the dominant question is who acted, who brought about an event or state of affairs; along the way we try to determine whether coercion or ignorance or some other extenuating factor diminishes responsibility.

Role-responsibility covers different ground. Here the dominant question is who occupies a role or office, and what responsibilities these social institutions or practices confer upon the occupant. Parents, department heads, and citizens incur positional or role-responsibilities, things they should do or are expected to do. This includes overseeing the activities of others, so role-occupants can be responsible for the acts of others, say those of a wayward child. Here one *takes* responsibility for actions or situations independently of whether one chose to perform that action, or chose to bring about that state of affairs.

Both act-responsibility and role-responsibility can be nailed down more or less legalistically. We find out who chose what, or who did what, or determine from the public record what requirements were implicit in the position occupied by the person whose responsibility is at issue. In its third domain, however, responsibility is harder to pin down. If I am responsible as a matter of character—"self-responsible" that is—then I will accept responsibility for my acts and I will be sensitive to the position responsibilities that I incur as I take on jobs or assume the open-end responsibilities of citizenship, say, or of parenthood. But a responsible character or self embodies more than act- or role-responsibility.

A deeply responsible person has moral aspirations and sensitivities to suffering and injustice that far exceed what can be caught within the nets of act- or role-responsibility. These aspirations and sensitivities become traits of character or sensibility. They become clusters of virtues that unfold narratively as the story of our identity. They trace out a self with overarching and interwoven aims that serve as essential background and supplement our grasp of the specific self that takes on roles or that acts. We become "crystallized particulars." Self-responsibility is, in part, responsibility to and for this particular identity, to and for the interweaving cares, resolves, and relationships that course through one's life, bequeathed by tradition, history, and others, and shaped through self-articulation. A familiar example will illustrate such self-responsibility.

SELF-RESPONSIBILITY: THE CASE OF SOCRATES

As the Judge surely agrees, Socrates is a paradigmatic ethical and responsible figure, answerable for who he is. He's responsible for things he's done, and responsibly fulfills the varied requirements of the offices or roles he holds. Yet his good character is more than this. Socrates finds himself saddled with responsibilities toward Athens that are based on relationships largely inherited, and not a matter of choice. He sees his integrity in terms of responding *to* those unchosen situational demands. His case reinforces our native intuition that many duties and moral demands come *upon* us, rather than being invented or selected by choice.

Socrates speaks movingly in the *Crito* of his bonds to Athens and its traditions. The laws and practices of the place are like parents to him. They give him birth, and provide nourishment and protection for his flourishing. As the place he's grown to cherish, we might say that Athens is Socrates's "chosen city." But Socrates has not deliberately picked Athens from an array of cities to be the place that he respects, in which his identity will be rooted. Athens is his city because he recognizes a debt of gratitude for the way he's been raised by it. He *acknowledges* a value deriving *from* the city, *from* the community. He is receptive to the demands of the place.

The Judge writes of the ethical, self-responsible individual: "He has his place in the world, with freedom he himself chooses his place, that is, he chooses *this* place.[48] "Accepts" or "acknowledges" his place, or "receives this place as his own," are phrases that fit as well as "chooses his place." But "selects his place (from an array)" is no fit at all.

Socrates's loyalty to Athens is best clarified by bringing out his recognition of links to Athens that are already well-established. Alternative accounts have some weight. Acts he has performed (or failed to perform) ground his loyalty. He has participated in the life of the city, and so owes it respect. His loyalty is partly based on default. He failed to leave Athens; therefore he owes a debt to her. His loyalty might be partly grounded on the recognition that his physical residence is role-related. He filled the role of resident; therefore he has a debt. But Socrates puts most weight on the idea that the practices of the place have *raised* him to full self-hood.[49]

A responsible self will answer for things it has not chosen, by virtue of who and where it is. Upon receiving his sentence, Socrates answers for the good in Athens by returning it to good, not evil. Earlier, at his trial, his response to the mistakes and foolishness of his city was responsible. He took upon himself its shames not as something he had chosen, not as something for which he was to blame, but as something that demanded his moral critique. Taking on the burden of critique showed the extent to which his character was morally responsive *to* the plight of Athens. He is responsible *to* and *for* Athens. Self-responsibility now becomes articulated as responsibility for others, for ideals, for history and tradition.

RESPONSIBILITY FOR HISTORY AND MILIEU

Say that I, like Socrates, identify with the country within whose borders I reside. I feel proud or exhilarated by some aspects of its shape or past, and repelled by others. These reactive emotions betray the fact that I take some responsibility, perhaps vicariously or imaginatively, but nonetheless decisively, for the way the country has evolved. I may be proud of the havens it has afforded and repelled by the oppressions it has committed. This pride or shame is centered on a wide historical community to which I find myself attached, a community which includes groups, victims, and victors far removed in time. Some of these will be known to me only collectively or as general types. Acknowledging these ties expresses the need to take the boundaries of my self (and hence my responsibility) out beyond the acts I alone have performed or the roles I occupy.[50]

Establishing the history of my community or my country as part of *my* past will expand my responsibility. This acknowledged past predates my birth. Nevertheless, it is something that I find myself *already* involved in. Here is how the poet William Carlos Williams puts it: "...only by making [America] my own from the beginning to my own day, in detail, should I ever have a basis for knowing where I stood."[51] Taking up the past as my own is to find my ground and footing.

Character as self-responsibility looks simultaneously outward and inward. There is outward responsiveness to one's situation, including one's past and the history of one's community. There is also inward responsiveness to the self one takes oneself to be. "The individual is then aware of himself as this definite individual with these aptitudes, these tendencies, these instincts, these passions, influenced by these definite surroundings, as this definite product of a definite outside world. But in becoming self-aware in this way, he assumes responsibility for it all."[52] Assuming responsibility for self presupposes that I can be more or less transparent to myself, responsive to my deepest inner promptings, and morally attentive to my context and historical location.[53] And it includes, as Kierkegaard's

Judge has it, taking responsibility for one's "definite surroundings," and for oneself as the unwitting "definite product of a definite outside world" constituted by traditions and a past established prior to one's birth.

Although the idiom of self-choice can highlight the taking of responsibility, choice cannot be cited as the basis for self-responsibility. The basis in the case of responsibility for history and milieu is simply my avowal that I will be answerable for and show moral sensitivity toward shames or prides lying deep in the past and beyond the grasp of my control or choice. Nothing deeper can or needs to ground it.

Say we tried to ground the idea of self-responsibility by positing a phantom *prior* choice of self. If that choice is a responsible one, then the choosing self already *is* responsible. And if that prior choice does not issue from a responsible self, then *what* it aims to choose (say, responsible selfhood) cannot derive its special virtue (responsibility) from that act of choice itself. *Who* (or what) could have effected this choice if not a person with character and responsibility intact? And what could be the *target* of this postulated "choice"? Do sensibilities, virtues, or principles and their interpretation (the likely ingredients of moral selfhood) come package wrapped like "policies to vote on," or "products to be delivered?" If not, what would choice of *self* be like?

There are familiar arguments against "given essences" (say, "my essential and responsible self") and against value structures that are mysteriously already in place, ready to be seen or found. To speak of Socrates "finding" or "seeing" himself as already answerable or as receptive to values already in place *may* sound like philosophical naiveté. Yet Socrates can find himself in Athens, in its past, in his "chosen home." He can find himself (or receive himself) in a straightforward sense that does not carry with it the baggage of mysterious ontological "givens," of essences that are historically unconditioned, or of factors that restrict freedom.

We can take the self that's found or received as a fluid mix of capacities and aspirations and convictions, of relationships and roles, of character traits and sensibilities, more or less in and out of environing strands of culture and convention.[54] Finding or recognizing oneself is having a pattern of these self-strands crystallize in a particular way one can acknowledge as one's own.[55] As we will see in the next chapter on Kierkegaard's reading of the *Book of Job*, this moment of transforming recognition engages imagination.[56] It is a moment of meaning-acquisition. Self-recognition and self-receptivity resemble Job's receptivity to world-conferral as he shutters before the majesty of the Whirlwind's Voice.

QUESTIONS REVISITED

The receptivity model of self emerges in Judge Wilhelm's letter almost accidentally. Here I've worked to fill out its capacities as a constructive alternative to the model of self-choice. The idiom of receptivity captures our sense that values, convictions, selves, are largely *given* in experience, already there awaiting our acknowledgment. The role of invention, projection, or selection by the self then becomes relatively peripheral. And the receptivity model has a further advantage. It dissolves the issue of how a premoral self can muster power sufficient to achieve an ethical status. Resources for self-acquisition are *conferred* by tradition, by community, even by a deeper Source. This avoids the paradox of brute choice vaulting a self into existence.

Of course self-reception adds new paradoxes. How can anything have the power to *offer* moral selfhood or value to a receptive (premoral) self? How can anything *be* a moral (or meaning) source? But is this enigmatic source *more* opaque or unintelligible than the enigmatic self that chooses itself? Perhaps the deepest issue is which questions must remain unanswered.

In *Sickness Unto Death* Kierkegaard (or the pseudonym Anti-Climacus) introduces a model of self-acquisition and self-loss that can serve to some extent to coordinate the models Judge Wilhelm leaves in tensed suspension. This is a model of "relational self," of self as an ensemble of juxtaposed opposites relating to a grounding power or source. The tension between choice and receptivity is not explicitly addressed by the mock-philosopher Anti-Climacus. But this contrast is implicit in his formula for self.

Anti-Climacus views selfhood as a "relation relating to itself and grounded in another." The juxtaposed factors in relation referred to in this formula leave choice and reception poised in dynamic equilibrium. One such pair of related factors is Freedom and Necessity. And at another level in his relational schema, the self endorses or avows a relation to itself—hence "chooses itself." But it also finds itself—or "receives itself"—as "grounded in another." We must defer exploration of this model.[57] But it seems that Judge Wilhelm's tensed suspension of idioms remains even as it becomes transformed within Anti-Climacus's model of relational self.

REPENTANCE AND DESPAIR

The esthete must recognize that he is in utmost need. And in the Judge's view, "A" must *choose* (rather than reject) his despair.[58] Being in despair is a familiar state. We understand how someone might fall into it from deep affliction. But what could motivate *choice* of despair? If one had options in response to one's afflictions, why not chose hope, or resistance, or resignation? The enigma expands when the Judge urges the esthete not only to choose despair but to "repent back into the family, back into the [human] race."[59] How do despair and repentance connect to becoming a moral, responsible self?

There is an inevitable gap between what the moral self *requires* of itself and what its actual performance and motives are. To acknowledge despair is to acknowledge this gap. The ethically mature self knows that it is perfect neither in intention nor in accomplishment, though it rightly aims at both. It recognizes complicity in acts and intentions that occurred before its maturity, and even in its familial or community past. It can hold itself accountable for states of affairs it had no part in bringing about.

History, experience, and maturity, will raise the level of moral demands one strives to satisfy. This feeds the sense that such faults as etch our lives lie well beyond repair. To choose despair is to repent oneself "back into the race." It is to become aware of and answerable for a continually expanding moral burden. This crushes pride and makes indifference evil. As the Judge has it, moral effort can be sustained in such potentially debilitating circumstance only by repenting first back into the race, recognizing that one's burden is shared; and second, repenting back into God, a God providing hope for lives beyond repair. This falling back upon one's simple fault-lined humanity and upon a God who sustains it provides strength to continue moral efforts in circumstances that would otherwise be morally unbearable.[60]

To "choose despair" does not mean that to become an ethical, answerable self one must suffer misery. Yes, one must suffer something, in the sense of being open to the allure of value, to affection, or to affliction. Each of these can involve a painful vulnerability of self. But none of these have intrinsic links to misery. One lets go of assertive, selective will. In the only language the esthete can understand this appears to be letting go of hope. The Judge knows this, and so counsels the esthete to choose despair. Properly understood, however, heeding the Judge's counsel does not destroy all hope but makes room for a patient, "suffering" ethical resolve and trust. "It is a grave and significant moment...when one receives oneself..., when in an eternal and unfailing sense one becomes aware of oneself as the person one is."[61] Situational responsibilities and demands are allowed to come upon one, to be embraced and acknowledged, inwardly and in action.

Assertive will—the will to self-sufficiently choose oneself—stands in the way of letting roots reveal their proper salience for embrace: roots in community, family, friendship, and worthy activities, whether religious, educational, artistic, or political. In the willful attempt to create myself from nothing, or in the willful attempt to erase or be indifferent to the wider self I am, these roots are severed from their essential environing ground. Then self-decline sets in. Despairing of assertive will lets the proper set of my identity stand forth, ready for reception.

GETTING BACK THE WORLD
Kierkegaard on the *Book of Job*

[Texts can speak]...as living bodies having the power...to astound, to silence words on the tip of the tongue, to confute and disconfirm, to show things in an utterly new light, and by so doing to bring down in temporary ruin the pillars that uphold the self.

—Bernard Harrison, *Inconvenient Fictions*[1]

In 1843 Kierkegaard eased into print the slim volume of discourses containing what I'll call the Job Discourse. In that year he also published *Repetition*, a short book obliquely related to *Job*, as well as *Fear and Trembling*, and the two-volume *Either/Or*—not to mention two other short volumes of discourses. By any standard seven volumes in a single year is a prodigious effort. He wrote as if his life depended on it.

If as Kierkegaard avers Job is an exemplar, a "teacher for humankind," then we might expect a full portrait. Yet the brevity of the discourse, barely a dozen pages, and its relatively narrow focus on an early short passage, disappoint this expectation. *Repetition*, published six weeks earlier, is not a great improvement. It too provides only a partial account of Job, incomplete for more complex reasons. *Repetition's* pseudonymous author, Constantine Constantius, does little more than allude to Job; and although the nameless youth who writes Constantius letters is more expansive in his talk of Job, he has a view of Job skewed by youth and the romantic heartache of first love.[2] Unlike Abraham or Socrates, to whom entire books are devoted, Kierkegaard breaks up his portrait of Job, distributing its fragments over several works. This leaves us with the task of assembling the pieces, filling in gaps as best we can.

A prologue and epilogue written in straightforward prose serve as the framing folktale for the *Book of Job*. The prologue sets the stage: the divine court with an identifiable villain. The "Satan" is a prosecutor or accuser bringing a case against Job, questioning Job's motives for faithfulness. The fact that the Lord hearing this case is willing to let the accuser torment Job gives us a simplistic, folktale account of the *cause* of Job's suffering. The epilogue gives a similarly simplistic "happy ending" where "all is made right," as the Lord restores to Job all he had lost, and more. The drama within this framing folktale begins with Job's afflictions, including his extended struggles with his friends, and culminates with the poetic outpouring of the Whirlwind's Voice. I indicate below my reasons for attending to the central drama ending with the Voice, and declining the easy answers that the folktale epilogue and prologue provide.

I'll take my cue for interpreting both the *Book* and Kierkegaard's discourse on it from the three-part verse in Job (1:21), that Kierkegaard himself picks out to prompt his reading. The verse is this: "The Lord gives; the Lord takes; Blessed be the name of the Lord."[3] Considering the restoration provided by the resounding Voice from the storm, this verse might be expanded to read, "The Lord gives, takes, and then gives back again"—though in the immediate context of its utterance, Job could not presume to anticipate a restoration of all he had lost.

Seeing *Job* in light of seeking and receiving back what he had lost would link the discourse to the greater body of Kierkegaard's work. Cycles of possession, loss, and return recur throughout his authorship: Constantine Constantius attempts to *regain* the experience of an earlier journey to Berlin, an experience now lost; the young man, his friend, yearns to *repossess* a love now lost; Abraham has, loses, then *regains* Isaac; Job is blessed, loses all, then gets it *back*.[4] "Repetition" is the term of art Kierkegaard adopts to depict this pattern of loss and subsequent return.

The Danish word for "repetition," *Gjentagelse*, also means "retake" as in a cinematic second or third "take." Hence it is close to the idea of dropping an initial approximation in favor of a version done better, or being richer in meaning. The idea of repetition is itself repeated, modulated differently in different texts. Kierkegaard's esthetic, dialectical, psychological, ethical, and religious authors all have their various opinions, or "takes" on this concept. The Judge (in *Either/Or*) avers that true love renews itself in repetition. "Repetition" is opposed in *Concluding Unscientific Postscript* to the Platonic idea of "recollection." The thin book *Repetition* opposes this idea to the Hegelian idea of "mediation." Theologically, repetition is the pattern of God's incarnation into worldly suffering and then His subsequent return, bringing also a new world. Having these several texts— *Either/Or, Repetition, Fear and Trembling*, and the *Postscript*—in mind as one goes back to the Job Discourse is itself a kind of repetition, a renewal and revision of the meaning in the Discourse in light of these other works. And of course the Discourse itself is a "repetition" of the *Book of Job*.

MEANING ACQUISITION

In *Either/Or* and other early esthetic works repetition is a central philosophical motif. But it most often slips in informally, without much fanfare. There is musical repetition and the repetition of the dance. Kierkegaard also uses the example of reading: "The repetition of the reading of a book, of the enjoyment of a work of art, can heighten and in a way surpass the first impression, because one...immerses oneself more deeply in the object and appropriates it more inwardly."[5] In such cases, repetition is linked to meaning-acquisition, to *increasing* stores of sense, stability and life within the world of esthetic appreciation and performance.

Esthetic repetitions can be intensified to illuminate religious themes. The "first immediacy" of art is paralleled by the "second immediacy" of religious experience. Both the knight of faith and the knight of resignation in *Fear and Trembling* perform dance steps, ballet leaps.[6] Kierkegaard warns against conflating esthetic and religious spheres. A merely esthetic reception of biblical texts or Sunday sermons is an all-too-common decadence. Although a religious reception of a text, or of a familiar notion like love, is worlds apart from a merely esthetic reception, both are forms of what Kierkegaard calls "immediacy." In both religious and esthetic consciousness, meaning strikes directly, unmediated by reflective or discursive judgment.[7]

Repetitions animate not only esthetic and religious life, but ethical spheres of life, as well. The esthete in *Either/Or* finds the rhythms and familiar habits of married life a boring prospect. The anticipated novelty of uncommitted café life is a better bet. But Judge Wilhelm frames the daily repetitions of married life quite differently. For him, the repetitions of married life are time when meaning is renewed. Companionship or marriage includes the rhythmic ways of sleep and walks and eager conversation, the returns of familiar griefs and loves and stories. Conceived as richly ceremonial, not *pro forma* gestures, these repetitions actively incorporate and deeply animate our lives.[8]

At a basic level, repetition shapes experience by keeping focal patterns salient against their backgrounds. For example, when working through a difficult line of verse, recognizable words emerge from lettered ink. If they fail to jell as poetic line, they will fall away, lacking sufficient stability or vibrancy to be sustained within a field of meaning. But if instead they crystallize as poetry, then words lift off the page in new relief. The *same* words—and yet restored to life. They are restored, as Kierkegaard would have it, through repetition.[9]

In ways reminiscent of Hegel's account of the dialectical development of ever more satisfying concepts of experience, Kierkegaard makes it essential that repetition not annul or erase the initial perception. For example, the increase in understanding that may occur in hearing the story anew does not replace the story with something else (say, an abstract philosophical doctrine or theoretical interpretation). Meaning is renewed in repetition, not secured through subsumption under a theory, law, or doctrine.[10] But contrary to Hegel, at least as Kierkegaard reads him, when meaning is deepened (rather than trivialized) by repetition, this supplement is conferred by something transcending the first, now deepened experience—not by an uncovering of what was immanent all along in the experience. Repetition brings out supervenient qualities in the look and the reality of things. It marks an uncoercible recognition as some unnamed (and finally transcendent) force crystallizes a new richness in something familiar and quite specific: *this* face before me, *this* melody or mountain pool.

SELF AS CRYSTALLIZED PARTICULAR

An otherwise mostly meaningless natural particular (a random pile of rocks) may acquire meaning through repetition within an esthetic frame (an Ansel Adams portrait of a tallus slope). Or some random particular (a stone) may acquire meaning through repetition within an autobiographical frame (a piece of granite that as a three-year-old I used to jump from). Repetition crystallizes the meaning of particulars by placing them under or within a frame—natural, moral, esthetic, or autobiographical. Persons, selves, or souls are rich, complex particulars crystallized in stories, in narrative frames. *Job* displays a complex deepening of self (or soul) that comes about through repetition and through shifts in enclosing narrative frames.

In "recollecting yourself," he says, you return to your experience, transforming it by "the addition of a sharp," thus repeatedly raising the key signature of the (initial and repeated) melody.[11] The narrative flow of self gets increased in intensity, mood, and timbre. In his *Journals*, he puts it this way: "The presuppositional basis of consciousness, or, as it were, the [musical] key, is continually being raised, but within each key the same thing is repeated."[12] Musical key is "the presuppositional basis" of the field within which melody is played out, varied, and renewed through repetition. The particular selves we are and become may have a constancy of motif (or cluster of motifs) over time which develops through change in the "presuppositional basis" of the pattern of our emerging selves. On this view, change in self is not *primarily* change in "content" or "motif" but change in frames containing or applied *to* a self, as a new key is applied to or "contains" existing musical material.

Let's imagine that central parts—"motifs"—of my biography are in place by age eighteen. The meaning of these motifs nevertheless will change as I change, as the frame of marriage, or middle-age or of age itself supervenes upon these earlier motifs. The reality of my youth looks and in fact is deepened, renewed, as my later life unfolds, Kierkegaard's stage-view of development is an elaborate refinement of this idea. Self attains meaning newly crystallized through stage- or frame-shift, deepened as an ethical-religious frame supervenes upon the life of an esthete.[13] The first truly personal repetition is then the move from esthetic indifference to ethical responsibility for oneself and for manifold relationships with others. The "presuppositional basis of consciousness" undergoes a shift in key. We discover, or receive, the engaged moral self, a self that is exemplary, deep, and rich.

Selves in general might be layered narrative clusters including the several stories we tell ourselves over some span of natural life; these stories themselves are modulated by esthetic, ethical, or religious frames—and including, too, the several stories others might tell of our cares or growths or failings. These "other-generated" stories are also modulated, by esthetic, political, or religious frames. Our "true self" (or soul) would then become the richest, most truthful narrative imaginable: the God's eye view of our particularity swiftly crystallized through the multiple frames and contents of self- and other-generated narratives. Soul would form within the repetition of God's gaze: a freedom-granting, judging, forgiving, loving eye, a telic power or shadowed face in which we find our ground.[14]

The *Book of Job* displays the work of repetition on several levels. Job becomes a particular self and a prototype for others through a development we can describe as repetition's work. The Whirlwind's work of restoring a world to Job can be seen in terms of the imaginative frame-shifts characteristic of repetition. In particular, the final Theophany of the *Book*, the poetic Voice from the Whirlwind, delivers a world of crystallized particulars. Their reception is the world's return for Job, and is the outward sign of his inner restoration. The Epilogue recounts a suspiciously materialistic Hollywood ending, where Job's worldly goods are returned, and even doubled. In contrast to the poetic splendor of the Whirlwind, this folktale ending is one we should not trust, for reasons I give below. Let us turn to Kierkegaard's discussion of Job.

REPETITION AND PROTOTYPE

At the start of his *Discourse*, Kierkegaard reminds us that not all teachers have a teaching: some teach not by leaving doctrine or discovery but by being themselves particulars so meaning-laden as to be prototypes for later generations. Job is such an exemplar. He teaches us ways of loss, struggle, and restoration through living out that cycle.

The utterance that Kierkegaard takes as text, "The Lord gave, and the Lord took away: blessed be the name of the Lord," may be proverbial wisdom, embedded in tradition, and accessible even to a child. But for these words to gain their proper stature they must be more than platitudinous, consolatory proverbial wisdom. It is not enough for these words to be merely honored or promoted or repeated in a touchingly esthetic delivery. However earnest the teaching, lecture, or discourse may appear, these words must be rooted—repeated—in the being of the self who thinks or speaks them. Job must *embody* them in his action, so that words and life become a seamless web, inside and outside of a single fabric: "[T]he statement itself is not the guide, and Job's significance consists not in his having said it, but in his having acted upon it…[I]f someone else had said it, or if Job had been someone else, or if he had said it on another occasion, the saying itself would have become something different."[15] A "prototype" or exemplar is one whose *words and conduct merge over time as a particular of special depth.*

The *Discourse* continues by elaborating the idea of "acting upon" a statement. To act upon these words is not merely conforming one's action to the precept, or adjusting one's life to exemplify the meaning of the words. The crux is "acting in asserting." If the words merely mirror his identity, we would have two particulars—words here, life there—in a symmetrical relationship. But Job is singular and one. By "acting in asserting" the gap between words and who Job is becomes closed.[16] We have a single crystallized particular.

VIRTUE, VISION, AND CHARACTER

The unity of a human life, Job's or our own, comes about through the stability of our virtues as they unfold narratively. But this stability is dialectical because any virtue-based identity is also marked by inherent instability, or discord. This instability, or "fear and trembling" of a developing self is rooted in three features of virtues we pursue.

First, any virtue we embrace creates a painful *gap* between an aspiration or ideal and our actual practice or condition. A fissure of vulnerability appears between where and what we are and what we seek or would be. Second, our embrace or appropriation of any virtue is always partial or by degrees. Therefore, there is always doubt that our commitment is deep, that our understanding is pure, that our grasp is solid. Related to these doubts, there is, third, the experience of destabilizing frame-shifts in our understanding of any virtue. That is, apart from our doubts about our understanding at a given time of some particular virtue, such as love, with maturity we find over and over that our conceptions can undergo sea-change, massive modulation. In these cases the lack of confidence in our grasp of what love amounts to is less a doubt about the detail of the conception than a realization that the conception *in toto* may have to be revised. A Kierkegaardian stage-shift can be taken as a thorough-going revision of the very conception we have of an array of virtues.

A virtue-based identity beckons us to where we would be, and this is partially specified by an inclusive line of sight embracing our ideals. This is moral-religious vision, both the looking or sighting (initiated from our end) and the ideal or sight (received from elsewhere) radiantly or dimly there.

In a good and virtue-saturated life, truths are known, beliefs are fit, desires apt, and action conforms to principle. The additional ingredient of moral vision both locates the moral perspective appropriate to one's situation and highlights one's failings or distance from one's ideals. Kierkegaard shows various ways that Job's response, although still containing the utterance of these words, "The Lord gives, the Lord takes," might nevertheless have failed—through stoicism, for example. The verse Job utters cannot mean for him a resignation that puts all in the hands of a natural Fate. His words must be rooted in a life whose unity is captured in the exemplary vision of *faith*.

Faith means taking the things of the world in a certain manner. In contrast to stoicism, it means taking them as blessed, just as Job blesses the Lord who gives and takes. But how can a man as afflicted as Job is, nevertheless affirm the inexhaustible meaning of the particulars around him, or of the particular he is? As if by design—in fact if we credit the prologue, *by* design—Job's capacity to maintain a faithful vision is put on trial. We can conceive this trial as a battle between two competing frames or visions for understanding suffering and affliction. The battle takes place on many fronts, between Job and his friends; between Job and the Lord; within Job himself; and within us as we read this unsettling, inconvenient scripture. The frame-conflict is between the folkloric prologue and epilogue and the more complex (and profound) central drama, culminating in the Whirlwind's Voice. The moral-religious difference between these frames is this: in the folk tale, all suffering is either deserved or justified in the long run by some sort of restitution, worldly or divine; the poetic central drama denies this misleadingly simple view of suffering. It denies the overly reassuring prosaic moral of the folktale, that in the end all accounts will be fairly squared.

From the start, we know that Job is a well-assimilated, respectable, pious man. We are meant to accept his innocence. How this innocence has been sustained is a matter put beyond our ken. Put otherwise, what repetitions preceded, and so brought about, the crystallizations we confront at the opening of this tale must be taken more or less uncritically as setting up the props for the story about to unfold. Every story or play begins more or less arbitrarily, in the sense that there can never been an exhaustive account of what tale precedes the initially "given" frame. On pain of infinite regress, it starts in the middle of things, amidst a larger, and so untold tale. And from *our* end of things, as readers, we likewise start in the middle of things. This lack of closure on "the total story" for any reader, anytime, does not foreclose the availability of crystallized narrative-encoded meanings available to us here and now.[17]

We might suppose, then, that this innocent, pious and previously untroubled man is now tempted by the commonplace view that somehow his recent terrible afflictions are fair allotments in the cosmic scheme of things. Yet he also knows in his bones that this is false, that there is nothing he has done to deserve this pain. His friends gather to scold and remonstrate. There is no coherent place within *their* assumptions for the fact of undeserved suffering. Either Job is wrong about himself and shields some inner fault, or else the enclosing frame must yield. Job prefers to push the frame in bitter protest. With increasing anger and vehemence, he rebels, rejecting his friends' shameless accusations and calling God to account.[18] "Surely I would speak to the Almighty, And I desire to reason with God" (13.3). He demands a hearing and reasons. The battle to acquire a new vision, a new frame, is underway.

As Job's protest intensifies, the stability of the initial frame is broken. Its final overthrow occurs with the appearance of the Whirlwind's Voice. This marks the raising of Job's consciousness through altering its "presuppositional basis." If Job were merely his successfully assimilated social identity, then his great losses would diminish his identity to zero. What is the good of a faithful servant of the Lord if wealth and home, if children and health, are lost—and if those one took as friends look on with scorn? Job's identity shifts. His consciousness is raised up so that his identity is decidedly not equivalent to his social status and wealth, and cannot rest on the assumption of his friends that he has brought his sufferings upon himself through some fault. But how does this shift, from a stage where he protests his innocence to a stage where he protests no longer, occur? In particular, how can a *Whirlwind* effect such change-in-world—and at what price to Job's freedom?

Here we carry the interpretation of Job beyond the bounds Kierkegaard himself sets in the discourse. But this expansion flows naturally from the groundwork we've laid. Repetition will be the key to the Whirlwind's power to return a world to Job.

IMAGINATION, WHIRLWIND, AND RENEWAL OF PARTICULARS

Frame-shift supervenes. It does not occur at our command. As Kierkegaard has it, Job's soul, through his suffering and rebellion, becomes fertile soil receptive to new growth. But the planting of new fields for him to husband is accomplished by the eloquence of a storm, a wonder carrying its own powers of persuasion. Job must be readied. "The ears of the troubled are formed in a special way"[19] But the Voice is not his own. The storm changes Job by altering his world, by transforming his vision of it through the poetry of the Whirlwind's Voice. The Voice delivers sacred song, the crystallization of new meaning in familiar things.

We might ask whether the Whirlwind is the *cause* of the frame-shift Job undergoes, or rather the *occasion* of the shift—perhaps a celebration of a shift independently caused.[20] But the perceptions, declamations, and questions central to the *Book of Job* belong in the conceptual field of meaning-shift and meaning-acquisition. They fit not at all, or only problematically, in the conceptual field of causes and effects. Kierkegaard's notion of repetition describes a give and take, an ebb and flow in fields of significance and meaning. As in the unfolding of a song, we are interested not in causes but in shifts of mood, timbre, rhythm, and idea. From the standpoint of meaning-shifts or acquisitions, the final Theophany neither causes nor is the occasion of frame-shift. It simply *is* the frame-shift. There is simply no gap between Job's shift in consciousness and the streams of melody from the storm, from the stars. Self and world are simultaneously and reciprocally articulated in magnificent verse.

We can follow meanings as they restore or animate a life independently of knowing what *causes* are at work in such repetitions. The Lord in *Job* is the Source or ground of meaning gained. If additionally he is First Cause, this would need to be argued from the text. And if the text supports the Voice as Cause as well as Source of meaning, then we need a metaphysics or theology wider than the *Book of Job* provides. Next, we'd need to look outside the text. We'd need scaffolding for a structure broader and more intricate than either the causal or the meaning-nexus alone. For we need a scheme or structure rich enough to coordinate each meaning or meaning nexus with (or within) its causal partners. Do we have an inkling what such an encompassing scheme would be like?[21]

In a slightly different context, Charles Taylor has contrasted "relations of subsumption" (where an event to be understood is subsumed under a rule or causal law) with "relations of renewal" (where something to be understood is "carried through" or "renewed" in a field of wider events).[22] He claims these two sorts of relations map incompatible routes to understanding.

Applying this contrast in the present case, the Whirlwind's Voice is not the *cause* of something, or itself caused, an element subsumed under a causal web. Instead, the Voice is a revision or repetition or renewal of themes already present in the wider context of the *Book of Job*. The Whirlwind spins out something that in retrospect is waiting behind the false words of the "friends," behind the insistence of Job's protest, behind the speeches of Elihu. The Voice comes alive, is understood, through establishing "links of renewal." These links are forged through interpretation, through placement of the Voice within the larger tale of Job (and within the larger story of our humanity) in such a way that meaning jells. As poetic verse springs from simple ink, so the Voice sings forth the consummatory vision that it is.

When Job confronts the Whirlwind, it is not quite his *moral* imagination or sensibility (narrowly construed) that is activated, nor quite his *esthetic* sensibility or imagination (again, if narrowly construed).[23] It is his *religious* imagination (or sensibility) that is energized.

Knowing what we must do, what reality demands of us, or even seeing that a world has been conferred, presupposes that our sensibilities, whether personal or moral or religious, have been activated. They are activated not just by a belief or by a feeling, as familiar theories of moral motivation might claim. Rather, it is imagination as a dynamic unity of belief and feeling, a full-fledged sensibility, that presents paths that beckon, alternatives with allure, voices of inescapable requirement, and capacity to receive world-conferral.[24]

In verse after verse of unrelenting majestic power, the Voice recounts the music of creation. Job can now share the Lord's righteous pride, awe, and amazed delight in this display. By calling out the wonder, the inexhaustible richness of *this* hawk, *this* shower of hail, *this* necklace of distant stars, the Whirlwind crystallizes their particularity with a force Job cannot resist. He yields. Misery no longer floods his consciousness. In this, the blessing earlier conveyed *to* the Lord is now *returned*. Job gets back a world.

Job is given repetition of what he already knew. Had he not observed the sea or sky or land before? It is renewed now under the frame of inescapable grandeur and power, symbolized by the depth of the sea or the power of the ox. This frame thoroughly displaces the overall assumption of universal justice in worldly punishments and rewards and delivers a reality so rich in meaning as to overwhelm his sense of suffering:

> Can you command the dawn?
> Like clay the form of things is changed by it,
> They stand forth, as if clothed with ornament.[25]

Job comes to *see* the form of things dawn anew, clothed in ornament.

This sight is reassuring, a glimpse of truth or reality, not just an exposure of his weakness before raw power. Harrison nicely captures this moment of perception on Job's part through a paraphrase of the Lord's massive declamation. At least in one stream, he means to say: "I made the world and *it is real*: truth and falsity mean something in the sense of being beyond human wishes and conventions ..."[26] Job's outrage is not simply crushed, for a new frame replaces the old. This frame-shift is a move *away* from consciousness awaiting explanations or arguments, and *toward* consciousness receptive to the inexhaustible meaning of particulars. It is not a step in argument or explanation. In fact it completely sidesteps Job's demand for argument or explanation. The change in consciousness marks a change in framing assumptions, or a change in world. In terms of logic, the Lord completely changes the subject. Initially, this appears illegitimate, dialectically. But perhaps changing the subject is a permissible move if discussion otherwise deadlocked is thereby moved toward the good. In any case, this much is clear, that after the Whirlwind's appearance Job no longer finds his suffering bright-lit and centerstage. It retreats to shadows in the wings.

Job's freedom is not diminished by some tyrannical power play from above. He rises up, tears his robe, and shaves his head. In these responsive gestures, in his later bitter interrogations of the Lord, and in his final recognition of his blindness, his "repentance" in dust and ashes, we have Job's free responsiveness, not blunt obedience to coercive power. Kant, perhaps more than any other philosopher, articulates our modern concept of moral freedom and autonomy. When he praises Job's integrity before the Lord, he has in mind at least Job's honesty in confronting the circumstances he endures, and Job's refusing servile acceptance of his pain as punishment.[27] Job is correct to rise up, reason passionately for his view, and demand reasons from the Lord.

Although the Lord respects Job's honest avowal of his innocence, He is unconcerned with, or finds ultimately absurd, the human wish that all human suffering be entered in the legal record, gathered for some trial in the near or distant future, at which point those harmed undeservedly will be awarded full remedy. Job is wrong to take the sphere of justice as the *ultimate and only* way his afflicted life can honestly be understood. Job initially supposes that there *is* a court both to hear one's complaint and to provide remedy for injustice or an account of why one's suffering is deserved. If there is no such court, or no access to it, then some suffering, however terrible and undeserved, will not be subject to redress, will remain beyond accounts—and beyond the frame, beyond the consciousness, from which the "friends" reside and speak.

UNJUST SUFFERING AND THEODICY

The *Gospels*, we might say, add to the Joban sense of creation's raw and variegated power a supplementary promise of comfort for those who suffer undeservedly, without thereby necessarily reintroducing a final court of appeal. It is commonly assumed that the *Book of Job* provides an answer to the horrors of Job's suffering, a response or verdict from the standpoint of a divine court in terms of justice or fairness. But Job's sufferings aren't answered in these terms. Let me fill this out.

Consider the resonance of Job's suffering with the suffering the esthete lives through—and the storm he anticipates—in the book called *Repetition*. *Repetition's* young man is romantically afflicted, and from his plight calls out to Job for comfort. This would-be modern Job (as the esthete no doubt presumptuously takes himself to be) seeks a "repetition," a restoration. He seeks the object of his unrequited love. Were he to attain the repetition he seeks, however, at most *poetic* justice would be done. We may be thankful if we have received love enough, and sad if it is lacking. But there are no obvious legal remedies of justice for love lost (although justice may be invoked in protest of intentional harm). Not everything we seek or need is owed to us by principles of fairness or desert. More important, even if we could conceive of a just remedy for one deprived of love, the case of Job is not the "poetic injustice" of unrequited love.

Crediting the prologue to the *Book of Job*, Job suffers because the Lord unjustly *uses* Job, under provocation of an accuser. Job's suffering occurs, as the introductory folktale has it, because the Lord feels compelled to make a point to a third party. The Lord is taunted in this courtroom scene with the accusation that his "faithful servant" Job is faithful only because he has so far escaped true suffering. Unleash some torment upon him, and surely Job will disavow his faith!—or so the accuser suggests. The Lord accepts this challenge, and allows Job to suffer terribly. He must prove to a skeptical prosecutor that Job will be faithful despite his undeserved afflictions. Whether or not that point is made no subsequent rewards can right the balance in moral terms on Job's behalf. His is *innocent* suffering.

The restoration of Job's world cannot show, after all is said and done in light of his rewards, that Job's suffering becomes morally *justified*. This holds whether we take the restoration to occur with the poetic outpouring of the Whirlwind, or more superficially, with the folktale prose ending that has Job's material wealth restored twofold. The latter "repetition" is superficial in moral terms precisely because Job's indignation is so obviously *not* answered by the epilogue. That Job is justified in his protest cannot be obscured by a belated and inadequate "payoff" in restored wealth.

Whether God is fair or just in permitting Job's suffering is fiercely debated in the *Book*. So it is natural to expect that this question of justice will be finally answered. And it is but a short step from this expectation to the presumption that the Lord's final appearance in the Whirlwind and the epilogue in fact displays the justice that Job seeks. But the Lord does not at last address the question of suffering in these terms. Job is given meaning in his world but *not* along the lines he sought. There is no attempt at explanation why his suffering is fair or just. Instead, we see Job's consciousness deeply altered in ways that bypass the *need* for explanation, and that make the issue of his suffering cease to press.

Theodicy, defined as answering the question of God's justice, is set aside. Of course, forgoing theodicy is not to urge that when all is said and done God is *unjust*. It is putting aside the frame of mind preoccupied with the question whether God is just or unjust. Such preoccupation may be innocently misplaced, because the issue can never be given a satisfactory resolution. Or such preoccupation may itself be morally harmful. The moral danger of attempting a theodicy is that a sweeping justification of all suffering, in the nature of the case, must appear patronizing and insensitive to those who suffer. Furthermore, it threatens to distract us from a morally more pressing concern: how to respond sensitively, fully and without presumption, to those who are afflicted. There are frequent warnings in the Job Discourse against a presumptuous search for *explanation*—where instead a simple moral-religious *response* to suffering is called for.[28]

In summary, the *Book* does not explain (and thereby risk the evil of passing off as "justified") the reality of unjust suffering. Hence it offers us no verdict (from the divine point of view, and along the lines of fairness) either on the massive whole of human experience or on the more extensive range of what lies beyond the pale. Judgments of fairness are reserved for select parts within the pale. In *Job* the question of God's acquittal before the highest court remains unresolved, perhaps even respectfully but decisively rejected on grounds of impropriety. And I take it that in this regard Kierkegaard's *Repetition* and Job Discourse remain true to their original.

To make sense of Job's loss, his protest, and the restoration of his world, we need a supplementary set of orienting coordinates: the familiar axes of justice and injustice—justice challenged, justice restored—will not do. The coordinates of Kierkegaardian repetition provide a key. Meaning is challenged, then restored. Job is caught within an untidy plurality of frames that challenge his identity and his world. In "repetition," we watch frameworks shift from bewilderment to resignation to righteous indignation. And we see these shifts culminate not in a hoped-for renewal of justice but in a human vulnerability, a suffering. But this is a suffering whose ache is mitigated. Job is quieted, shuddering before powers that both renew a world and break the tides of misery.

TRANSCENDENCE AND IMAGINATION

The Otherness of the Whirlwind's Voice marks the supervenient phase of meaning-acquisition, and leads us naturally to the plane of transcendence. As Kierkegaard has it in *Repetition*, "Transcendence is at the borders of the wondrous."[29] M. Jamie Ferreira provides insight on such religious transcendence, "the wondrous," and the frame-shifts that occur in repetition:

> The need for transcendence refers then not merely to the transcending vision of imagination—the vision which goes beyond what is given and succeeds in being inclusive. It refers also to a transcending of imaginative vision itself, as mere vision. The transcendence which is contrasted with [in Kierkegaard's phrase] *circumnavigating the self* can thus be understood partly in terms of otherness as such…and partly in terms of transcending the imaginative contemplation of possibilities. Transcendence in the latter case issues in a doing rather than merely a vision.[30]

This passage suggests several sectors or levels of imagination's link to transcendence—or alternatively, sectors of transcendence itself, accessed through imagination.

The transcendent is what transcends our immediate context—as imagination opens possibilities for understanding or action that transcend the actual position we're in. Such possibilities might be relatively idle, fanciful. We can call this first level (or sector) the "imaginative contemplation of possibilities." Cultivating this sector is the preoccupation of the Kierkegaardian esthete, who imaginatively reviews pictures of the self he is or might have been or could become—enjoying snapshots, as it were. But this brand of imaginative transcendence or distance yields only a tourist's view: dreamy ruminations that are relatively removed from active life-engagements. We'd have a pleasant, even witty or nostalgic, circumnavigation of the self.

But imagination is also the field within which one can sort fanciful possibilities from "live options," the latter marking out a second sector of the transcendent. Here we are presented with paths to be seriously considered preliminary to action. Moving on within imagination we have a third sector, not of possibilities that are "live options" but of brute necessities, demands that bear down upon us, transcendent values that confront us as unequivocal requirements.[31] Here, the transcendent is the source of a value-frame that gets applied *to* our given context, calling for decision. We know we *must* do this, or *can't* do that.

Reviewing the passage above, a fourth sector of the transcendent appears where "*mere* vision," as the contemplation of possibilities, whether as fancies or as "live options," is itself transcended. As subjects we are confronted "in terms of *otherness as such*." I propose that "otherness as such" is experienced as *world-conferral*. Interpreting "otherness as such" in this way expands Ferreira's account. She writes: "Note that for Kierkegaard the 'other' we are called upon to appreciate imaginatively and respond to is as much within us as outside us—the other is fundamentally the self we are to become when we are called to become what we are."[32] In *Job*, the otherness confronted must resonate within us, as well as sounding "outside us," as Ferreira points out. But insofar as "otherness as such" is linked to world-conferral, the "other" we respond to is more than "self." What Job confronts as "other" is not "the self he is to become" but the empowering and mysterious Ground of what he is to become. It is a presence far transcending any conventional notion of self-identity, self-presence, or the self one will become. "Otherness as such" is not a crystallized particular.

The Whirlwind's Voice is a primary candidate for exemplifying imagination's access to this final sector, for it represents neither ideal possibility nor live option nor a necessary demand for action on Job's part. It presents reality restored, a world renewed *in toto*.

DEMANDS, WILLS BENT, AND WORLDS CONFERRED

Response to a transcendent demand may change a world, as in the case of God's demand for Isaac, or in the demand made on the esthete by Judge Wilhelm to "choose yourself," or in the Socratic demand to examine one's life. If a person's world is changed by these demands, such world-change is at least partially effected through the hard labor of an agent's particular response to these demands. Both self-choice and self-examination present a daunting *task* for the receptive individual. But the Whirlwind does not present Job with a task or a demand for action.

We can clarify the contrast between response to a demand and conferral of an entire world by linking repetition to limits and to will: "Only where there is limit can one come back, demand back or seek again...where we demand back, we effectively set a limit."[33] Coming back, getting home, is a return to familiar bounded things, even if these particulars, as Kierkegaard takes it, are gifts from beyond a bounded world. And demanding back asserts our limits, sets the limits of our tolerance for things unframed, beyond the pale. Demanding too much, exceeding the limit of what we can properly demand, we find our will rebuked, bent back.

Ferreira mentions *coming* back, *demanding* back, and *seeking* again. Wanting or willing plays a different role in each of these modes of repetition. An esthete may want to *come* back to an experience in order to relive it. This is close to *seeking* the experience again. Surely Job both seeks and *demands* that some sense be restored to his existence.

If I *come* back, success rests importantly on my *decision* to return. In contrast, if I *seek* return, success may be less a matter of my will than of external factors, circumstances, or obstacles. Finally, if I *demand* back, success depends on the *will* of *another*. Can we locate the Whirlwind's Voice as falling within one of these modes of repetition?

First, it is the *Voice* that effects renewal of a world. The world's return is not *Job's* coming back or doing, or Job's *resolve* to get back the familiar. In contrast, my effort and resolve surely are at work as I respond to the Socratic injunction "Know thyself!" or to the Judge's "Choose thyself!" or "Receive thyself!" Meaning flows not from Job but from Another.

In his Discourse, Kierkegaard warns against "the eloquence of horror"—the speaker, we might suppose, being more concerned in such a case with *his* quite moving rhetorical eloquence than with the actual horrors of the other's suffering.[34] So, too, it seems appropriate that the eloquence from the Whirlwind, the eloquence not of horror but of wonder or of "immensity," should be delivered not from Job's lips, but from a source that is Another. Job honors realities he cannot presume to voice himself—realities that include but also poetically outstrip our narrowly encoded conventional meanings.

Second, Job's getting his world returned is only problematically related to his *seeking* or *demanding* restoration. He fails utterly to get *what* he seeks or demands, that is, an *explanation* for his plight. The world's return is not dependent on his power of resolve or on his resources for world-production. It is dependent on his vulnerability to world-reception. The world's return is transcendentally bestowed.

Let's distinguish between the "how" and the "what" of Job's seeking and demanding. It is plausible that the Lord responds to Job's integrity, to *how* Job pursues his case. He responds to the *fact* that Job questions, and to the fact that he *abjures* other alternatives. But the Lord does not respond to the "what" of Job's demand. The substance of Job's demand is for an account of why he, Job, suffers. But he is not given this account. Job's integrity is displayed in *how* he pursues his case, alone and on his own behalf.

If I seek or demand something rightfully mine, and a neighbor acknowledges my demand by restoring it, I can be said to have bent my neighbor's will through my demand. But perhaps, even though I demand the return of my ladder, my neighbor returns it because she has no more use for it, and it clutters her yard. My demand for its return is then relatively incidental to my getting it back. Her will is not bent. Or suppose that she is indignant at my demand, and responds by throwing it back on my porch, destroying a railing. Again, her will is unbent, though a demand and a return are linked. If the ladder is thrown back, the return has a twist. I get back my ladder, but more importantly, her will is bent on bending *my* will.

So with Job. He demands. He gets back. And his getting back is related to his seeking and his demands. Although Job has not bent God's will, God responds to Job's will. Yet He doesn't answer Job's demands. In getting back his world, Job's will is bent. But unlike the case of the ladder thrown, the bending or the melting of Job's will is not destructive but restorative. The power that smites or quiets him is the power that returns his world. The power that empties his will makes space for the reception of a cosmos wondrously stocked with richly crystallized particulars.

Job's will to argue is surely humbled as he confronts an overwhelming natural and supernatural force. His will is quiet, but quiet before the great height of starry skies, the wildness of sea-beasts, the wonder of sleet and dew and sunrise, the raw might of a bull, the gentle curve of *this* hawk in flight. All this is his world, as much as suffering is. And as these splendors reappear, his eyes now see where before he had been blind. His protest melts away, settles in dust and ashes before the grandeur of a world returned in terms eclipsing pain.

Job's final words, including his "repentance in dust and ashes," are often translated from the Hebrew in ways that make the image of a servile, broken spirit all but inescapable: "I abhor ('abase,' 'despise') myself, and repent ('recant') in dust and ashes."[35] But neither the original text nor the dramatic context require anything approaching the sort of self-loathing, shame, or humiliation contained in these versions of his closing utterance. These lines have been rendered equally, and much more plausibly, in terms that erase the image of a self-abhorring Job, finally broken by brute power. In awe, he is "dissolved ('emptied,' 'smitten')." Before the power of the storm. As before the power of great music, he stops, confesses: "I melt away ('am quiet') in dust and ashes."[36]

Repetition is bestowed. And the Lord has shown that Job's demand, in this, the *last* analysis of suffering, is beside the point. Job has not demanded his fortune returned. He has demanded reasons. "Surely, I would speak to the Almighty, And I desire to reason with God." (13.3) Job is denied reasons. "Who is this that darkeneth counsel by words without knowledge?" (38.2) And Job is given more than fortune and more than reasons. He is given understanding. This occurs as he is given a new world, a world in which reasons and fortune are differently framed, and have acquired new meanings, more precious than before.

FAITH AND SIMPLE SHOPMEN
Fear and Trembling: One

[I]t is advantageous (to morality) to "work out one's salvation with fear and trembling," a hard saying which if misunderstood is capable of driving a man to the black-
est fanaticism.

– Immanuel Kant[1]

Crimes and Misdemeanors, A WOODY ALLEN FILM, HAS A RATHER EASYGOING
meditation on Abraham. An elderly "Professor Levy" appears on a TV monitor,
apparently in the middle of an interview or lecture. He wonders out loud how
the God who introduced us to a moral universe based on care could so quickly
turn uncaring, demanding that Abraham sacrifice his son. His worries, delivered
in a thick Eastern-European accent, are put this way: "The unique thing that
happened to the early Israelites was that they could see a God that cares. But here
comes the paradox. What's one of the first things that that God asks? That God
asks Abraham to sacrifice his only son to him." Apparently the biblical story is
flawed—or we are flawed—and the failure is of imagination, for he continues,
"…[I]n spite of millennia of efforts, we have not succeeded to create a really and
entirely loving image of God—this was beyond our capacity to imagine." This is
a doubtful approach to the Abraham-Isaac story.[2] But whatever we may think
of it, the film reminds us that Abraham is still an issue, at least for Woody Allen
and his viewers—not just a problem for Kierkegaard, or for the imaginative and
quirky "freelance" writer, Johannes de silentio, whom Kierkegaard produces as
the pseudonymous author of *Fear and Trembling*.

There are clear similarities between the ordeal of Abraham and Job's ordeal.
Kierkegaard had both in mind at this stage in his authorship, publishing his "Job
Discourse," *Repetition* (replete with allusions to Job) and *Fear and Trembling* nearly
simultaneously. Job discovers, or rediscovers, that the simple moral scheme of
divine rewards and punishments adopted by his friends is false. The God of
Abraham, too, puts conventional morality at risk. It is not as if God were asking
for an ear of corn. The ordeals of both Job and Abraham raise skeptical questions
that are nearly impossible to set aside. Perhaps Job is merely broken, a victim of
raw power rather than one who undergoes a transformation where receptivity
to the wonders of creation displaces ordinary questions of justice, rewards, and
punishments. And perhaps, in his readiness to sacrifice his son, Abraham is not

the hero or knight of faith that Johannes de silentio so admires, but rather a hor-rifying relic "we moderns" must unequivocally dismiss. In the following two chapters, I wish to pursue specific themes that have been raised by critics of my earlier work on *Fear and Trembling*.[3] I begin with the role of the pseudonym, Johannes de silentio.

JOHANNES AS ARTIST

Fear and Trembling is a complex narrative that engages a number of dialectical issues. In fact, Johannes de silentio subtitles his work "A dialectical lyric." Kierkegaard presents Johannes as an artist and dialectician attempting to come to terms with the Abraham story. How can he comprehend a figure who alter-nately dazzles and dismays him?

Johannes must express his deepest convictions, not so much regarding what Abraham should do, but about what the figure he confronts amounts to, what Abraham can mean to him.[4] He works to display and relieve the tensions between taking Abraham as a murderer and taking him as the father of faith. He has the privilege of leisure and disengagement which is denied Abraham. This allows Johannes to try out different scenarios for fit, finding the one that best captures the moral-spiritual mood or attitude or stance his subject Abraham evokes.

In an early section of *Fear and Trembling* titled "Attunement," Johannes warms his poetic and dialectical sensibilities to meet the task. He readies himself for a response adequate to his subject, Abraham, and to the lyrical and dialectical stan-dards of his craft, standards which he holds dear. He needn't decide what would be right for *him* to do in Abraham's place. In any case, God will not appear to him as he appeared to Abraham. His job is to deepen and clarify a picture of Abraham in his ordeal.

Although he is clearly an artist and thinker, Johannes calls himself "not a philosopher" but a "freelancer."[5] He warns us not to expect a finished System, or the promise of one, in the bits and pieces of his work. Despite Johannes's dis-tancing himself from presenting simple doctrine and the clear evidence of his imaginative literary engagement—looking at the story first from this angle, then from another—there is an inevitable urge to rush headlong to dispute Johannes's philosophical theory. But where *is* this doctrine or thesis?

About one-third of the way through *Fear and Trembling*, a central question is raised. Can ethics ever be legitimately suspended—in deference to a religious command? This question appears only after a preface, an "Attunement" section, where Johannes sketches four versions of the Abraham story in which Abraham would fail as the father of faith, and an extended "Speech in Praise of Abraham," where Johannes struggles with his role as a writer reporting on such a complex phenomenon as Abraham. The question whether ethics can be suspended is fur-ther delayed by a lengthy and lyrical "Preamble from the Heart," which contrasts the stance of resignation of worldly loves with the more complex stance of faith. So the issue whether a "teleological suspension of ethics" is possible turns out not to be the first thing on Johannes's mind.

Philosophers or theologians are understandably eager to get their teeth into the question of Abraham's deference to God's command. But this threatens to make the issue of a suspension of ethics the single bone of interpretative contention. However, if the bulk of *Fear and Trembling* skirts this "thesis," then perhaps it is not the book's paramount concern, or not its single concern. Why not take the "Preface," "Attunement," "Speech in Praise of Abraham," and "Preamble from the Heart" as serious investigations, allowing their musical, lyrical strains to register a dialectic of questions or ideas? We can shed the ascetic stance that makes poetic reflection an unfortunate or merely ornamental distraction.

Is it trivial to ask, as Johannes does, how a poet can commemorate his hero without upstaging him, or how mere words of praise can save a hero for eternity? Is it merely small talk to ask, as Johannes does, how so many words can be spun about a hero who is in some sense unintelligible—beyond any adequate account? Johannes poetically invents a jaunty shopkeeper knight of faith. Is it of no deep concern how both Abraham and shopkeepers can be knights of faith? Why does silence shroud the knight of faith? Avoiding the poet's task of capturing the full scene in dialectical lyric leaves these questions, much the heart of *Fear and Trembling*, under dust, forgotten.

What lyrical-dialectical light Johannes can shed comes through imaginative narrative portraits, spread out as variations on a suite of themes. As Kierkegaard has Johannes tell and retell the Abraham tale, we are lead imaginatively through corridors of the moral self sequestered from easy public view or assessment. We probe the subjectivity of the self. And to probe these obscure regions we resort to sketches, to metaphor and narrative. We invent and develop figures of speech, illuminative parables. We tell "Just So" stories, and toss off passing "folk theories."

Though these portraits and poetic explorations are dialectically related, they can not be reduced to simple doctrine, or pro and con arguments. Abraham and his variants are situated figures midway in a journey. Articulating what Abraham is about occurs through articulating his environing world. At key junctures Abraham must keep his gaze outward on the conflicting requirements of his context, not just inward on his convictions or on his freedom. Likewise, Johannes, at key junctures, must look outward toward his hero, toward his would-be exemplar, not inward toward his wants, interests, or convictions. Articulation of conviction, inwardness, or identity comes about through attention to something both outer and other than itself.

The Whirlwind at the close of the *Book of Job* presents a poetic, lyrical vision of convictions in transition. In the present case, the way to probe Abraham's frame of mind is to sketch the turmoil he is undergoing. The illuminations these dialectical narratives cast are not statements lined up as steps in a juridical argument, or as considerations leaning toward a judgment. They do not add up to a verdict we might recommend to "any rational, reasonably well-informed agent (or spectator)."

Adopting Charles Taylor's phrase again, we could say that these portraits and elaborations persuade not by establishing relations of derivation or subsumption but by establishing relations of renewal.[6] From this viewpoint, moral change (and the practical reasoning involved in understanding such change) is a special sort of renewing transition. Such understanding, Taylor claims, is rooted in "biographical narrative," where we understand change in self and self-conception retrospectively. As Kierkegaard might put it, such understanding of transitions is displayed through dialogue between exemplars of moral-religious standpoints. Kierkegaard's development of this point through a pseudonymous authorship is a major innovation. It is a lasting contribution, we could say, to metaethics.[7]

Let me pause to make two further points about Johannes's lyrical approach to Abraham's subjectivity. First, it does not entail a nihilistic subjectivity of "anything goes." Johannes the artist knows the likelihood that he may be mistaken in knowing what Abraham is really about. Whatever the artist's degree of confidence or conviction, he is also persistently open to a critical self-scrutiny.

Johannes de silentio aims to bring out Abraham's inwardness, to establish, as Taylor would put it, the "first-person" point of view in moral dialogue, encouraging it in one's own case and for one's interlocutors, as well. To make a subjective standpoint explicit, or as explicit as can be, opens the possibilities for serious engagement. A commitment to articulating personal visions is not endorsing a shallow subjectivity that leads to isolation or self-defeating contradiction. As Stephen Mulhall puts it, from this commitment

> it doesn't follow…that such personal visions can only have meaning or validity for the person who creates them. Insofar as they are articulated in a natural language, they are in principle open to the comprehension of others; and insofar as they are articulated with the aim of deepening our understanding of a particular moral source, their creator has a vested interest in striving to avoid the merely subjective—formulations in which all that she is really talking about is herself or the idiosyncratic quirks of her experience.[8]

Neither does such emphasis on subjectivity preclude moral agreement or consensus. Taylor speaks of shared "horizons of significance" that make serious moral dialogue possible.[9] And Mulhall expands this point: "[When] judgements of…relative moral worth are…indexed to a personal biography [as Taylor claims], then even when another moral agent is brought to agree with them, that agreement should be seen as mediated by the confluence of two individual perspectives rather than consisting in the joint recognition of a perspective-independent reality."[10] This, as we have seen, is related to Kierkegaard's insistence on a reader's responsibility for interpreting the subjectivity of the figure presented, as well as her own position, by her own best lights. Kierkegaard interposes neither the impersonal authority of logic, nor an impersonal reason. Nor does he interpose his own authority as somehow holding the master evaluative key to a figure's moral-religious sensibility, its adequacies or its deficiencies.

The second point about Johannes's approach is this. The moral-religious arena is wide and complex, never reducible as a general matter to the personal alone. Even though Johannes may find Abraham at a personal impasse, there are better and worse ways of getting through that impasse. He may be hard pressed to articulate Abraham's way of resolving his situation, but not everyone has achieved Abraham's moral maturity. Only those who have gained the plateau of the ethical, on Kierkegaard's view, are in a position to undergo a spiritual trail where a personal, "subjective" decision is called for. A compulsive shoplifter, or someone prone to lash out angrily at the smallest provocation, would be flat wrong to construe their situation as calling for an expression of their deepest convictions—that is, an occasion to steal or lash out in anger. As Johannes de silen-tio puts it, the knight of faith cannot be "a straggler or vagrant genius."[11] Later, in *Concluding Unscientific Postscript*, Johannes Climacus adds that the sort of personal suffering the religious soul must undergo is off-limits to a "robber, thief or mur-derer."[12] Straightforward, universal moral prohibitions apply here unproblem-atically. The moral-religious life is not exclusively a matter of subjective resolve, and Kierkegaard's artist-dialecticians know this.

KNIGHTS AND SIMPLE SHOPMEN

Johannes de silentio provides numerous sketches of Abraham. But he also tries his hand at sketching quite ordinary unterrifying exemplars of faith. He introduces faithful housemaids, professors, and ordinary shopmen—folk who do not *look* like "knights of faith." And they seem to cope without taking great moral or religious risks. *They* do not confront demands to sacrifice their sons. Yet they truly are such knights, despite the fact that they pass unnoticed.

There is a comic interlude early on in *Fear and Trembling* where Johannes de silen-tio unveils this unassuming sort of knight. "Here he is. The acquaintance is struck. I am introduced. The moment I first set eyes on him, I thrust him away, jump back, clasp my hands together and say half-aloud, "Good God, is this the person, is it really him? He looks like a tax-gatherer!" Yet it is indeed him."[13] He looks like just another tradesman. But Johannes assures us that he is a knight of faith, and imagines a simple test to make the point.

The shopman journeys not to Mt. Moriah but simply home from work. On this trek he pictures the tasty meal awaiting him. If he should be denied the feast, he would resign himself to its loss. He would not bewail his fate. From earlier accounts, we recognize that this resignation is not enough. Because he has faith, the shopman also believes he will get his meal back even as he resigns himself to its loss! This was what made Abraham the father of faith. It was not enough that he resign Isaac, that he sacrifice his son. That moral-religious "movement" had to be accompanied by a simultaneous trust that Isaac would be returned. It is this "second movement," a belief in "repetition" or restoration, that is crucial to the faith Johannes de silentio admires.

We have seen how Job has his world restored, earning a "repetition" despite his great suffering. And Abraham must have trust that Isaac will be restored, even as he raises up his knife. But a shopman trusting that his meal will be there—is this a wicked *parody* of faith? Perhaps Johannes is tossing us a distraction. Yet I think this comic interlude and other allusions to unterrifying knights of faith are serious in intent.

Johannes approaches the gap between knights "visible" and "invisible" by degrees. The story of unrequited love in "Preamble from the Heart" recounts the suffering of a young man who, like Job and Abraham, faces devastating loss. He must resign all hope of winning his princess, his eternal love. This tale does not represent the full suffering of faith, however. It is only an intermediate case. The lad can resign his love (as Abraham resigns Isaac), but he cannot make faith's essential *second* movement. He cannot believe his princess will be returned. He becomes a "knight of infinite resignation" but still a step behind the knight of faith.

We can vary the case, imagining the afflicted youth is blessed with true faith. He not only resigns his love, but also believes in its return "on the strength of the absurd." Nevertheless, he would look pale beside Abraham, because Abraham must "suspend the ethical," act in apparent defiance of parental love of Isaac (even as he loves Isaac and hopes for his return). However the lad could believe in the return of his beloved without suspending ethics. So his ordeal would remain easier than Abraham's, even if he had faith. *Ethically*, there will be nothing outrageous in his faith.

Then we encounter shopmen knights. What is required of such "invisible knights" is a willingness to resign worldly things believing they will be restored. "Invisible knights" seem improbable because on the surface they are so ordinary, so unlike Abraham. Nevertheless, they serve a crucial purpose. They challenge the view that faith requires doing something morally outrageous in blind obedience.

Abraham's terrifying readiness to act shocks us alive as no shopkeeper's faithful virtue could. Yet as Johannes Climacus warns in the *Postscript*, there may be something deceptive in *Fear and Trembling*'s terrifying "outward shriek." That shriek, intensified as we complete the journey to the mountain and confront the upraised knife, deafens us to more telling but quieter motivational phenomena, what Johannes Climacus calls the "abyss of inwardness."[14]

Faithful shopkeepers remind us not to be distracted by the "shriek" of an upraised knife. Abraham then becomes a figure journeying through the "abyss of inwardness." Probing this abyss is testing the quality of an ethical-religious stance, scanning and refining the depths of inward discord and resolve. As Kant has it, the only thing good without exception is the moral will, not any sacred list of moral dos and don'ts, or calculation of social outcomes. The arena of this moral will is deep and hidden, difficult to decipher or to judge.

Job's inwardness is eloquently voiced in speech after speech addressed both to his "comforters" and to God, while Abraham's inwardness is starkly *unvoiced*. Not until Johannes poetically *gives* him inwardness can we begin to sense what might lie within.

Through a series of lyrical thought-experiments, Abraham's journey becomes dream-like, an image waiting to be read. In "Attunement," we hear this journey to the mountain through the clouded memory of an old man, a man who muses on a tale he heard in childhood. Then, still in the vein of "once upon a time," this man finds himself moved to spin further tales upon this tale. Later Johannes wonders lyrically at "invisible" shopkeeping knights of faith. If Kant and Kierkegaard are right, if *this* is where our moral-religious gaze should rest, then housemaids and other hidden knights of faith can be preferred to the distracting "shriek" of Abraham's anticipated deed.

As Johannes will unveil it, the story is a chilling metaphor for movement away from a simple "outward" code morality toward a more complex moral stance where purity of heart, purity of will, becomes the central focus. It is a metaphor of transformation any person can (and should) undergo, not a test reserved for heroes. Serving maids and shopmen can undergo inner struggles in the midst of which it may seem to them that codes are broken, that civic virtue falls flat, that ethics and moral identity are at risk *en masse*. And it may seem even to them that

God opposes ethics. But it is an illusion that God shatters all ethics, however bold Johannes is in luring us toward this fiction. In the end, Johannes brings us back to ethics properly understood, to a "post-suspension ethics" that is not at odds with the divine.

KANT AND INWARDNESS

In *Conflict of the Faculties*, Kant considers a father who thinks that God requires the sacrifice of his son.[15] In this passing allusion to Abraham, Kant assumes that Abraham hallucinates, for religion cannot be allowed to supersede morality. For Johannes de silentio, however, an Abraham who hesitates or doubts that God has spoken will be a failed Abraham. But the matter is not as simple as deciding which of two domains, the religious or ethical, is highest. Kierkegaard has not simply inverted Kant, making religion supersede morality.

God expects Abraham to love Isaac unreservedly, so Abraham's parental love is as much a *religious* as an ethical requirement.[16] And Abraham's love of God involves the *moral* expectation that God will keep his promise that through Isaac Abraham shall become father of a people. The religious and the moral are not easily severed, even in the context of *Fear and Trembling*.

Abraham faces conflicting demands—the demand to love Isaac, and the demand to obey God; and he faces conflicting expectations—the expectation that Isaac will be lost, and the expectation that Isaac will be returned. This describes a transition within an ethical-religious sphere. A *kind* of ethics gets dethroned while a superior, more complex sort gets installed. A "teleological suspension of ethics," in this view, focuses a moment of conflict in our *conception* of ethics. The demand for Isaac becomes the occasion of a gestalt-shift. If not its jus-tification, the *intelligibility* of this need for a shift in orientation would be redeemed—retrospectively in terms of the richness of the shift effected.[17] Only having worked *through* the transitional crisis, would we be in a position to under-stand the "contradictions" inherent at the moment of transition.

If the "contradictions" of transition are initially rendered as the opposition of familial and religious duty, this can be seen as heuristic and experimental, a mat-ter of elaborating a moral and religious psychology rather than constructing a social ethics. The Abraham story neither depicts a civil, political, or legal con-flict, nor asks how public moral codes accommodate the sort of crisis the story depicts, nor how a municipal judge would handle problem cases where duties collide. Johannes's task is to understand the hidden labyrinths of a faithful soul.

In an offhanded comment in *Either/Or*, Judge Wilhelm reflects on an issue par-allel to Abraham's dilemma. He reflects on benevolent parricide in pre-literate tribes, deciding that moral assessment should rest on the quality of inward virtue, not on outward conduct. The question is whether the children, in these cases of apparent murder, have the *intention* to help their parents.[18] Tribal sacrifice, in his view, cannot be approved merely on the basis that it is a traditional social cus-tom, a publicly endorsed "universal" practice.

If we take this parallel seriously, then Abraham cannot be absolved on the ground that child-sacrifice or obedience to God were moral or religious expec-tations in his time. For both Kant and Kierkegaard, mere rule-following, how-ever desirable as training, is primarily premoral behavior. An ethics of conventional, even "universalized," rules of "Right and Wrong" is presumed to be in place. Constraints on liars and cheats are essential, but the larger issue remains the question of motivation. Rule-based morality threatens to make a fetish of thoughtless, passionless, conformity.

Say one needs to be shocked into a Kantian realization that conventionally "good" behavior is morally not good enough. In Abraham's case, being a conventional loving father is conventionally good, but not good enough to win a special *moral* accolade. An absolute beyond convention must be acknowledged, a vantage from which convention can be displaced to reveal something deeper. This absolute might be Kantian Reason, or Purity of will or a Source of all that's good, worthy, or moral. In any case, we need to drive a wedge between outwardly proper but non-morally motivated behavior, on the one hand, and pure moral motivation (whatever the outward expression) on the other hand. We could do this by telling a story that made the outer expression appear evil, while raising the possibility that inner motives were properly aligned. The Abraham-Isaac story seems to do just that. It depicts an outward action utterly abhorrent while an inward motivational stance gets bolstered by divine approval and necessity.

Despite the risk of letting *Fear and Trembling* become too palatable, or of letting Kant become too wild, I will extend this interpretative line which joins Kant to Kierkegaard. The Kantian interpretation of Kierkegaardian inwardness will not get started, however, so long as we take the central issue in *Fear and Trembling* to be whether Abraham should obey God. If the obedience/disobedience issue remains forefront, the matter of inwardness will seem irrelevant. But obedience is *not* what is central to Johannes de silentio's account.

AGAINST OBEDIENCE

Faith can't mean obedience to God, whatever the cost, for three of the four Abrahams sketched in *Fear and Trembling*'s "Attunement" obey the command to sacrifice Isaac, yet each is mocked by Kierkegaard as false.[19] There are other false Abrahams, Abrahams who obey yet fall far short of faith: in one imaginary case, Abraham resigns Isaac, "dull with grief"; in another he is too quick to comply, taking a "winged horse" to Moriah; in still another variation, Johannes has Abraham set out, but *God* kills Isaac, relieving Abraham of the task and thus leaving his faith, but not his obedience, in question.[20] Willingness to obey God picks out nothing distinctive for Johannes's accounts.

Obeyers can be unfaithful, as in Johannes's example of a knight rushing too hastily to the mountain. Consider, too, that the faithful need not be obvious obeyers *or* refusers. Simple faithful folk are not *obviously* called to obey or to disobey. They escape the stark circumstances Abraham confronts. If the central issue were whether to obey or disobey, there would be a role in Kierkegaard's account neither for obeying-but-unfaithful Abrahams nor for simple faithful folk who never face head-on the issue of obedience or refusal.

We could even propose an Abraham who refuses God's demand, yet remains close to meeting the requirements of faith's double movement.[21] Sketching a not-quite-faithful Abraham would continue the pattern Johannes introduces in sketching an Abraham who procrastinates, or who fails by plunging the knife into his own breast.[22] If only by exclusion, these failed Abrahams illuminate where faith's center will have to fall.

Our present (imaginary) counter-Abraham believes that although his refusal suspends his obedience to God *in this instance*, nevertheless his faith is preserved, for he trusts he will "get God back." That is, he believes that his refusal in *this* case will not jeopardize his long-term faithfulness to God—or God's faithfulness to him. As our faithful Abraham's love for Isaac continued despite his resolve to obey God, so our counter-Abraham's trust in God continues, "on the strength of the absurd," despite his resolve to disobey. He gives up God and gets Him back.

This invention strips away the thought that only an *obedient* Abraham can shed light on faith. It is clear that "repetition," a trust in the return of what has been resigned—not brute obedience—is at the heart of Johannes's account of faith. The issue is *how* an Abraham, or a near-faithful Abraham, can sustain such faithful resolve, can gracefully move through giving up to getting back.

A counter-Abraham, a Maharba (Abraham backwards) who refuses to comply, is an imaginative embellishment in the style of Johannes de silentio, meant to shift focus away from whether Abraham does x or y, and toward the spirit in which he is moved.[23] Moving the focus from outcomes (whether x or y is done, or will occur) to the manner or the way an action is undertaken brings us closer to what Johannes finds important in faith. From the start, he makes it clear that it is Abraham's journey to the mountain, not the detail of the command or the restoration after, that most concerns him. The journey stands for a way of dialectical reflection, of threading through one's intentions, of clarifying one's soul, of checking the purity of its motivations. Maharba is willing to resign or "sacrifice" God, believing every moment he will get him back. A refusing Abraham cannot be entirely plausible, of course, because in the long run the knight of faith must have been first a knight of resignation. And if Abraham has already resigned the world, resigned his Isaac, then he cannot simultaneously cling to Isaac, in defiance of God's demand. But this is far from saying that a refusing Abraham fails simply because he disobeys. The upshot, then, is that a faithful Abraham could almost have made any choice—obeyed, refused—if only it were undertaken in the proper spirit.

The idea that the essence of moral worth falls on deciding yes or no about specific acts is deeply entrenched, blinding us to other aspects of a moral sensibility.[24] It is true that options are often well-defined, and the task is to decide for, or against, or to refuse to go on record either way. Ballot propositions work this way. Our religious identity can be crudely registered this way in questionnaires. We check "theist," "atheist," or "agnostic." And Abraham can be described this way: he must "vote" for or against God, for or against Isaac, for or against ethics—or else he must somehow manage to refuse to go on record either way. But there are morally relevant possibilities that escape this simple yes/no/neither schema. One might forget the polling date, or fail to make up one's mind on an issue. One might vote "nay" wholeheartedly or cast the same vote whimsically. One might abstain in true composure, or feign composure while steaming wildly within. One might picket the polling place to protest the limited options available for one's decision.

Biblically, and in Johannes's retelling, we know that Abraham sets out for the polling booth, and we know exactly how he will "vote." These aspects of the tale are transparent, part of what Hannay calls the "framework assumptions"—too thoroughly transparent to play more than a background role. As we've seen, something else grabs Johannes's attention. He tells us ways of going *to* the booth, ways of voting "correctly" yet failing to have faith, how Abraham travels (or delays his travel) to the mountain. This is not to say it doesn't matter which path is taken—clearly it does. But how Abraham will "vote" is not the aspect under scrutiny. Faith lies in how Abraham travels (or refuses to travel), in the way his soul, his passional-imaginative state of mind, is misted, set, or moved…*as* he journeys to the mountain.

TRYING ABRAHAM

God is no tyrant forcing people through a test of absolute obedience. The question is not whether they will do absolutely anything for Him. What, then, is the motivation for putting Abraham through this shock? If it's plausible to think that we need to be shocked out of moral complacency, having God invisible in the lives of professorial or serving maid knights of faith will not serve to dramatize that need. The very placidity of their lives makes us all too comfortable, all too sure that we non-Abrahams have arrived at faith without bother. But if Maharba or Abraham or Job are useful for their shock effect, we still must ask what more substantial lessons follow. Being startled awake, what do we see?

We need to see something that can be present beneath a range of acts that includes Abraham's journey to the mountain, Maharba's refusal to budge, a professor's trek to the library, and a shopkeeper's jaunty homeward march. The most likely candidate for something lying beneath these various acts is a certain motivational stance. We are forced to grasp the Kantian insight: that conventionally approved action can pair up with impure motive, and pure motive can pair up with the conventionally inappropriate. But there are other issues latent here.

Focused through Johannes de silentio's narrative lens, the Abraham-Isaac story works at several levels of resolution. We can ask our array of faithful knights not only to reveal their motivational stance but also how their aspirations lie. Here the focus shifts from a plane beneath the level of their public acts (their underlying motivations) to an elevated plane of orienting value. The values that our shopkeeping knights embrace resonate within the ambit of the human. But the Abraham-Isaac story lifts the source of essential human concern above and away from Isaac, away from Abraham. Judge Wilhelm acknowledges a "higher source" from which his identity can be received. Job acknowledges a transcendent source from which crystallized particulars and worlds emerge. Abraham acknowledges a source higher than any worldly power from which his Isaac will be returned. As we have seen in our discussion of Job, this is the realm of the transcendent available through imaginative vision. At its height, it offers powers of world-conferral.

Abraham must relinquish (or show that he has already relinquished) Isaac as the unique center of his world. Worldly attachment, on this view, cannot serve as the unique center of aspiration and devotion. Resigning Isaac is resigning such worldly attachment. Outwardly, from the position of civic or parental virtue, this looks absurd. We witness no saving inner-transformation, only a brutal crime. What saves Abraham from this crime is placing his trial on the plane of orienting value, and giving that plane—that allegorical space—a certain narrative structure. We've sketched that plane as a space which permits Abraham not only to honor God's command, but also, and all the while, to believe that he will get Isaac back. And we've filled in this paradoxical structure as having trust in a source or center of value such that Abraham can believe that losing Isaac is as absolute center is not to lose his son outright.

Relinquishing Isaac as absolute center of value means that Abraham must relinquish any claim to possess, master, or control the meaning Isaac will have as the aged patriarch advances toward his death. Isaac was to be the promise of his immortality, the consolation of his mortality, the continuance of his seed. Abraham must be weaned from any presumption that in this way his future can be foreclosed. He cannot presume to master history through selfless care of Isaac.

Isaac must be loved and weaned. Hence the repeated refrains in the opening "Attunement" section of a mother "blackening her breast." Thus she softens an inevitable weaning. She preserves her maternal love even as she denies her child succor. The motive for this denial is acknowledging the infant's inevitable independence, a center of meaning beyond her power of possession or control. This denial and acknowledgement will seem dangerously close to losing the child and the world outright. Hence fear and trembling. But the knight of faith knows in his heart, as Abraham does, that Isaac is not lost, even as he journeys toward the mountain. If not as the absolute center for his life, Isaac nevertheless will be returned. In faith, Abraham relates absolutely not to Isaac but to Another.

Descending from the plane of transcendent orienting value to the Kantian motivational plane, we recall that it can be all but impossible in actual lives to discriminate between mere compliance with "moral" norms and a proper moral motivation. Is this particular act—say of kindness—done in proper spirit rather than from fear or intimidation or the desire to please or to win approval? Unable to rest our case on actual lives, we retreat to stories made to order. We shift the medium of inquiry. We allow a lyrical dialectician to use the Abraham story to dramatize a point.[25]

Johannes de silentio shakes us from the idea that the key to moral or religious earnestness is in the public sphere where we discover and can then conform to a lucid list of rules. Johannes puts our eyes on underlying motive and transcendent orienting vision. We confront the transcendent as Job did, in terms of world-conferral.

Abraham's task is to decide what to do. Johannes as a spectator cannot have his assessment of Abraham be determined by Abraham's thinking about his situation, for Johannes has an independent evaluative perspective to maintain.[26] Yet as he himself confesses, it is unclear what standards of assessment he should adopt. Is he confronting a crime, something holy, some irrational surd lacking all intelli-gibility? He is at a loss to find an answer he—or we—could promote as correct for Abraham on the basis of some code "all reasonable and well-informed persons" share. Johannes is left, even in retrospect, without a clue, without a decisive principle to jell his evaluative convictions. And things are no better viewed from Abraham's standpoint. Are we sure that were he to be placed again under spiritual trial, his experience in the first trial would make a difference? Is there anything about the first outcome, God's restoration of Isaac, that would make a future request for Isaac's life easier for Abraham to resolve? So Johannes and Abraham are struck with fear and trembling.

If there is an evaluative impasse here that makes appeals to general or universal considerations indecisive, then what gets Abraham through this ordeal? A coin-toss wouldn't do. Perhaps one alternative begins to take on a compelling salience vis-à-vis its contraries. This is not the discovery that one principle ought now to be accorded more rational, objective weight, nor the discovery of a latent strength in a principle. It is instead a discovery about one's situation and about who in truth one is. Abraham finds his identity jell, move toward closure around his deepest convictions. Rather than reaching a deliberative, juridical verdict, Abraham discovers, as Andrew Cross puts it, "what kind of life he can conscientiously affirm."[27]

If one of the alternatives facing Abraham takes on a moral salience that produces a practical necessity, this descries something about moral identity and integrity, about moral psychology, sensibility, and perception. Abraham's crisis shows that a moral theory cannot come to grips with practical necessities if it only looks at the relative authority, priority, or stringency of moral principles or considerations, in their familiar context of quasi-legal deliberation. Abraham must resolve or reaffirm an issue of identity. What he does—whatever it is—must express who in truth he is. Renewal of identity—the sort of Kierkegaardian "repetition" we've discussed in *Job*—becomes the key to an individual's weathering this sort of moral-spiritual impasse.

There is a standard view of reasoning one's way through moral obstacles that pictures a neutral agent adopting the objective "view from nowhere."[28] This objective evaluator "adds up" considerations, reaches a verdict about the overall balance, and acts in keeping with that verdict. Objective rightness of action results from carrying out this process faultlessly. But Abraham resolves the turmoil of his ordeal quite differently. He begins not as a relatively neutral agent but as someone with conflicting passions, convictions, and loyalties. The latter appear to him not as considerations in a justificatory argument under construction before the public eye. They are contending forces in the tumult that his life, for the moment, has become. The resolution will be a stance and act and value-encasing vision that is true to all that's best in his life and soul, as he sees it.

How deeply and authentically can Abraham express—or form or discover—his convictions regarding his son, his God, his integrity generally?[29] This seems a better way to put the question than having Abraham's task be how to tally consequences or ponder how a principle could be bent to fit his case. A requirement such as "fathers should love their sons" or "the faithful should obey their Lord" must be fully transparent to Abraham. Even to suppose that Abraham needs to consider them would betray a prejudice against him. He needs no coaching here. In fact, we know that such general considerations are transparently in gear, because it is exactly these general considerations that structure his ordeal.

If we have been reading Johannes correctly, then Abraham gets through this crisis without throwing reason or moral sensitivity to the side. His response undermines a "considerations-verdict-response" scheme of problem-resolution. But Johannes de silentio leaves us with an alternative scheme of crisis-resolution, one which brings to the fore moral salience, moral perception, and the task of articulating moral identity. From this angle, the "teleological suspension of ethics" is not only the suspension of one broad sort of ethical stance in favor of a richer construal (though it is indeed this). The teleological suspension is also the suspension of one common view of moral conflict-resolution, a view based on quasi-legal deliberation, in favor of a broader, deeper model of transition through moral discord to identity and resolve.

Fear and Trembling covers any number of issues in addition to the question of the status of ethics, and the question whether a divine command can suspend it. It covers the double movement of giving up and getting back, of worldly resignation and of worldly reconciliation. And it displays moral turmoil that an Hegelian pedant might call a teleological suspension of the ethical, a shift in moral perspective that can convey the terror of a command to do the murderous.

ABSOLUTES AND ARTISTRY
Fear and Trembling: Two

> The light work sheds is beautiful light, which, however, only shines with real beauty if it is illuminated by yet another light.
>
> – Wittgenstein, *Culture and Value*[1]

CHRONOLOGICALLY AND CONCEPTUALLY, *Fear and Trembling* IS A TRANSITIONAL text. Placed between *Either/Or* and *Concluding Unscientific Postscript*, it deepens the notions of integrity, freedom, and receptivity introduced by Judge Wilhelm, and complicates his contrast between particularity and universality. In turn, these notions undergo further modulation in the *Postscript*. Such dialectical revisions from one text to the next undermine initial versions of a concept as they prepare the way for new ones. *Fear and Trembling*'s "shriek of horror," for example, creates a chasm between the Judge and Abraham.[2] But shopmen knights soften the apparent breach, creating continuity. And both figures prepare the way for the *Postscript*'s skeptical yet faithful Socrates.

I work *back* to the Kierkegaardian text from contemporary perspectives, but I also seek the text as Kierkegaard would have liked to have it seen. I'd like to cross between Kierkegaard's local perspective and our own, remaining true to both.

This means I provide commentary on Johannes de silentio's commentary—interpretative variations on Johannes de silentio's original interpretations.[3] These are meant to lure us to grounds otherwise left uncharted or forgotten. I test Abraham by charting counter-Abrahams, test the absolute by charting an array of absolutes, and test a strictly unintelligible hero by charting a (somewhat) intelligible hero. I try to rescue Johannes from obscurity by breathing life into a ghostly frame—then, perhaps some skeletal features will emerge. Finally, I try to locate *Fear and Trembling* midway on the path toward a fully Christian position—say that laid out in the *Postscript* as "Religiousness B."

FAULT AND FORGIVENESS
One strategy for avoiding *Fear and Trembling*'s "outward shriek" is to focus, as we have in the previous chapter, on a shift in moral orientation from an ethics of rules and acts to an ethics stressing purity of heart or will. Another strategy for avoiding the "outward shriek" and moving toward the "abyss of inwardness"

is to bring out the importance of remarks Johannes de silentio makes toward the end of *Fear and Trembling*. In the long run, Kierkegaard wants to move us toward a readiness for Christianity. This means he must at some point raise the issue of sin and forgiveness. In fact, near the end of *Fear and Trembling*, Johannes de silentio does mention sin, though almost as an aside. Johannes apologizes for not saying more about the subject. He sees it as outside his purview given that he takes Abraham not to have sinned. Nevertheless, these disavowals may be a cover.

Ronald Green argues that the secret message of *Fear and Trembling* revolves around sin and forgiveness—especially Kierkegaard's need for forgiveness.[4] Roughly, the idea is that Abraham's sacrifice of Isaac is parallel to Kierkegaard's sacrifice of Regine Olsen, his betrothed. Kierkegaard broke off his engagement abruptly and apparently without reason. The parallel requires that we see the Abraham story as illustrating Abraham's need for forgiveness. Is there a *general* need for forgiveness—as opposed to a specific need when one has acted wickedly?

In *Religion Within the Bounds of Reason* Kant traces an antinomy in our moral consciousness. Moved by reason toward moral perfection, we also harbor a "propensity toward evil."[5] The very elevation of ideals can frustrate satisfaction, but when their pursuit is joined by a countervailing tendency, satisfaction seems all but impossible. The natural temptation, then, is to trim down our moral sights. Short of that, we become vulnerable to despair of reaching our aspirations, and so we despair of any effort toward them.

A solution to this moral "double bind" or "practical antinomy" would be faith in or hope for divine forgiveness, which would remove the bite from ineradicable fault. We would know we had fallen short of our ideals, but would feel less than condemned for this shortcoming. In Kant's view, there is no certainty of this release from judgment. But embracing it lessens the risks of cynicism or despair. This makes the general need of persons for forgiveness more plausible than it would be if we thought divine forgiveness became an issue only if we were especially wicked. It lets us see how shopkeeping, invisible knights could seek forgiveness, even though they escape any outward brush with crime or blatant evil.

There is a *Postscript* passage calling for "a more religious expression" of the teleological suspension, which Ronald Green calls to our attention.[6] The suspension of judgment which forgiveness represents could be exactly this "more religious expression." Kierkegaard (or Johannes Climacus) now looks back from the standpoint of the *Postscript* and reveals a wish to *revise* a strand of *Fear and Trembling*. Climacus might have said, in reviewing *Fear and Trembling*'s content and reception, that this sin-forgiveness subtext is present, and that readers have in their shallowness and haste simply overlooked it.[7] But instead, Climacus finds the suspension of ethics in *Fear and Trembling* to be incomplete, defective, and in need of *another*, "more religious expression." So perhaps *Fear and Trembling* is to be read as incomplete, as necessarily transitional.

Expanding the idea of a teleological suspension in the direction suggested by Johannes Climacus would move the Kiergaardian discussion of Abraham closer to a specifically Christian center. And it would link the text to Kierkegaard's life crisis. We know that Kierkegaard perceived himself as laboring under a moral cloud, perhaps inherited through his father, and perhaps related to his treatment of Regine. Inexplicably, he was breaking off his engagement even as he wrote of Abraham sacrificing Isaac. Thus forgiveness as a suspension of judgment could merge three targets into one. Whether *Abraham* suspends the ethical, whether *Kierkegaard* suspends the ethical, and whether *God* will suspend the judgment bearing down on Kierkegaard, become a single issue: whether a general forgiveness is available. On the face of it, however, what Abraham needs is not forgiveness in advance for a deed not yet performed, but a suspension of the moral law as it operates for *humans*. He needs permission to sacrifice his son. Or, as we could put it, he needs *moral permission* to obey God. What could this mean?

A suspension of ethics does not need to be a suspension of a specific ethical prohibition, say, against killing one's son. It can mark suspension of a general moral orientation. If the willingness to sacrifice Isaac is roughly equivalent to a willingness to suspend a broad moral stance, then some of the terror of the "upraised knife" will be diffused. The more general ethics meant to be suspended could be a Hegelian assimilationist view of ethics. Furthermore, if we link this suspension of a broad ethical stance to faith's double movement, then we can expect that the apparent suspension of parental duty (and other duties generally) is linked to the simultaneous assurance that paternal duties (and Isaac) will be returned. One believes every moment that one has *not* forfeited one's status as a parent, or as a moral being. And if faith is appropriately fulfilled, then in addition to the loss of an inferior (perhaps assimilationist) construal of duty, something else will not be lost: love for a child, one's worth as a parent, one's worth as a moral being. Ethics can be suspended only on the presumption that it will not be lost.

The bestowal of Isaac to Abraham includes a bestowal of all that Isaac represents. Abraham's isolation from "the universal" is emphasized in faith's first movement, the act of resignation. But in faith's second movement, the familiar and consoling resources of a social matrix, "the universal," are returned. In their "post-suspension" status, reason-infused convention now has a *limited* Kantian or Hegelian import. We have reason and convention within the bounds of faith. A world Judge Wilhelm could embrace remains, and remains important to identity. It provides structures through which a worthy particular humanity can be expressed.

One might be unpersuaded by this reading. But consider the alternative—not suspension-as-forgiveness, but suspension as permission to act radically against the moral grain.

If one reverts to this view, then the Abraham example illustrates, at best, an exceedingly narrow range of cases. Extraordinary cases are bad precedent for conduct, even when the balance of worldly costs is not so one-sided as it is with Abraham. In worldly terms, he has absolutely nothing to gain and everything to lose. So my conclusion, once more, is that the Abraham case does not provide a model of a "real-life" situation where a specific ethical prohibition can be suspended. Instead it models a "real-life" alteration of moral-religious consciousness. Abraham's journey symbolizes a shift in an ethical-religious standpoint that might be underway or already accomplished in relatively unheroic and quite typical circumstances—say in the outwardly tranquil lives of shopkeepers, housemaids, or professors.

Targeting extraordinary cases, like that of a refusing Abraham or related tragic ones like Agamemnon's, is a useful way to zero in on the general area where a faithful Abraham would fall. We come to know faith's center by discovering our misses. Nevertheless, seeing the target may be difficult. Sarah, friends, and observers remain aghast that Abraham, "on the strength of the absurd," responds affirmatively to God's raw and wild demand. Johannes, likewise, is alternately amazed and aghast. He finds himself finally silenced by the unintelligibility of Abraham's resolve. It will not reduce to a rule like "Just obey your God." Hannay captures the darkness of Abraham's resolve by calling it an encounter with "the absolutely Other."[8]

DILEMMAS

Johannes goes to great length to distinguish tragic heroes from knights of resignation or knights of faith. Tragic heroes are caught between two universal requirements—that is, requirements that are public and neither of which, taken singly, is opaque or difficult to grasp. Thus we can see Agamemnon as caught between the requirement to save his city and the requirement to protect his daughter. We can give a rationale for both. But a knight of faith is subject to at least one requirement that is opaque and particular. There is no general or universal requirement to sacrifice a son. And the requirement, delivered from God to Abraham in his particularity, is nonpublic, a private requirement.

Showing Abraham to be "higher" than the tragic hero does not mean he is "more accessible" as an exemplar, or more helpful in providing confidence amidst moral devastation. Quite the contrary, Abraham's dilemma is worse than the tragic hero's. It represents no "real-life" guarantee that worldly joys and pleasures will certainly be restored. The knight of faith clings only to the *possibility* that value can be restored—"on the strength of the absurd." So *Fear and Trembling* leaves enormous room for unalleviated moral pain. Here, tragedy unrelieved by Christian redemption or forgiveness remains not just a possibility but a human likelihood.

In Hegel's view, Agamemnon escapes his dilemma because his ethical framework gives him unambiguous advice. He knows that "political duties, absolute duties of thought" override "duties of sentiment," such as the claims of family ties. Kierkegaard uses Abraham to *break* any temptation to assimilate faith to tragic cases. As against Agamemnon, Abraham acknowledges an absolute that is higher than "absolute political virtue." He encounters a demand that transcends the ethical framework of duty altogether, a "God beyond the barrier of intelligibility."[9] Yet this God provides unambiguous guidance. Thus Abraham is not caught wondering what to do. As Hannay has it, the problem is not uncertainty about what he, or we, ought to do. The issue instead is whether Abraham *wills* to do what he unquestioningly *must*.[10]

In my book *Knights of Faith and Resignation*, I sketched Abraham's ordeal as involving more than the question whether Abraham wills to do what he knows he must. In my view, Abraham confronts a clash of considerations that neutralizes definitive moral guidance, and puts him in the dark. Not just his will, but guidance too is put at risk.

God both requires that fathers protect sons and that believers obey all divine demands. So this God-connection rubs against familiar Kantian and Hegelian requirements of reason, both because the demand for sacrifice seems, on the face of it unreasonable, and because even if it were reasonable, it would conflict with another equally powerful requirement. Each requirement seems to defeat the other. This challenges the presumptions of an omnicompetent rationalist morality, whether Hegelian or Kantian, for even if both demands on Abraham were intelligible and within reason, putting them together creates an impasse, placing Abraham in this sense "beyond reason"—beyond reason's capacity to extricate him from this trap. And the claims of an omnicompetent moral reason can be challenged from other angles, as well.

RELATIONS TO AN ABSOLUTE

Can it be that for Kant or Hegel divine requirements merely duplicate humanistic moral law? By means of Abraham, Kierkegaard drives a wedge between respect for the moral law and worship of a Source of all value. If there were no such distinction, then all worth would have a human source. The credentials for all value would be delivered to the heavenly desk *from us*, requiring, at the level of the divine, only a redundant rubber stamp. This casts God as merely an efficient office clerk.

How are we to conceive of an "absolute" that lies deeper (or higher) than those mundane values whose worth is apparently reduced to our desires or will? In our earlier discussion of Judge Wilhelm's models of choice and reception, we saw the respect in which value may be, not willed or chosen, but given for our receptive embrace. Charles Taylor speaks of "absolutes" and Bernard Williams speaks of "categorical demands," each naming something "external" to our desires or will that can found a self.[11] Attachment to these "absolutes"—responding to their demands—confers orientation, stability, and identity, whether secular or religious.

To a talented but wayward esthete, a stuffy municipal judge might recommend marriage as a timber of identity. But in the Kierkegaardian long run, such civic virtue, though part of an array of potential absolutes—points of orientation for an emerging self—can't count as *the* absolute. The sort of identity-conferring commitments Judge Wilhelm has in mind transfers *some* intelligibility to a more strictly religious concern, say the idea of an "absolute relationship to the absolute."[12] But Abraham marks a divide between family and divinity, a breach which removes God from an array of potentially competing and more mundane absolutes. If "the absolute" is radically Other, an object of brute unmediated confrontation (as it indeed appears to be for Abraham), then it cannot be one of several qualitatively distinct values, differing from others only in being raised to a higher order of significance. God is *the* Absolute for Abraham.

The absolute to which Abraham is attached might be placed beyond the bounds of Kantian reason (at least beyond the reach of the categories of reason that provide us with legitimate knowledge). But reason does more for Kant than provide structures for access to knowledge. A Kierkegaardian absolute would not necessarily fall outside the orbit of Kantian *practical* reason, or "regulative ideals."[13] It is worth considering an argument Kant himself makes for an Absolute in some sense beyond the bounds of knowledge.

Kant posits a faith in the proportionality or symmetry of the universe, which requires that rewards be matched to moral worth.[14] The extent of our knowledge of evil in the world and consequent susceptibility to moral despair prompts us to posit this cosmic moral symmetry. Without such symmetry, moral will would be demoralized. Faith in this symmetry functions as a regulative ideal, required by practical reason. It inspires moral action despite our knowledge that in *this* world goodness goes unrewarded and the wicked prosper.[15] Kant allows practical legitimacy to such an ideal so long as knowledge cannot show decisively that such hope is illegitimate.

Striving for the highest (most complete) good is to strive for a virtue combined with happiness; yet each goal taken separately eludes achievement. Striving for happiness alone, we fall to the level of hedonism (a morally impermissible, improper end); striving for virtue alone, we aspire to a stoic, god-like self-sufficiency (a morally vain and also unattainable end). To continue these aspirations is to reap a double failure. Worse, it's clear that moral worth is not rewarded by happiness in this world. Yet we cannot escape a drive for repair or resolution of these paradoxes. One way to meet this drive for repair is, as Kierkegaard would have it, to postulate a God "on the strength of the absurd," that is, squarely facing the rational irresolvability of these antinomies. "It becomes clear...that the only way in which an existing individual comes into relation with God is when the dialectic contradiction brings his passion to the point of despair, and helps him to embrace God with the 'category of despair' (faith). Then the postulate [God] is so far from being arbitrary that it is precisely a life-necessity. It is then not so much that God is a postulate, as that the existing individual's postulation of God is a necessity."[16] We may thus hope, as Kant has it, that this God can provide a measure of resolution for pursuing virtue in our worldly struggles. It can now be a "life-necessity."

INTELLIGIBILITY AND EXTRAPOLATION

An antinomy of practical reason is intelligible in the sense that its structure can be laid out and that it is motivated by what Kant calls a need of reason. Abraham's antinomy has parallels to Kantian practical antinomies. He must strive to satisfy God's moral law ("Love Isaac!"); and he must strive to satisfy God's status as an independent *ground* of moral law. God's precarious or "contradictory" status as a ground or source independent of the law he grounds or delivers is dramatized by Abraham's ordeal. This story seems to pit one face of God, the unassuming more or less redundant reinforcer of the moral law, against a contrary face, God as unconstrained by any human conception of reason or value, as a source who may command Abraham to perform an act contrary to moral law, as a power radically Other. Then there is the further difficulty that God first promises Abraham that through Isaac he will become the father of his people, and that God then requires that Abraham kill Isaac.

The "repair" (as Hannay puts it) of such antinomies or "contradictions" comes through faith, but it is nevertheless rooted in a *need* of reason.[17] Reason discovers its own gaps and discovers that it cannot close them, and discovers painfully that it needs them closed. Faith spans the gap.

Our grasp of the possibility of repair is delivered not as the straightforward outcome of argument but symbolically, in narrative images. Kierkegaard provides such symbols in his portraits of the Judge, of Job, of Abraham and Socrates. Yet these are incomplete as discursive accounts of faith. Each image leaves loose ends, questions unanswered, further issues to explore. These portraits lead us toward the core of faith, but that is just to bring us to a place where charts no longer serve. Dialectical, lyrical ruminations are preliminary reconnaissance. They confer some intelligibility on a position at the brink of reason, and confer some intelligibility on what it would be like to discern the other side.

For Kant, the necessities of practical reason include a space for hope and for imaginative "archetypes" that provide guidance in ways other than reference to a rational principle. In the *Prolegomena*, Kant allows a "symbolic anthropomorphism" to shed light on a supreme being strictly beyond the range of reason.[18] He reads the *Book of Job* as depicting God's test of Job's "sincerity." Job succeeds even through outright rebellion, while his "friends" are hypocritical and dishonest.[19] This shows that although Kant places "religion within the bounds of reason alone," he allows himself to hazard what sort of God or absolute might lie *outside* the bounds of reason. A God who tests Job's sincerity is declared superior to one who rules through intimidation alone. So reflective excursions "beyond reasons" must be partially intelligible.[20]

By providing a God well beyond the reach of reason alone, Hannay describes Johannes as putting an invigorated Abraham back on his pedestal (thereby knocking Kant and Hegel off theirs).[21] But if Kierkegaard succeeds in placing God beyond the reach of reason alone, is the God so placed utterly unintelligible—a God now radically Other?

If we can distinguish degrees of adequacy in the accounts of Judge Wilhelm, Johannes de silentio, Johannes Climacus, or Kierkegaard, then there must be some intelligibility to the absolute each confronts and strives to capture in poetry, dialectic, or edifying prose. The "absolutely other' must be intelligible enough to let us judge that Kierkegaard's thoughtless adversaries entirely miss this quality of the divine. And even if God *is* on the far side of intelligibility, the project of *seeking* Him may not be.

The *Postscript*'s "Religiousness B" offers a Christian position beyond the standpoint of *Fear and Trembling*. It holds out the possibility of forgiveness against the unrelenting stringencies of the ethical. Of course, Hannay reminds us, we can know neither that the absolute will deliver this forgiveness, nor that its deliverance would take the form of easing the stringency of the ethical. But a "guilt-forgiveness" scenario is meant to be responsive to an earlier flawed standpoint (as the *Postscript* is responsive to the "flaws" of *Fear and Trembling*). Hoping for forgiveness, therefore, must be intelligible in the sense that it is intelligibly distinct from a "mastery-self-sufficiency" scenario, say, or an 'obedience-reward" scenario, or a "pleasure-perdition" scenario—even granting we can not *know* that there is such forgiveness.[22]

If it is important to maintain distinctions between stages or life-views, especially between "Religiousness B" and earlier stages, then God cannot be utterly beyond intelligibility. Perhaps there are persons who have no idea what counts as final forgiveness, or no idea of the need for or the availability of forgiveness. If so, then the Kierkegaardian task is to elucidate these ideas, by whatever means. What thought and imagination we can muster will aim at making something blurred or absent more intelligible—all the while aware that there are no guarantees we will succeed.

Consider Kierkegaard's intentions as a writer. Can authorial labor survive *as* authorial labor if it cannot make its end—to chart a path toward "an absolute relationship to the absolute"—somewhat intelligible? For the theory of stages to make sense, for the idea of an authorial labor that moves us toward the brink of intelligibility to have a grip, there must be some sort of intelligibility-access to the absolute that we sense we are approaching. Furthermore, we should have grasp enough of our goal to know what sort of brink we are approaching. There must be contrasts between the brink of remediable ignorance, the brink of transitional confusion, the brink of an antinomy of reason, practical or theoretical, and the brink of intelligibility. Each abyss calls for a different cognitive-affective response. If God were *utterly* Other, we would have no way of marking these important contrasts.

HOW REAL IS JOHANNES DE SILENTIO?

We come full circle to the question that opened our discussion of *Fear and Trembling* in Chapter 4, the question of Johannes's status not just as an artist, but as one whose lyrical talents are essential to the philosophical and dialectical issues of the text. Can Johannes bring us closer to the God of Abraham than otherwise possible? Or does Abraham's God remain absolutely other, resistant to our attempts, and Johannes's, to grasp?

As we've seen, in *Fear and Trembling* an obedience-engendering belief in God is not a premise to be questioned or proved but is instead a framing assumption of the narrative. But if we are to make sense of this assumption *as* a frame, then we must sense what lies outside the frame. God as Other, as an outer limit to the understanding, is not an idea left coolly unexplored by Johannes de silentio—as if it were a raw, imponderable irrationality, about which nothing could be said. Indeed, Johannes declares outright that Abraham is unintelligible to him. Nevertheless, it's also true that Abraham and the absolute to which he is attached is alternately focused and then blurred, first something quite beyond any grasp and then something looming in the offing.

To the extent that the framework assumptions of "God-and-obedience" are hard-edged in the accounts in *Fear and Trembling*, the appropriately matching author is a stripped down, minimalist Johannes de silentio. Johannes's job is simply to provide, in Hannay's word, a template.[23] The "God-and-obedience" frame locates Kantian and Hegelian targets for destruction, so it's best to have the frame laid out unobtrusively by a low-key stylist, shrinking toward invisibility. Eyes can then attend the target undistracted either by the fumblings of the archer or by the antics of a target-setter. But just as surely, Kierkegaard wants to display dialectical efforts to sustain this frame, to honor its requirements, to test its shape. The vehicle is Johannes's presence as a clever and showy poet-dialectician.

That something is a framing assumption does not put it beyond inquisitive attention: we may ask what it frames, how porous or unbroken that frame may be, exactly where it is placed, and how it works. A hard-edged frame provides a lucid and nonporous boundary exactly placed and resisting imaginative elaboration, pondering, or interpretation through embellishment. Yet Johannes tosses off Abraham-alternatives far outside the frame of simple obedience: Abraham can plunge the knife into his own breast, or fail to comprehend the task. And

Kierkegaard has Johannes treat the framing requirement badly: Abraham complies too fast or slowly, desperately or wavering, deceiving or betraying Isaac. We ask if Abraham *will* obey, and also how he will *carry out* his will. As framing assumptions, belief and obedience can fog, shift in aspect, as horizons may. They are neither simple nor hard-edged, and in any case need constant thoughtful work to keep in proper clarity and place.

Johannes is wrestling Abraham toward a moral-religious position richer than Kant or Hegel can readily accommodate, but which we can decipher, in spite of obstacles Johannes himself throws up. Perhaps it includes aspects of a Kantian moral position rendered in archetypes delivered to the imagination to inspire moral dispositions of hope and fortitude. Or perhaps Kierkegaard's Absolute will fall outside even this expanded Kantian frame. In any case, the position aimed for would tolerate moral conflict and protect a moral source other than the moral law or reason. It would secure a Source of motivation deeper than respect for moral law or even respect for persons as ends. Here faith (a religious component) would bring a provisional moral outlook based on role and rule sharply into question. But it would also provide resources for *restoration* of the moral. There are dark spots to record. Yet one must nevertheless approach and chart the edges of this dark, if not hint at light within.

KIERKEGAARD OUR CONTEMPORARY
Postscript Themes and
Postanalytical Philosophy

I must deliberate from where I am. Truthfulness requires trust in that and...not the obsessional and doomed drive to eliminate it.

– Bernard Williams, *Ethics and the Limits of Philosophy*[1]

PHILOSOPHY PERIODICALLY TAKES A TURN OR EXPANDS IN UNANTICIPATED WAYS.
No one could have predicted the course of philosophy after Kant, especially the
reactive stream which leads through Hegel, Kierkegaard and Nietzsche and on
to Heidegger and other defining figures of twentieth-century European philosophy. On a smaller scale, we might see a similar turning point in recent philosophy
after Wittgenstein in North America and England that is also decisive and unanticipated. There is an unmistakable expansion in the range of topics deemed worthy of attention. Themes pre-viously relegated to literature or psychology or
some other exile are now quite fashionable: the expressive articulation of the self,
the role of emotions, passions and desires, the question of life's meaning, the
importance of death, the shift from Cartesian uncertainty to existential anxiety.
The label "postanalytical philosophy" has gained some currency as a mark of this
shift.[2] An alternative, which keeps the analytic stream alive, would be the label
"romantic analysis," for the shift includes explorations of love and death, tragedy
and lost community, and the discovery of philosophy in novels, drama, and
poetry. These philosophers—say, Bernard Williams or Charles Taylor, Harry
Frankfurt or Martha Nussbaum, Richard Rorty or Stanley Cavell—have deep
roots in the analytical tradition, although their interests may overlap with those
of European phenomenologists or existentialists or deconstructionists.[3]

May aim has been to bring Kierkegaardian figures onto the contemporary stage
and to listen for dialogue among these figures. It has also been to bring their polyphonic articulations into contact with a contemporary philosophical audience
for whom issues of attaining self are vibrantly alive. There has been some recognition of Kierkegaard and the themes of his moral-religious psychology among
"postanalytical" or "romantic-analytic" philosophers. Cavell has written on
Wittgenstein and Kierkegaard, and acknowledges Kierkegaard's presence in his
work.[4] Hilary Putnam has recently paired *Concluding Unscientific Postscript* with
Wittgenstein's *Culture and Value* and *Philosophical Investigations*.[5] In addition, a num-

ber of other analytically trained scholars have taken up Kierkegaardian themes explicitly.[6] Despite his rather scanty explicit recognition, however, Kierkegaard's shadow looms large behind the theme and focus of a broad spectrum of contemporary "postanalytical" debate.[7] This becomes clear as we take up central themes in Kierkegaard's *Concluding Unscientific Postscript* in the context of this contemporary work.

The central banner in the massive dialectical and satirical work penned by Johannes Climacus is "Truth is subjectivity." For classical analytical philosophers, this is a blatant oxymoron. More generally, stripped of context, the idea seems to feed the malaise of an excessive and defeatist moral and cultural relativism. But read in context, the banner is constructive. Through his pseudonym Johannes Climacus, Kierkegaard links subjective truth to the *Socratic* task of self-articulation. This can be shown by developing unexpected parallels between a rich framework of self-formation or subjective agency that we find in the writing of Frankfurt, Taylor, Nagel, and others, on the one hand, and on the other, a family of *Postscript* themes that are tied up with subjectivity.

In taking up the *Postscript*, I focus on Kierkegaard's—or Climacus's—Socratic voice, setting aside his specifically Christian concerns. Of course, subjectivity is for Kierkegaard the key to Christian faith—at least on first appearance. In the long run, even with regard to Christian faith, the formula may be ultimately revoked or qualified.[8] But in any case, subjectivity plays a central role in Climacus's portrait of Socratic existence.

As a first approximation, we can take Kierkegaardian subjectivity to summarize the ideas that we are fundamentally reflective, responsible agents capable of higher-order care; that we lack foundational certainties on which to base action or belief, and are thus fundamentally at risk, reliant on faith, whether secular or religious; and that we are immersed in but not reducible to our traditions and social roles. In Judge Wilhelm's admonition to the esthete we encountered the thought that subjective beings are beings capable of self-choice or self-receptivity crucial to self-responsibility. Now we can elaborate this idea, first broached in *Either/Or*, from a new angle. A model from Harry Frankfurt will prepare us for the approach to self-responsibility adopted by Climacus in the *Postscript*.

SELF AS HIGHER-ORDER CARE

As Frankfurt has it, persons are distinctive in virtue of their capacity to have desires *about* their desires, cares *about* their cares, reflections *about* their reflections.[9] My life can be viewed objectively, by myself or others, as a collection of various activities, desires, beliefs, and projects. Registered passively in consciousness, these are first-order facts or data. A second- or higher-order belief or desire would be one directed at such first-order data. I can register the fact that I want to leave the room, though I am speaking before a class. Additionally, I can have a belief or desire about that initially given data. I could desire not to want to leave the room, or think the want to be foolish or disavow it. I could take the fact I am speaking before a class with some wonderment, apprehension, or pride.

For Frankfurt—and for Johannes Climacus—human selfhood is distinctive not in virtue of our capacity to organize our beliefs in rational theory, or in virtue of our being aware of or self-conscious about our beliefs or desires or projects.

Such "objective self-consciousness" might describe essential human nature for an Hegelian. But for Frankfurt, the crucial mark of selfhood is the ability to have desires *about* desire, to have care *for* our cares. And then, to have such second-order care or desire be effective: a self will generate action expressive of such higher-order care.

An individual who either fails to exercise or lacks the capacity for higher-order care is not yet a self, but an onlooker, a spectator or voyeur. There is no core from which responsible action can flow. Like the esthete in *Either/Or*, there is no rudder or ballast to stabilize or orient this "proto-self." It is a life adrift. We find no underlying cares or projects to define its integrity.[10]

Of course, possessing self is typically a matter of degree. We may "thoughtlessly" indulge a passion for gossip or fast cars, or "thoughtlessly" let ourselves be consistently late for appointments. When something an individual does or endures appears to lie outside the range of their higher-order desire or care, we could say, to use Frankfurt's term, that the individual is to that extent a "wanton." The task of diminishing the degree to which we are wanton is, for both Kierkegaard and Frankfurt, the ongoing task of selfhood. Caring for my cares and projects, evaluating their relative worth, investing in some while discouraging or terminating others—these are the higher-order, subjective activities of a being who can gain or lose a self.

SUBJECTIVITY AND COMMUNICATION

Turning now to *Postscript* themes, we can put Frankfurt's model to work. *Becoming subjective* or cultivating *inwardness* is for Kierkegaard becoming a self, that is, increasing those areas of life subject to personal evaluation and revision, and decreasing those areas in life in which we are "wanton."[11] This is a process of exercising higher-order care, or in Kierkegaard's words, "*double reflection*," that is, reflection on reflection.[12]

Concerned reflections *on* our reflections, on our desires, ideals, and emerging identities, locates subjectivity—the space where selves develop and reside. Second-order reflection aims to determine how an initial reflection about a belief or feeling, about a desire or an ideal, conforms or conflicts with our underlying identity-projects. Such second-order reflective care is both evaluative and performative. It raises the *issue* whether to continue or to decline beliefs or passions or paths of action that I find myself immersed in; and in raising the issue, it also attempts to actively resolve it.

The data I initially confront is typically already evaluatively structured: I confront a roadside accident and think, "How terrible!" But the second reflection, crucially tied to selfhood, takes up that initial reflection with a specific self-relating question in mind: Granted this initial response, from the standpoint of affirming or neglecting my self-defining cares, what will my *response* now be? Here the question may answer itself, not in a further reflection but in a self-constituting response. In our earlier discussion of the *Job Discourse*, we heard Kierkegaard claim that a key to Job's response was his "acting in asserting." In the present context, we have an "acting in reflecting."[13]

Take another familiar *Postscript* claim. "The objective accent falls on what is said; the subjective accent on how it is said."[14] *What* I say can reflect things true of the world and of myself as part of the world, seen from a detached, impersonal point of view. Such objective truths are not unimportant. But of equal or greater importance, especially in a self-forgetful age, is *how* I take these initial "givens"— wants, beliefs, or facts that are the "objective" content of first-order representation or reflection.

If the subjective accent is on the "how," this can be a how of appropriation, how a speaker's words are integrated into her wider intentions and self. But it can also be a how of communicative reception: how someone addressed takes in (or refuses) what may be conveyed. So at least three focal points are central to "double reflection," or to the wider context of outward expression and communication. There is first the "objective message," then the "subjective" relationship of the sender to the message, and finally the "subjective" relationship of the receiver to the sender and to the message. These distinctions prepare us for the *Postscript* motif of "indirect communication."

INDIRECT COMMUNICATION

What I convey to another may be largely content—my credit-card number or the answer to a mathematical puzzle, say. If all we ever wished to communicate were simple facts of this sort, there would be little place for subjectivity or for Johannes Climacus's concern for indirect communication. Even simple facts, however, may be conveyed in contexts that undermine the appearance of straightforwardness. My card number may be a code for something quite different and portentous. It may carry "subjective meaning" *indirectly*—indirectly, because the meaning is conveyed by vehicles whose import at one level may be contrary to or differ from import at another level.[15] Thus there may be hidden import not available to just anyone. It may carry *subjective* meaning because what is conveyed may matter essentially to my moral-religious identity. Take the case of reporting numbers on my credit card. If indirect communication is at work, I must convey the numbers intending them as a code. I will have a reason for speaking in code rather than directly, and the numbers I send must be received as such a code, as containing something portentous, by whomever I address.

We should distinguish two sorts of portentous subjec-tive "content" that might be indirectly communicated. Some cases will resemble the credit-card case. I communicate what seems to be a direct matter of fact or doctrine. But beneath appearances, there is available to someone suitably prepared and alert, quite another message that is "subjective," crucial to their lives and mine, and which for some appropriate reason should not be broadcast for easy public consumption. We might think of Kierkegaardian pseudonyms as "speaking in code," which we must then decipher. But there is a deeper sort of indirect communication at work in the *Postscript* that does not merely involve deciphering codes. In a nutshell, there is still something beneath appearances made available to someone suitably prepared: but what is conveyed is *not* an ultimately decipherable message, but a power, capacity, or enablement. Here, linguistic communication is less the point than a communication of freedom.[16] In the language of *Job* and *Repetition*, we have a kind of world-conferral. Or in the image of Judge Wilhelm, we have self-reception.

Both types of indirect communication play on the fact that the manner of the communicator, and the manner of a receiver, can undermine or oppose the intended purport of a communication. The *way* I talk about philosophy, my friends, or my life, can oppose *what* I say about them. An underlying tenderness may betray "tough talk" or an avowed affection may be delivered unconvincingly. The "how" of communication is as much open to critique and evaluation as the "what."

If I teach "Though shalt have no disciples" in such a way that disciples gather around, or if I teach "The unexamined life is not worth living" as a random truth useful for mindless duplication on exams, then I have failed to communicate an appropriate second-order concern. The outcome, as Climacus would say, is comic. My audience will not have gathered, perhaps because *I* have not gathered, a proper concern for *how* those truths are to be taken—taken up in a life. I will have failed in two ways.

"The unexamined life is not worth living" is like a code that can be deciphered. We embark on a hermeneutical task, unraveling what's important about the motto, and trusting that the decoding will "click" for our students, our audience, or ourselves. We learn to hear the peripheral meanings that resonate in an utterance, not just around its explicit "content," but in the uttering itself, its overtones, its setting (in this case) in the life of Socrates. And a measure of our success or failure will be whether he or she whom we address can participate to some relevant degree, in the proper spirit, in this analytical or hermeneutical conversation. And in addition to talking, writing, or reflecting about the dictum in proper subjective passion, we also anticipate or hope for a deeper integration of the motto into the fabric of another's life. Thus we can succeed or fail to have conveyed a life-enablement, a capacity for *living* in a certain way.

The ability to decode a communication is distinct from the reception of a capability. So there are at least two worries for Johannes Climacus to contend with, whether the issue is understanding Christian doctrine, a Socratic admonition to examine one's life, or the Judge's admonition to "Choose yourself!" And the worries appear even with regard to a communication as weighty and entire as *Concluding Unscientific Postscript*. An appropriate how or manner of saying must be communicated. But a how of freedom, capacity, and doing must also be conveyed.[17]

Fearing that such a freedom has not been conveyed, that he has produced only fodder for academic conversation, at the close of the *Postscript* Climacus threatens to take back, revoke, all that he's written. If the intended enablements—say new access to freedom and self-responsibility—have not been communicated, the writing will have failed. And it's not so easy to say how he could be assured, or assure himself, that such enablements *have* been conveyed. If the overriding aim of his writing is to *enable* us to become ethical, to become Socratic, to become Christian, then whatever refined dialectical analysis or interpretation he provokes may be only another objective distraction.

SUBJECTIVE TRUTH

The central *Postscript* banner, "Truth is subjectivity," now falls neatly into place. For Hegel and Kierkegaard, truth is a property of statements, but more importantly it is also a goal to pursue, an essence to achieve. To call subjectivity truth is to set a goal of personhood, of ultimate fulfillment.[18] Subjectivity is an essence to be true *to*. To be true to who we are and should become is to live subjectively, to live lives of self-responsible agency, irreducible to social role or tradition, at considerable cognitive risk. The moments of relative ease promised to the esthete by Judge Wilhelm are not unknown to Johannes Climacus, but the voice of Socratic passionate critique that he projects is also full of suffering, and disappointment. The fierce dissonances of Abraham and *Fear and Trembling* lie just beneath the *Postscript*'s comic surface.

We fall short of the ideal of subjectivity by collecting objective truths, theorizing about them, or mindlessly repeating fashionable opinions—without facing our self-becoming. We might collect pleasant experiences, "circumnavigate the self" in idle fancy, drift into and out of social channels, or indulge in cynical detachment. All or any of these (and there are endless others), pursued to the exclusion of Socratic care for the soul, are flights from subjectivity.

We are far from finished with the contrast between objective and subjective truths, but it should by now be apparent that "truth is subjectivity" does not announce a challenge to epistemically objective truths. It demands that we *care about* what may be objectively true, in the interest of securing personal responsibility and integrity.

SELF-CONSTITUTING ACTS

A more difficult *Postscript* motto reads as follows: "There is a how that has this quality that if it is truly given, the what is also given."[19] How can a proper passion deliver us a true belief or statement? A hasty reading—one which would make Kierkegaard an instant irrationalist—might be this. If subjective truth is nothing more than sincere belief, then a passionate sincerity insures that *any* specific belief, no matter how absurd, will become true if only I believe it with sufficient passion. But Climacus himself refuses this reading. For just one example, no amount of passion on a believer's part could make it true, he says, that God will appear as "a very rare and tremendously large green bird…whistling in an unheard of manner."[20]

At an opposite extreme, there is a relatively unimportant range of cases for which this claim would hold straightforwardly. If I plead innocence in the proper passion, an objective truth can emerge: it can become true that the statement "his claim to innocence was sincere" is objectively true. But this is not the internally related "how" and "what" that Climacus wants. I think we get closer to Climacus's concerns if we take the "what" that a properly given "how" can deliver not as a true belief or statement but as a *true self* or *way of life*.

Reflective agency is at last partially self-constituting. We can lift ourselves by our own bootstraps—with the assistance of others, of luck, and ultimately in Kierkegaard's view, of an enabling Power. But how does this partial self-formation take place? An analogy with John Austin's notion of performative utterance—say, a promise—can help us here.[21]

Unlike an objective statement, a performative utterance does not reflect or mirror reality. Its aim is not fidelity of representation but fidelity of action. Promises constitute relationships, produce bonds between persons, link past and future, create and sustain community. Like legal oaths, marriage vows, or personal commitments, they both express and produce lines of meaningful connection that structure self and world.

If promises are, in Climacus's sense, subjective acts, then they can be more or less true to, and more or less productive of, an underlying integrity. They are public, rule-following, and in that sense "objective." But more important, they are expressive embodiments of care—and care *about* our cares. They embody the specific intentions of responsible agents, and in that sense they are subjective. Our aim as persons, we could say, is not merely to preserve statements faithful to the world ("objective" truths), but to engage in subjective self-constituting activity. This will preserve both subjective *and* objective truths, preserve goals distinctive of the selves we are, and preserve the reality of beings engaged in self-constituting activity.

Any one of an individual's wants, beliefs, or feelings can be seen as a potential identity-segment more or less central to the self. As such, it awaits further integration into, or alienation from, the self. This integration or alienation is accomplished through promise-like activities of avowal or disavowal, confirmation or rejection.

To illustrate, consider friends renewing or relaxing ties, moving closer to or farther from each other. There are outer ceremonies, invitations and refusals, that cement or break up these ties. And there are inner dialogues that each friend conducts alone, mulling over and rehearsing the bonds and tensions of the relationship. So with the acts that tie or untie an identity segment to a central core. There are public acts of avowal, owning up to or taking responsibility for some act or some position. And there are also "inner" dialogues in which we confirm or disconfirm, directly or deviously, our identification with sub-parts of our self. Acts of care or commitment and the associated inner dialogue can renew or diminish the connection of a potential identity segment already somewhat related to the self. There is a way of caring for a patch of earth, for a philosophical text, for those we hold dear, which sustains identity and world. There is no guarantee of a "return" on the care I "invest." And I cannot *aim* to obtain such a return. Clearly the self-responsibility Judge Wilhelm promotes is at issue here, as is the sort of "crystallization of particulars" that is central to the power of the Whirlwind's Voice in *Job*.

Just as community and friendship are created and sustained by ongoing acts of commitment and their fulfillment, so self is sustained and altered by ongoing acts of care. *What* I am or become, as Climacus has it, is the outcome, in part, of *how* I approach my self and world. If I believe with sufficient passion that I will not betray my friend, that very act of commitment may help jell my loyalty. Therefore a belief I hold about myself—here, that I am a committed friend—becomes true in the holding of it.

EXISTING "IN THE TRUTH" AND TRUST

Once we have Climacus's "what" and "how" properly aligned, it becomes clear that whether I live truthfully, "exist in the truth," as he has it, is a separate matter from the truth of my beliefs—granted that both are of utmost importance. Climacus brings this out in a passage that delights his critics while sometimes troubling his sympathetic readers:

When the question of the truth is raised subjectively, reflection is directed subjectively to the nature of the individual's relationship; *if only the mode of this relationship is in the truth, the individual is in the truth even if he should happen to be thus related to what is not true.*[22]

The contrast between a "how" and a "what" in this passage appears as the contrast between a purely cognitive, "objective" relationship (say, to a belief), and a subjective relation of care or commitment (say, to a project, goal, or self-conception). Hence I can *act* truly, be true *to* myself, or be "*in* the truth," regardless of the truth or falsity of a related cognitive belief. For example, I may believe my friend is trustworthy (an "objective what"), and act in such a way as to reaffirm and strengthen the bonds of friendship (a "subjective how"). In renewing the commitment, I will be acting or existing subjectively *in* the truth, relating truthfully to *her* and to *myself* and to the *ideal* of friendship. The public or "objective" checks on these "subjective truths of passion" are that my intentions *are* pure, that I in fact *value* my friend, that she figures *importantly* in my life, that my present act is appropriate in spirit and content to the continuance of the relationship, and so forth. But all this is compatible, as Climacus avers, with my being related to what is *not* true. Perhaps it's not true that my friend is trustworthy. If I am deceived, then I am an individual "in the truth even if [I] should happen to be thus related to what is not true."

Objective and subjective truths do not travel on the same tracks, though they can work in tandem. The sense in which I can truly (or falsely) renew my friendship places truth on a different track than the sense in which it is true or false that my friend is trustworthy, or that friendship is a good thing. Nevertheless, objective truths and subjective truths can reinforce (or undermine) each other.

Objective facts can figure in our assessment of whether our friends are trustworthy, whether we are sincere, whether a goal makes sense, or whether something is an appropriate means to the realization of a goal. This does not exclude subjective truth. To the contrary, existing *in* the truth sensitizes us to the importance of friendship, the urgency of integrity, even the importance of fact gathering. If subjectivity holds priority here, it is due to the importance of selfhood and of adopting self-responsibility as a goal, and due to the impossibility of the alternative: that is, the impossibility of delaying such commitments until the arrival of their objective warrant.

Perhaps there will always be a gap between beliefs we can objectively assess as bolstering a project or a care, and the confidence we must have in our loyalties and cares. In any case, the *Postscript* point can be put modestly in this way: whatever the links or gaps between objective truth and a truth we can exist *in* or be true *to*, possession of objective truth does not suffice for a full, responsible life.

Subjectivity entails trust. There is no certainty that my care for certain projects or the commitments I make will in fact do the job. Care precedes, and often *must* precede, cognitive delivery of its objective warrant, even when such warrant is retrospectively available. Thus caring rests on a kind of faith. Self-formation is also linked to faith because its focus is an ideal from which we necessarily fall short. It is striving for something whose attainment is necessarily partial and uncertain. As Kierkegaard has it, subjective truth is "an objective uncertainty held fast in an appropriation process of the most passionate inwardness."[23] In the best of circumstances, I will be denied the certainty that what *seems* to matter most to me in *fact* matters most in the larger scheme of things. Apart from an already existing trust in the ideals of self-responsibility and the worthiness of striving for them, there is little reason to believe that my cares will achieve their aim—a "truthful" subjectivity.

UNCERTAINTY AND JUSTIFICATION

Subjective passion, a constantly renewed commitment to those activities, people, principles, and ideals that are part of my life, can create and sustain the core of my integrity. We measure the integrity of a Socrates or Jesus by their refusal, at certain points, to yield. When challenged, they reveal the certitude of conviction: "Here I stand: I can do (or be) no other!" But such impressive resolve is not a report of epistemic certainty, nor does it create one. My salvation may rest on such conviction. But such saving, inescapable commitments are, for Kierkegaard, the very model of objective uncertainty.

It is a deep if disturbing fact that the very beliefs we embrace, and must embrace, as the foundation of our integrity, are beliefs we can also see, in moments of detachment, to be objectively insecure. Whatever matters to me, on which my integrity or salvation may depend, the basis for its mattering to me can be made vulnerable to doubt. What would it be like to discover basic truths, premises that were both absolutely certain themselves, and the basis from which one could give proof of the conviction, say, that life is worth living, of the trust that rationality is worth pursuit, of the confidence that love is worth cherishing?

Bernard Williams speaks of "ground projects," commitments that give meaning and point to our lives, but whose importance rests on something other than an argument that such concerns *must* matter.[24] Impartial reason is inadequate for founding the personal, subjective side of life, for justifying or grounding those cares that constitute our deepest convictions, those cares that make integrity possible and life worth living. In *Moral Luck*, Williams makes a number of points that have a distinctly Kierkegaardian flavor. Consider the following regarding the dangers of too great an allegiance to "the impartial system." "Life has to have substance—so the impartial system can't be all, and at the limit it will be insecure." And later: "The intuitive condition is not only a state which private understanding can live with, but a state which it must have as part of its life, if that life is going to have any density or conviction and succeed in being that worthwhile kind of life which human beings lack unless they feel more than they can say, and grasp more than they can explain."[25] As we will spell out in the following chapter, there are varieties of objectivity, not all of which must collide with a Kierkegaardian subjectivity or with what Williams calls an "intuitive condition" in which we "grasp more than we can explain." Nevertheless, there is a sort of objectivity related to what Williams calls "the impartial system" that *can* be pernicious, draining meaning from the "density and conviction" of our lives.

An objectivity that preemptively drives us from the context of our everyday cares and practices, if left to run its course unchecked, will inevitably deplete our lives. Thomas Nagel has described this process as repeatedly taking a skeptical step backward from our lives, becoming ever more detached from the cares that actually inform them.[26] We ask, "Why does *that* matter so much?" Given a response, we repeat the questions. In fact, our questions can easily outlast our answers. At some point, we just have the cares we do. Across much of our lives, they motivate justly and effectively without deep theoretical derivation. Ironically, the very search for such a justifying, theoretical derivation, requiring us to take more and more detached positions, can empty a life of its ordinary significance. The initial convictions that we set out to rationally ground seem, through the very process of examination and every more detached attention, to lose their previous weight. There are occasions where greater detachment is precisely our greatest need. Nevertheless, as both Nagel and Kierkegaard passionately aver, we must also grant those contexts wherein, and respects in which, the subjective standpoint is legitimate because inescapable for life.

In a number of classic essays, Charles Taylor takes up the issue of how our inescapable convictions can be weighed when they conflict. This weighing amounts to balancing "strong evaluations," identity-conferring convictions. It is the process by which self-responsible persons preserve their integrity through resolution of discordant aims or goals which deeply matter.[27]

Confronting a crucial choice about what to do or to become, we turn over our cherished convictions, attempting to grasp their relative significance, but without having any fixed independent standard that could assign comparative weight. The dilemma may be friendship versus vocation, the claims of civilization versus the call of wilderness, the familiarity of the more cautious route versus the thrill of the more adventurous one. Of course, often such "either-or" situations can be mediated. But sometimes they are intractable. One alternative may nevertheless, as in the case of Abraham's crisis, become salient, overshadowing its competitors. But digging through the self for clarity is not an easy process. We must remain true to a but dimly sensed image of our integrity, knowing all the while that no timeless certainties exist from which a solution to our dilemma can be derived.

For different ends, and from different perspectives, Taylor, Nagel, and Williams provide sustained critiques of a preemptive objectivity that would banish personal, subjective concerns, that would deny importance to a particular, necessarily partial outlook from the midst of an ongoing and uncertain life. They acknowledge the failure of reason, in any ultimate sense, to gird up our cares. In this, and in their interest in the structure of the caring self, they are profoundly Kierkegaardian.

IRRATIONALISM / HYPER-RATIONALISM

Epistemically and existentially, we are, in Neurath's celebrated image, afloat and underway on often dangerous seas, lacking fixed horizons or certain compass, carried in structures of questionable strength. But this does not foreclose the possibility of rational assessment of our plight or reasonable control of our direction. A modest, finite rationality can operate in the space between an outright irrationalism—the idea that reason has no role whatsoever to play in the subjective life, and a hyper-rationalism—the idea that our action and belief must be based on nothing less than the deliverances of a determinate, impartial Reason.

In all his works, but especially in his comic-dialectical *Postscript*, Kierkegaard displays an inspired passion for rational critique. As any coherent critique must, he heeds requirements of rationality like respect for consistency and truth. And he argues rationally and at length that a bloated Hegelian intellectualism is absurd, for it neglects our true condition. His critique of various foolish or incomplete forms of life appeals to our sense of what is fitting for a human being. To lack lucidity about oneself, to lack seriousness about one's projects, to fail to "choose" oneself are failures about which we feel shame. And even as Kierkegaard moves from critique of "the crowd" or esthetic ways of life toward elaboration of the pre-Christian religious existence of a Job, a Socrates, or an Abraham, reason still retains a hold. What else will pry real from fake devotion, better from worse religiosity? His pseudonymous works provide portraits bent on showing what faith or ethics or full selfhood would entail—portraits penned from specific points in self-development, and aimed at disabusing others, at other specific developmental points, of their illusions. His authorship becomes an extended exercise in rational elaboration and critique.

We have noted the view of practical reason implicit in Kierkegaard's construction of a community of figures presented by pseudonyms, figures in mutual dialogue where ways of life are at stake, yet each is open to the other. Stephen Mulhall, in discussing Taylor's views, elaborates the centrality of responsible, first-person viewpoints in committed moral discussion:

> [W]hen one party to a moral debate presents her reasons for advocating a certain transition [from one standpoint to another], she should do so in a manner which acknowledges the personal, experiential and intuitional roots of her argument. If she were to present them as impersonally decisive, the form of her discourse would imply a belief that pure logic dictates a certain perspective on the issue at hand, when the reality of the matter is that the adoption or rejection of any ethical stance is a personal decision, an existential act, the responsibility for which one cannot avoid by sloughing it off onto logic.[28]

We may live without ultimate rational assurances or secure impersonal principles. But this fact should not be conflated with the view that rationality can play no part in our lives. Rationality does not require the presence of Archimedean points, objective certainties from which to raise a world or found a self. To be powerful, it need not be omnipotent. Adopting a subjective standpoint which acknowledges the experiential and intuitional roots of argument does not imply that objectivity has no central role to play. In particular, it does not imply that all options are equal, and equally ungrounded, for the passionate self. And it does not imply that an effective, deep critique of one's age, or of oneself, is vain.

A moderate, domesticated rationalism would be consistent with Kierkegaard's conviction and practice. It would not assume one's cares to be irrational until proved otherwise, or that reasonable conviction required a theoretical derivation. It would tolerate conflict between convictions, believing realistically that we can't assume that merely because two convictions conflict that one of them is necessarily mistaken. We may need clarity about their opposition, which may lessen it. A domesticated reason would honor one's ability to recognize strong critique before one has the tools to raise a theory explaining or justifying it. It would accept a circularity of mutually supportive cares (with any given care defended or defamed only by reference to others, themselves ultimately open to question). And it would hold a faith that this circularity of care need not be narrow or vitiating, and can trace a fullness of life—not just the dizzy circularity of a self-defeating mind. It would recognize that not all parts of a loose system of self-constituting cares (which would function, too, as a loose array of reasons) will be in question at once, and that our sense of direction and purpose, the best we have by our finite lights, will not be found perversely unknowable or askew. And finally, as we have noted, there is ample space within such a domesticated reason for reciprocal illumination of selves and their sensibilities in conversation and dialogue. Such a relationship, or ensemble of communicative relationships, is a partial ground for those activities and motivational stances that constitute the self in motion.

By chipping away at those misconceptions that have led analytical philosophers especially to dismiss him as an arch-irrationalist, I have tried to illuminate the vital core of Kierkegaard's case for subjectivity. And I have tried to bring out what is constructive in his picture of reflective agency by linking him with contemporaries who, if I am correct, share at least large parts of his vision of subjective, personal life. If, along the way, Kierkegaardians become surprised that leading North American thinkers sustain concern for subjectivity, that too is welcome. Unclarities remain about integrity and evaluation, about the productive capacity of care and the sustaining web of conviction that carries us through. But the burden of removing these unclarities does not rest on Kierkegaard alone. Others are also shouldering the load. Where, if anywhere, salvation or fulfillment may lie remains opaque. But the recurrent hope that knowledge or reason alone can free us from this encompassing dark is surely illusory—as illusory as the hope for release from the recurrent demands of reflective agency, of a deep and not irrational subjectivity.

A VIEW FROM HERE AND NOW
Subjectivity and Double Vision

The seductive appeal of objective reality depends on a mistake. It is not the given. Sometimes the truth is not to be found by traveling as far away from one's personal perspective as possible.

– Thomas Nagel, *The View from Nowhere*[1]

IF COMMUNICATION REQUIRES RECEPTION BY AN AUDIENCE PROPERLY PREPARED, it behooves us to consider not only how Kierkegaard's pseudonyms talk across their own divides, but also how we today might be prepared, or ill-prepared, to hear and even to extend that dialogue among Kierkegaardian figures. In the previous chapter, "Kierkegaard Our Contemporary," we focused on the *Postscript*'s Socratic voice and its parallels in recent "postanalytic" philosophy. This brought current discussions in moral-religious psychology into explicit contact with a central figure on the Kierkegaardian stage. In the world of the *Postscript*, and for Kierkegaard's wider world as well, Socrates remains the exemplary thinker—a subjective, existing individual. We now continue and extend the dialogue between Kierkegaardian concerns for subjectivity and current debates. The vehicle for testing our present attunement to *Postscript* themes will be Thomas Nagel's recent survey of philosophical issues, *The View from Nowhere*.

Nagel sees problems of consciousness and knowledge, of self-identity, of meaning in life and death, as varied expressions of a single problem: "how to combine the perspective of a single person inside the world with an objective view of that same world, the person and his viewpoint included."[2] Nagel holds that the major issues of philosophy are rooted in a fundamental tension between relatively subjective views from within an engaged ongoing life and more objective views from positions that are more detached. This surely parallels a *Postscript* theme: How to reinstate the truths of subjectivity without dispensing with the claims of objectivity.

General theory drives toward wider, more inclusive views that become increasingly less dependent on our own particular perspectives. As an unattainable limit, we approach a stance without the restrictions of personal perspective—something like the "absolute" viewpoint of Hegelianism or Rationalism. This is the illusory "view from nowhere." But our humanity exceeds our search for general, objective theory. We cannot forget that we are blessedly local, subjective creatures whose lives are firmly anchored in time and place, tied to friends, family and personal pursuits, and embedded in given physiologies, psychologies, and cultural histories. Understanding may push toward the general and detached, but it also requires that we take our subjectivity seriously: "…the seductive appeal of objective reality depends on a mistake. It is not the given. Sometimes… the truth is not found by traveling as far away from one's personal perspective as possible."[3] Could this mean that there are indeed subjective truths?

We rightly view the world from here and now. Bernard Williams makes the point with characteristic (and Kierkegaardian) eloquence: "I must deliberate from what I am. Truthfulness requires trust in that…and not the obsessional and doomed drive to eliminate it."[4] Encountering both the drive toward evermore detached standpoints and the equally insistent reactive pull toward the ordinary, particular, and local we crave some sort of equilibrium. But a conflict-resolving response to these rival views may seem out of reach or impossible. The challenge is to resist the nearly irresistible urge for premature closure, for simple belief, for stopping the clash by disowning one party to the dispute. Allowed to force simplicity in this way, philosophy becomes fiercely partisan and half-blind.

In Nagel's view, accepting a disharmony of perspectives, (what Kierkegaard might call the inevitable incursion of the absurd) leaves us closer to the richness and complexity of the realities we are and confront than reaching for the smoothed out, attractive simplicity of a familiar or faddish "solution." We live with conceptual and practical "either/or" situations. Perspectival conflict, even paradox, cloud our search for understanding, and so our lives.

As Nagel has it, an objective and a subjective self vie for dominance in Kantian-Kierkegaardian fashion; the realm of freedom confronts a natural, physical and biological order—paradoxically, we belong to both. The world may elude even our best capacities for understanding. The antinomies of metaphysics express rival intuitions neither of which we can discard, producing discord which has no obvious resolution. And there are prominent Hegelian-Kierkegaardian themes in Nagel's account, as well: the enigmas of death and personal difference and particularity, the desire for a total and impossible autonomy, the conviction that philosophy confronts not just linguistic or cultural confusion, but "real disturbances of the spirit."[5]

BIRTH AND DEATH

Early in the *Postscript*, Johannes Climacus raises death as precisely the sort of issue that existentially vanishes when the only framework one has at hand is an objective one.[6] Death vanishes existentially to the extent that I lose the capacity to take myself as an "existing individual," one whose existence matters both to me and in the scheme of things.

Subjectively, it is enormously important to me that I was born and am now alive as the particular person I am, though from a sufficiently objective standpoint it doesn't make much difference whether I exist or not. Other members of the species roughly like me would probably do just as well at whatever ill or good I leave behind. And from a detached enough standpoint, it may not even matter that others of my species exist. It may be hard subjectively to imagine the world leaving out the fact that I am the person through whom any such picture of the world is projected and whose life is at its center. But it is perfectly easy *objectively* to imagine the world existing in my absence, and to accept the largely accidental nature of my birth.

Similarly for my death. Objectively, it is an uneventful part of nature's necessary processes of decay, on a par with rotting fruit or digested salmon. Subjectively, it can be a minor (or major) catastrophe. It is also difficult to think clearly about. It is often noted, for example, that persons subjectively at least, are strongly future-oriented, their possibilities stretching out before them with an immediacy and indefinitely continuing openness that quickly disappears once we consider them objectively.

Nagel offers a possible explanation. With regard to ordinary objects, and our own bodies conceived objectively, their ending or demise is made easier to conceive because we take them as the realization of preceding contingent actualities—states of affairs that might not have been. What arrives contingently can as easily depart. But subjectively, Nagel suggests, things are otherwise. When we turn to consider ourselves subjectively, we discover no ground in terms of preceding conditions. We find it hard to date our subjective emergence as selves, as the particular persons we take ourselves to be. To ourselves we seem strangely groundless and timeless, our start, finish, and conditions of growth retreating, under subjective examination, into an increasingly opaque yet portentous penumbra. Perhaps this is a ground for the Kierkegaardian sense that we are inextricably linked to the eternal, to an elusive Power in which we find our ground.

Unlike our considerations of ordinary objects, whose existence is explainable in terms of prior contingent conditions "...the possibilities which define the subjective condition of my life seem not to be explainable in turn, within a subjective view, as the contingent realization of deeper possibilities."[7] Thus we can appear subjectively self-contained, even self-caused. Judge Wilhelm captures the abruptness of this self-formation in his idiom of self-choice. We must "choose ourselves." And from this angle our death seems relatively diminished, overridden, as it were, by the immediate sense of a future opening endlessly before us.

Is this a sketch of a would-be Kierkegaardian *temporality*—the radical openness of my future, as encountered, say, by Abraham, or Job, juxtaposed to the certainty of death? Nagel depicts this juxtaposition as a clash of standpoints rather than as a feature of existential temporality.[8] But he thinks it illuminates both the difficulty people can have in taking their own death seriously and the quite different (and opposed) fact that our future annihilation worries us far more than our past non-existence. This would be expected if our lives were predominately future-oriented projects.

SELF-IDENTITY

Nagel comes at the problem of self-identity not in terms of self-formation in the fashion of Judge Wilhelm, or of the pseudonymous author Anti-Climacus in *Sickness Unto Death*. He approaches it more narrowly in terms of a "dialectical" or conceptual puzzle.

One aspect of this puzzle is the fact that after I have given a complete inventory of persons who exist, and all the facts about them, there is an extra fact, or apparent fact, of utmost importance—namely, that one of those extant persons is *me*. Now this extra fact cannot be just another objective fact on a par with countless others. It is, as Kierkegaard would have it, the discovery of my subjectivity. A second aspect is less frequently discussed It is the discovery that the grand objective self surveying the inventory of the world is simultaneously not just an abstract one-amongst-billions surveyed (and hence no one in particular) but instead a specific, highly differentiated individual. It is puzzling both that I could be *any* particular person, and that *that* particular person is me. To take this seriously is to take subjectivity seriously.

When Kierkegaard speaks, as he does in the *Postscript*, of an *existing individual* falling through the net of any objective system or theory, in part he means that the person I take myself to be, my particular shifting and discordant identity, eludes this net insofar as I view myself as an active, responsible agent. But more generally, consciousness itself seems to elude objective treatment. We are surely familiar with the feeling of unfocused awareness, a feeling which happily disappears once we start functioning. Thereupon mind seems to become transparent, a kind of translucency without handles. And lacking handles, it evades the objective net. Say we turn from such subjective awareness to a wider, more detached and scientific perspective. Matters do not thereby improve. If consciousness is replaced in a more scientific view by the details of brain physiology, tangible behavioral outcomes, functional flow charts or analogies with computers it is even further removed from immediate, intelligible grasp.

Scientific objectivity leaves out crucial parts of reality. It cannot give us an account of what it is like to have consciousness, to have points of view, to have scientists or philosophers reflecting on or creating theories. Subjective "takes" on the world are an ineliminable part of reality, a reality which includes much more than what gets caught in the web of present sciences of the mind. Without consciousness, "we couldn't do physics or anything else—and it must occupy as fundamental a place in any credible world view as matter, energy, space, time, and numbers."[9] This brings us to a complexity in Nagel's use of the objective/subjective polarity that has relevance to our understanding of the *Postscript* discussion of this polarity.

OBJECTIVE / SUBJECTIVE

In parts of Nagel's discussion, objectivity means taking the scientific view (which reduces consciousness to physics, chemistry, or computer analogies). But in arguing that subjective experience is part of reality, Nagel suggests that subjectivity might itself have an objective aspect. Here, "objective" can no longer mean "scientific." It must mean an aspect of something that can be described from a point of view in some sense wider than a contrasting local one, whether or not that wider view is "scientific" or "physicalistic." Thus Kierkegaardian reflections on anxiety or resignation might be more or less "objective," depending on the relative detachment, the broadness of the stance from which he considered these subjective states. This seems right. An enduring appeal of Kierkegaard's writing is the depth, the acuity, the "objectivity" of his descriptions and analyses, perhaps especially of subjective states. Thus the objective/subjective contrast offers us a comparative "more or less" rather than a definitive "either/or."

A related aspect of Nagel's treatment of consciousness recalls Johannes de silen-tio's despair of understanding the knight of faith. Thus the author of *Fear and Trembling* finds himself, and in another sense finds his knight, reduced to silence. In a curious parallel, Nagel despairs of describing what it is like to be a bat. He's sure it makes sense to ascribe consciousness to such an alien (yet familiar) crea-ture, even though he is at a loss to describe in detail what this consciousness might be like. Specific embodiments of reality seem to outstrip our capacities for description and comprehension.

We are tempted to define reality as whatever our best theories or linguistic practices end up positing as real. This relativizes reality to the state, present or potential, of our theory or language, and betrays a curious pride in our surely limited conceptual capacities. Kierkegaard and Nagel are at one in this regard. Our conceptions of something transcending our cognitive capacities may be inef-fable or paradoxical. But it is certainly not senseless to picture the world as hav-ing a character we are not biologically or cognitively equipped to grasp. As the tone-deaf are to music, so we may be to some unencountered (or even unen-counterable) dimension of reality.

The objective/subjective polarity illuminates matters of birth and death, iden-tity and consciousness, and reality and our grasp of it. And Nagel sees this polar-ity at work within ethics. Objectively, it can seem that my personal moral intervention in the world is no more crucial than anyone else's. What counts morally is outcomes, not who effects them or what is done to accomplish them. For some, it is a truism that moral judgments should be formed from a position as detached as possible from personal standpoints.[10] But for responsible, subjec-tive selves, it makes all the difference that it is *I* who will (or will not) cheat or kill. Similarly, in many cases I will want to make judgments about good and bad, right and wrong, from where I now am, considering my intuitions, ties, and pro-jects—not from nowhere in particular.

Two short notes before we turn to meaning in life and moral issues in more detail. First, as we can see from these brief accounts, the clash between objective and subjective standpoints does not always amount to the same thing. With regard to knowledge, realism leaves a gap between subjective conviction and what reason raises as a possibility of error. With regard to birth and death, rival conceptions linked to objective and subjective standpoints compete, with con-sequences upon our self-conception and the way we lead our lives. This is also true of the issue of freedom and responsibility. The strain between personal moral ties to others and what might be required impersonally can be acute. We take praise and blame, moral responsibility, seriously; yet from a more detached standpoint our actions can seem little more than part of nature, as much exempt from moral appraisal as the fall of a rock or the cry of a cat.

Second, as we will discover (perhaps despairingly), advance in philosophy is less a matter of solving problems than illuminating them, less a matter of disposing of them than retrieving them, and less a matter of escaping their frustrating hold than facing up to their power to engage. Reason raises doubts it can't defuse, con-siderations it can neither fully refute nor fully acknowledge. If we are caught between subjective convictions of the everyday and objective possibilities of error or deflation of meaning, that fact must be faced, not peremptorily denied.

MEANING IN LIFE

Nagel points to the danger of letting all the small things that count from my relatively subjective point of view slowly vanish by adopting views at ever greater distance from the "thick" reality of the everyday. If by such backward-stepping I lose my concern for appearance, for my family, for the details of my work, then the move toward greater objectivity is indeed self-destroying. But it is difficult to accept the idea that in general when global meaning-loss occurs, I should attribute this loss to the theoretical drive of objectivity alone.[11]

Progressive detachment or loss of meaning can be a symptom of more mundane causes (social isolation or poverty, or the pervasiveness of evil, say), rather than the outcome of semi-autonomous pressures toward an increasing objectivity. And there may be deep reasons, detailed from countless angles by Kierkegaard's pseudonyms beginning with Judge Wilhelm, for avoiding the self-responsibility that subjectivity entails. Yet there must be selves to responsibly endorse any viewpoint, including the objective one.

Kant found the starry heavens fit objects for the scientific gaze, and also capable of filling his soul with awe. The world in *Job* articulated by the Whirlwind's Voice need not be defeated by physics or biology. And subjectivity can have its competitive edge in this rivalry, for the scientific standpoint cannot make sense of its own power to still, console, or to inspire the soul.

When meaning in our lives gets challenged in global, urgent terms, the remedy is not always a return to more local and ordinary "subjective" concerns. Job brought his personal sufferings to the attention of his God—to a more objective court, as it were—arguing that those sufferings should count in the wider scheme of things. He demanded that sense be established from that wider, more detached standpoint. And there is surely something right in the relatively "objective" response, voiced finally from the Whirlwind, a response mightily detached from what Job had taken his concerns to be. Suffering abates and meaning is restored as Job becomes conscious of a world wider than himself.

If there are "preverbal and precultural" philosophical problems or "disturbances of the spirit," surely one of them must be grappling with undeserved suffering. And it is striking that something like the objective/subjective polarity seems to be at work in the text of *Job*. Yet this text also suggests other Kierkegaardian strains in Nagel's account. Job attempts a comprehension of his plight (unsuccessful, as it turns out) first in moral terms, asking how, objectively, his suffering could be morally deserved. In addition to moral value or principle however, there are other possible points of equilibrium between the nihilism of utter detachment and the dangers of total subjective immersion. Here are two that Nagel suggests.

Humility "falls between nihilistic detachment and blind self-importance." It consists in "the recognition that you are no more important than you are, and that the fact that something is of importance to you, or that it would be bad or good if you did or suffered something, is a fact of purely local significance."[12] Second, there is "nonegocentric respect for the particular," which "cuts through the opposition between transcendent universality and parochial self-absorption."[13]

There is an unmistakable congruence between these points of equilibrium—humility and respect for the particular—and the lessons gathered in our discussion of Kierkegaard's "Job Discourse." In *Job* we see that subjective suffering can be mitigated by displacement of a moral context and opening to a larger one. Awe before the grandeur of creation, silence before the wonder of a squall or the repose of a hawk, can defuse or still one's complaint. A world of crystallized particulars is conferred and received. This looks like humility, and "nonegocentric respect for the particular." The example of Job also reminds us that the path toward detachment or objectivity is sometimes not so much voluntarily taken as something that one gets carried or pushed into, the position and vision arriving involuntarily, as it were. Nagel speaks almost entirely in active terms: the objective will *creates* value, a stance is *adopted*, we *return* to the ordinary. Yet there are powerful counter-intuitions here: that meaning can happen or be discovered unexpectedly, in insight that appears given to the receptive self. This is the contrast so pervasive in *Either/Or* between self-responsibility based on choice and a more responsive receptivity.

RESPONSIBILITY

In a way reminiscent of Johannes Climacus's dialectical maneuverings, Nagel seems to alternate between the view that the objective urge is all-consuming, and bound to end in nihilism, and the more salutary view that there are a number of relatively secure stopping places for a self in motion. Perhaps morality or humility or respect for particulars can provide refuge from the dangers of endless outward transit. The necessity yet insecurity of such stopping places is displayed in the area of responsibility. The esthete addressed by Judge Wilhelm could illustrate the case, but let me work with an alternative from Dostoyevsky.

Ivan Karamazov comes at the world as an outsider, screening himself off in a hidden corner of the second floor of a cafe to discuss good and evil, eavesdropping on his father's lechery, or collecting second-hand newspaper accounts of the suffering of children. He is portrayed as a removed, objective observer, wedded to enlightenment science, heartless and in despair. He is an easy double of Kierkegaard's "scholarly esthete," with an appropriate dash of Karamazov sensuality tossed in.

His brother Alyosha is equally aware of evil—perhaps more so, for unlike Ivan, he shares in the sufferings of others. But Alyosha finds himself positioned in the world of care, not out of it. He asks what can be done, given that one is *already* engaged, bound, and accountable to others through love. In this regard, he has acknowledged his roots in community, roots he does not create but which nevertheless mark out his responsibilities. If Judge Wilhelm were to speak, he'd say that Alyosha has "repented himself back into the family, back into the [human] race."[14] He is "self-responsible."

Between Ivan's objective detachment and Alyosha's subjective engagement, there appears to be little common ground.[15] And the appeal of Dostoyevsky's narrative rests on the truth of something like Nagel's claims. We are caught up in a personal world where responsibility is central, yet simultaneously, we can be driven outward, encouraged by the authority of science (not to say discouraged by the presence of evil) until the point of responsible action seems to disappear. As in *Job*, the objective/subjective polarity seems to have a broad explanatory power.

Although Ivan is detached with regard to action, finding no reason to enter a personal world from which he feels alienated, nevertheless he easily attributes evil to humans, holding them responsible. And he holds God responsible, too, for permitting such evil. So at the level of judgment of others, Ivan sustains sufficient engagement to ground his praise and blame. This is not true at the level of moral action; here Ivan seems immobilized. Perhaps his initial question locks him out of meaningful engagement. It is as if he asks: Given that I am *not* involved and see things as *happenings* from which I am largely detached, what reason can I possibly find to induce me to *enter* that bent and broken world?

The spot from which he asks excludes a helpful answer. Placed outside, he can't find reason—no one could—to join a world whose evil disgusts (and fascinates) him. He tells Alyosha that it's not God, but His world that he rejects.[16] He rejects participation in ordinary temporal life. In contrast, Alyosha's confessor, Father Zossima, does not ask Ivan's question, nor a question from Ivan's standpoint. He, like Alyosha, places himself differently, allowing a helpful answer to the question of evil to emerge. In its very asking, the question Zossima asks shows that he is *already* within the life of responsible, compassionate agency: Given that I am joined with others, linked to them through love and concern, what can I do to *renew* these ties?

ETHICS ONCE AGAIN

The mainstream Kantian and utilitarian tradition holds that the impersonal moral standpoint must always dominate more personal ones. Nagel denies this. He accords personal, subjective reasons the possibility of overriding weight against objective ones. This means, to make a Kierkegaardian application, that Abraham's personal ties to the divine can generate reasons that outweigh or balance more objective social one. But Nagel is less concerned with this than another more "esthetic" situation where the personal and nonuniversal may contend with the ethical.

Nagel characterizes objective or impartial reasons as "agent-neutral" and more subjective ones as "agent-relative." To say that values have some objectivity means that they can form the basis for reasons that are relatively detached from the personal perspective of the agent, that function as motivators and justifiers and that do not reduce to what I might want or feel justified in doing from a merely self-absorbed, subjective standpoint. Kierkegaard acknowledges this sort of objective reason when, in the *Postscript*, he says that a knight of faith can not be a common thief or murderer. The existence of such objective "universal" obligations creates one-half of the dilemma Abraham faces in *Fear and Trembling*. There would *be* no dilemmas, no fear and trembling, if these objective reasons were illusory.

Where can traits of character—Socratic self-responsibility—be located within the objective/subjective spectrum? Generosity, responsibility, or love involve a stance that is often personal and specific rather than detached and impartialist. Yet in such cases, action flowing from these traits or virtues does not seem to be *merely* personal or subjective.

There is an unfortunate abstractness in Nagel's characterization of the self. Rather than being "thick" with character and embedded in tradition and relationship, it is divided into parts, the objective and subjective self, each tending in apparent independence of particular social or historical or personal conditions to pursue its separate end: the former moving relentlessly toward increased detachment and deflationary theory, the latter, pulling back toward self-concern and nonmoral desire. But the moral life of the self—especially as that self is expressed through the categories of virtue and character, community and tradition—is richer than this relatively abstract bipolar design can easily allow. In this case a Kierkegaardian corrective is available, the development of self-responsibility and its virtues.

For Kierkegaard the required move is toward the concrete particularity of engaged selves. Apart from the familiar philosophical demand that moral reasons be general, impartial, and openly delivered, there seems little reason to withhold the accolade "moral" from a person's native concern for those nearby. Given that initially one's concerns are necessarily nourished in a provincial or local setting, it's natural to assume that concern continues to be nourished through particular personal ties. And it's not obvious, as some ethicists have thought, that having such particular concern, rooted in a history of loving care rather than in adopted principle, will entail a dangerous indifference toward relative strangers. But however this debate proceeds, there is another and wider point to be made. At the level of "moral phenomenology," Nagel's map seems incomplete. The phenomenon of particular loving response seems to be theorized out of existence, for such particularized response is neither, on its face, the application of an impartial principle, nor an "agent-relative" or "subjective" reason.[17] It is a response to the independent value of another self, a "crystallized particular." An adequate moral psychology must reserve some place for caring attentiveness to particular persons.

In a later passage, Nagel speaks of moral "conversion" as a possible response to the painful gap between doing what's right (impersonally, impartially) and the requirements of a personally satisfying and meaningful life. Alteration of consciousness away from "the good life" or the "esthetic sphere" might veer toward something more altruistically focused, toward impersonal and impartial benevolence as well as toward the civic morality of Judge Wilhelm. Or it could veer toward a sort of selfless devotion bestowed on friends, kin or special causes. These shifts can resemble Kierkegaardian stage shifts. Nagel's consideration of such "conversions" could be expanded in ways that would refine the objective/subjective continuum, providing lines for a richer moral psychology of the developing person-in-relationship. Nagel's remarks about humility and nonegocentric attention to the particular could provide the elements for a Kierkegaardian other-regarding attentiveness to the particular.

Nagel suggests that cultivating a sort of esthetic attention to particular objects can cause the distinction between subjective and objective aspects to disappear. He doubts one can maintain this attention for long, but for moments, attending to special beauty or grandeur can catapult one outside the unhappy shuttle between perspectives. It is natural to see this attitude as primarily esthetic, and therefore irrelevant to questions of ethics. "Ethics, unlike aesthetics, requires more than the purification and intensification of internal human perspectives. It requires a detachment from particular perspectives and transcendence of one's time and place."[18]

But must we accept this sharp contrast? We can become lost in our attention to the grace of a lively child at play. Or as we have seen in the case of Job, we can become lost in the wonder of sleet or stars. Is it clear, though, that there must be a categorical break between such "selfless" esthetic appreciation and a moral, caring attention to a child—or even to the heavens? Even Kant permitted a connection: "[T]o take an immediate interest in the beauty of nature...is always a mark of a good soul...."[19] And he continues: "[Aesthetic] taste makes, as it were, the transition from the charm of sense to habitual moral interest possible without too violent a leap...."[20] An esthetic viewpoint can seem naturally to slip into a moral one. And as Sylvia Walsh has argued, there is a sense in which an esthetic sensibility, or poetic way of life, underlies all of Kierkegaard's "stages on life's way," integrated into, and not merely in opposition to, the ethical or religious perspectives.[21]

Such an attitude may seem too passive, too "receptive," to be properly moral. But although action is often the foreground in our moral assessments, the background quality of consciousness and the environing world can be equally important. And an apparent "esthetic" passivity need not be assimilated to moral failure or vice. The other's reality can capture and draw out our loving concern; an alert receptivity is a precondition of being so drawn out. This receptivity is linked to humility and "nonegocentric respect for the particular." One opens oneself, as Larry Blum puts it, to an "unsought reality external to one's explicit projects and endeavors."[22] One develops, in the phrase of Henry James, a consciousness "finely aware and richly responsible."[23] Kierkegaard's stress on an individual's development of such a sensibility is descried this way by Alastair Hannay: "Kierkegaard aims to enrich his reader's sensibilities so that the narrow yes and no of the palate gives way to a sense for the kinds of considerations upon which choices and rejections of whole ways of life depend.... [T]he attempt to appeal to anything else, for example objective reason, argument, revelation, or any authority at all, is simply a strategy of flight...."[24] The flight from our finite lights toward a presumed view from nowhere is bound to fail, however insistent and persistent the impulse inevitably appears.

OBJECTIVE / SUBJECTIVE AGAIN

Let me now turn to the troublesome complexities of the objective/subjective polarity. In fact, there seem to be several polarities at work.[25] There are differences in what we could label objectivity of stance. In what I will call reflective objectivity, we step back from our customary assumptions and judgments momentarily holding them in suspense. We cultivate maximum openness and receptivity to new insight, data or ways of framing issues, prior to settling on a more fixed position. This is the sort of flexible and attentive stance that permits discovery, the growth of knowledge and the extension and enrichment of our lives. Kierkegaard employs such "reflective objectivity" as he clarifies subjective states and transitions.

Adversarial objectivity aims to expose fraudulence, ignorance, pretense, or presumption. We might speak here of frames of trust and mistrust. Reflective objectivity assumes a sort of preservative care for its object, presuming that there is something at hand worth caring for. Adversarial objectivity lacks this preservative care. From the standpoint of reflective objectivity, adversarial challenges are preliminary forays, always subordinate to the primary goal of a wider, more precise, or more viable understanding, knowledge, or orientation. Perhaps Kierkegaard's dialectical forays are primarily aimed at disillusionment, at breaking down defenses rather than in laying out positive or exemplary positions. In that case, his overall stance would be adversarily objective. But no doubt his aim is shifting, sometimes constructively reflective, at times meant primarily to undermine.

A third sort of objective stance could be called role or institutional objectivity. Here, we adopt a position, an ongoing stance integral to a role or policy, that requires that the self be detached from some of its particularity and some of its subjective concerns. There are conventional social rules constitutive of such roles that specify the forms that such objectivity must take. Judges, scholars, scientists, sisters, in different ways will find themselves bound by position-related duties. Such institutional or role-objectivity is essential both to a rational or good society and to the selves that compose it. It is what Kierkegaard (or Judge Wilhelm) would call "the universal." Just as clearly, a reflective objectivity can fruitfully weigh how much of an individual life, or how much of the life of a community, should be taken up by such role objective pursuit, and how the several roles we occupy should be weighed with regard to their relative importance.

Adopting a more objective stance removes some subjectivity from the field attended to. This use of the subjective/objective contrast marks the difference between methods or outcomes that are less reliable, or falsehood-tending and those that are typically more reliable, or truth tending. These uses of the subjective/objective polarity can nest in various ways. For example, within the objective, detached standpoint, there are more or less reliable or truth-tending, "objective" ways to organize the field of inquiry or understanding. If these distinctions have weight, then an account of objectivity or subjectivity will be neither simple to trace nor single in structure.

Furthermore, the drive toward objectivity is not a unitary force with inherently self-propelling and self-reinforcing momentum—the ghostly activity of abstract, deracinated thinkers. There is a social, political, and economic underlay to this pursuit. Technological, bureaucratic societies and market economies play into its advance as well. And lastly, there is the familiar Kierkegaardian point that spiritually we tend to flee the unbearable tensions of a subjective life by seeking an impersonal vantage-point from which the self is largely excised.[26]

UNFINISHING REFLECTIONS

Nagel doesn't think he has found solutions to most of the problems he wrestles with in *The View from Nowhere*. He believes some of them may be unsolvable. But we learn something by laying out the nature of a particular problem even if what is thereby clarified is the problem's relative intractability. This sense of the powers and limits of reflection is surely Kierkegaardian in spirit, as we have seen especially in our discussions of Abraham and Job, and of Judge Wilhelm's "double vision" of self-acquisition.

At one point Nagel speaks of the need for "double vision." In crucial cases it may be impossible to relegate one of a pair of conflicting standpoints to the status of "mere appearance," for that would strip it of the seriousness it must have in our lives. The measure of reality is partly the measure of what matters, and conflicting things can matter. "We cannot come to regard our ideas of our own agency or of the purity of our self-identity through time as mere appearances or impressions. That would be equivalent to giving them up. Though our intuitive convictions about these things emerge very much from our own point of view, they have pretensions to describe not just how we appear to ourselves but how we are."[27] Unable to give up either our subjective convictions or the realization that from a sufficiently objective standpoint they simply wash away, we develop a twofold vision. "Double vision is the fate of creatures with a glimpse of the view *sub specie aeternitatis*."[28]

If we are fated to live out this doubleness, we should nevertheless probe our motivations for attaining a "glimpse of the eternal." They may be quite pure and defensible. Or it may be that the allure of the utterly objective viewpoint is the attraction of invulnerability, a status denied mortals. It may be the quixotic project of containing and protecting the self through denial, part of a drive to escape the messiness of the world and the terrors of undeceived selfhood. Martha Nussbaum has traced one powerful strand in our tradition (what we could call the Platonic flight from embodied particularity): the pursuit of a harder "objective" self-sufficiency to escape a painful yet precious human vulnerability.[29]

Is acceptance of "double vision" just a perverse refusal to pare down, sublimate, or integrate, as the case might dictate? For many, the heroic course is to accept a scientific objectivity and its consequences as the "realistic" course. As one celebrates or accepts the death of God, so one must now announce and celebrate the death of Self or Mind or Freedom—not to mention the death of Philosophy itself. Others seek negotiated truce, patchwork settlements that mask the failure to face the deepest conflicts in our conceptual schemes. Perhaps worries about Consciousness, Freedom or Self or the Divine should be ceremoniously buried or allowed to diminish, to become lost in the cultural clutter, amusing relics of another age.

Yet the more Socratic or Kierkegaardian tack, and the tack that Nagel takes, is to acknowledge our pervasive ignorance, confusion, and layered self-deceptions, to marshal our capacities for clarity in the struggle against these conditions, and to trust that such excellent if benighted labor is neither needless nor thankless. As Climacus put it in the *Postscript*, the labor of an existing individual is to "interpenetrate one's existence with consciousness, simultaneously to be eternal, far beyond it, as it were, and nevertheless in a process of becoming—that is truly difficult."[30] It is, he says, the paradoxical attempt to be "at two places at the same time."[31] This is Nagel's faith, and Kierkegaard's, that even if delivered only as a double vision, there is truth and value to be found.

MUSIC OF THE SPHERES
Kierkegaardian Selves and Transformations

The self-relating self can be...a family, or a sisterhood, or a string quartet.

— Stephen Crites[1]

An abundance of feeling...as complex as any trio or quartet that was ever meant to express love and jealousy, and resignation and fierce suspicion, all at the same time.

— George Eliot[2]

MUSICAL MODELS AND MOTIFS ABOUND THROUGHOUT KIERKEGAARD'S VARIED compositions. To link his moral-psychological themes and musical structures or motifs promises a great return, For musical figures are not just ornamental in his writings.[3] They provide essential clues to the philosophical and religious structure of his thought—in at least three ways. The discourse on Mozart's *Don Giovanni* and "the musical erotic" in *Either/Or*, for example, is a discussion of music that is immediately relevant to our understanding of the esthetic sphere of human existence.[4] Second, there is Kierkegaard's subtle imitation of musical form or structure. The richest example here is *Fear and Trembling*, upon which we might dwell a moment.[5]

The subtitle to this work is "Dialectical lyric"—a kind of philosophical poetry or song.[6] Its unfolding structure seems symphonic or operatic: there is an opening program note (or preface), a tuning section which sets the stage, a lengthy overture, three dialectical acts or movements, and a closing coda. The section immediately following the program note has a title best translated "Attunement."[7] This captures the idea of setting a mood or atmosphere, as the Danish *Stemning* (mood; atmosphere; feeling; tuning) would suggest.[8] It also rings of "tuning up"—readying audience and performer alike for an ensuing performance. Our mood and sensibilities are tuned by a quartet of Abraham and Isaac tales. Kierkegaard—through the voice of Johannes de silentio—sounds variations on the Genesis story of God's terrible command to Abraham. These abbreviated, disturbing, and distorting "attunements" are rehearsals, false starts. We hear a virtuoso warming up, practicing in the wings. By their dazzling obscurity, these exercises tease our dialectical and musical ears, preparing us for longer renditions yet to come. Following "Attunement" is a lengthy introductory section titled "Preamble from the Heart,"[9] which I'd call the overture. Then three dialectical "Problems" overtake the lyricism of the heartfelt opening. The first asks, "Can there be a Teleological Suspension of the Ethical?" The third act or movement is a lengthy discourse on silence. An "Epilogue" or coda closes out this musical performance. If nowhere else in his voluminous production, surely here Kierkegaard anticipates—and fulfills—Nietzsche's call for a music-playing Socrates.[10]

So music informs Kirkegaard's thought both as an explicit topic of discussion and as an implicit structure for a work such as *Fear and Trembling*. Finally, music can provide analogical models for interpreting some of Kierkegaard's more abstruse dialectical discussions.

Our discussion of the "Job Discourse" and repetition modeled change in the consciousness (or its "presuppositional basis") on change in musical key, along lines Kierkegaard himself suggests. Here we return to the issue of transition between life-views or moral-religious outlooks. Judge Wilhelm vacillated between "self-choice" and "self-reception" models of transition into selfhood in *Either/Or*. This transition, and transitions between life-spheres generally, can be modeled musically, as we shall see. And not just transitions, but selfhood itself yields to musical interpretation. This becomes especially apparent when we consider *Sickness Unto Death* which opens straightforwardly with a "musical" definition of self. In this late pseudonymous work, we find Kierkegaard refining and expanding the tentative sketches of self produced in his earlier pseudonymous works. Idioms of self-choice or self-reception are now incorporated within a more expansive relational view of self.

Penned by the mysterious author Anti-Climacus, *Sickness Unto Death* sketches Kierkegaard's most complex portrait of moral-religious discord and resolve. This portrait is introduced abstractly in a notorious definition of self as a "relation relating to a relation."[11] As the epigraph for this chapter suggests, the formulation can model a number of things besides the self you or I might happen to be. Among them, as Stephen Crites insightfully suggests, it might model a conversation, a labor union, or even a string quartet.[12]

As Socrates reaches an impasse in discussion of a soul in *The Republic*, Plato employs a startling strategy to clarify a person's inner life or character. He asks us to picture a community, a complex city, a "self writ large." This enlarged model of self allows Plato (or Socrates) to discuss a soul indirectly by considering something perhaps more accessible and familiar, the more visible political life of selves in community. This parallel discussion of self and city will hatch paired lines of insight. A reader of *Sickness Unto Death* might equally be aided by an enlarged model of self. The abstract formula for self laid out by Anti-Climacus can be expanded not to city size, but to the scale of a performing musical ensemble. This "self writ large" might give insight into self, and also into self-like spheres—musicians who weave, round out, communal faith and spirit.

I have hopes for several lines of thought. To project self-structure onto a wider stage can clarify the complex of relations constituting a particular self; it can clarify the complex of interpersonal relations making up a Kierkegaardian "life-sphere" or "stage of existence;" and it can clarify the strains that both self and self-sphere undergo in movement from stage to stage. Finally, I hope this more expansive prospect may lift, if only momentarily, fogs that shroud the glad suffering of a religious life—its pained convictions, lucid patterns, and uncanny, dark serenities.

SELF AS RELATIONAL FIELD

If persons are selves, then perhaps self is something that develops *through* stages—a common thread, winding through, and thereby linking, transformations. We might picture a self moving "dialectically" through Kierkegaardian esthetic, ethical, and religious stages. We'd have the self as a most important and primordial *something* that takes on various moral or esthetic features, or subscribes to various stage-defining moral or religious principles. But however natural and obvious this construal may seem, it starts us on the wrong foot. What could this primordial self be—apart from the relationships defining some stage or plateau in development? Could it be a pinpoint, perhaps a spot, of will or choice? Perhaps that spot vaults from sphere to sphere, leaps from this stage to the next over a chasm of deep uncertainty! True, this is a familiar picture, championed by many expositors of Kierkegaard, including most recently Alastair MacIntyre in *After Virtue*.[13] A look at *Sickness Unto Death*, however, presents quite another view of self. There it is mapped not as a substance or a central spot of will but as a complex *relational field*. In an infamous opening passage, we find the formula: "self is a relation which relates to itself."[14]

Imagine not Crites's string quartet, but a sextet with alto/alto, tenor/tenor, and bass/bass parts sharply juxtaposed. Anti-Climacus describes self as such an ensemble of juxtaposed pairs, pairs with abstract names: "freedom and necessity, the infinite and the finite, the eternal and the temporal."[15] These are the "voices" of his self ensemble. So named, they form pairs in antithesis, in apparent disharmony. We might think of each term as defining a limit which when linked to its contrary describes an axis—say, a continuum between freedom and necessity. The point of making such an axis would be heuristic. It would play some helpful theoretical role in describing the tensions and unities of a functioning self. Given the apparent opposition between these relational terms—"factors" or "poles" of self—the self ensemble we have been imagining would require, in concrete orchestration, pairs of severely contrasting coloration. Perhaps the opposition of each pair might be caught, comically, by scoring oboe with fugelhorn, tuba with contra-bassoon, cello with krummhorn—each instrument then assigned notes at the extremes of its normal register.[16]

What will make this musical ensemble more than a chaotic noise machine is to have each individual voice relate to its given partner, to create some sort of synthesis of these opposite pairs. Furthermore, the pairs, as pairs, must be mutually relating—tenors must relate to bass and alto parts, as well as to each other. Furthermore, each voice, we might say, must conceive of itself as participating in the *ensemble's relation to itself*—conceive of itself *as* an ensemble. This is a relation over and above the relations of any voice to another, or to another pair, or to the aggregate of other voices.[17] Somehow the group must become more than a lifeless, bland collection. Anti-Climacus calls a mere aggregate of pairs a "negative unity," a unity that falls short of the requirements of self or spirit.[18] To become a functioning, flourishing whole in a fluid unity we need a set of relations that relates positively, actively to itself *as* a flourishing ensemble. This threefold set of juxtaposed factors or vectors relating positively, actively, to itself, *is* relational selfhood, self as ensemble.[19]

One thing is evident immediately from this construal. Self, so far described, lacks any *element* of central command, lacks any discrete point of will or choice. So far, the ensemble is its self-relating, and nothing more—not in particular, its relation to an independent director. Nor is there a factor that might be thought to "possess" the field of these existentially contrasting pairs. In later sections, I pursue at length the implications of this fact—the absence of a concrete center of self—for construals of Kierkegaardian stage-shifts that emphasize "arbitrary choice" of life-sphere. For the moment, we can say that crossing the threshold into selfhood can not require an independent *choosing* self (or faculty of will). An individual constituted by a set of tensed vectors will just *become* that field relating *to* itself as self ensemble. Before filling in the details of this phenomena, however, there's a further complication to face.

GROUNDING POWER

Anti-Climacus has given a fairly opaque formula, which by now should be less opaque: "[Self is not just]...a synthesis of the infinite and the finite, of the temporal and the eternal, of freedom and necessity...but of the relation's relating to itself."[20] He then proceeds to add a third level of relationship. He declares that a self must relate to something outside itself, to a constituting power: "This...is the formula which describes the state of the self when despair is completely eradicated: in relating to itself and in wanting to be itself, the self is grounded transparently in the power that established it."[21] So a nondivisive, non-despairing self is in "downward" relationship to itself and to God as a power in which it is transparently grounded.

If self becomes self only as it finds itself willingly in a transparent relationship to God as a constituting power, then what would this mean, musically construed? The "selfhood" of our ensemble must be "grounded transparently" in something deeper. This might be the score in which performance finds its roots. An ensemble grounds itself in a text that gives it division of labor, notes to sound, direction, entrances and exits, authority and subordination. But some great ensemble playing proceeds in the absence of a printed score. And scores, at best, require extensive interpretation. Perhaps we could say that some potential, or possibility—an "idea" to be realized, "the music-to-be-played," or more opaquely, "Music"—is the power in which the sextet must transparently ground itself (or find itself grounded). Before the moment of fully realized ensemble—say, as audience or artists anticipate an opening chord or voice—such grounding power will seem something to await, on which one fully depends, something to be discovered, full of contingency, metaphysically of uncertain yet crucial status.

Anti-Climacus does not characterize God as a person-like something with supernatural attributes. He writes instead that God is "that all things are possible."[22] If God is the power that grounds our agency as selves, then by this formula, He is also the ultimate field of possibility. The divine is radical freedom. A functioning ensemble must also be grounded in such freedom. As we listen to (or play) great music, we know, paradoxically, that "all things are possible." As audience, we can be placed in wondrous expectancy, even when the piece about to be played is familiar. So also for performers. Whatever the discipline or training or practice preceding a performance, once the opening phrases spin out, then wonder, surprise, and contingency can mark the emerging spirit of the piece—

and ideally *should* be present. This sense of possibility as wonder or ripeness for the new is a requirement, we might say, both of attentive performance and attentive audition. It is a power both audience and artist will welcome as a grounding power—something that will provide the very life of this particular music, no matter how many times it may have been previously brought to birth. Yet this field of contingency, freedom, or creation is strangely wedded to its opposite, necessity. Even as the piece unfolds freely, winding into regions uncanny or unknown, whether as audience or as performers, we sense it just as strongly *find* itself. Even as each phrase is radically born anew, so it is repeatedly rediscovered to be as it *must* be. Music, as ensemble, will ground itself transparently, freely, in its destined future—in what it must forever be.

If our rendering of relational self is still on target, then perhaps the ultimate field, context, or authority for our being, whether as individuals or as actors in concert, is something that appears contingent, separate from the mastering struggles of our will. Salvation, then, must rest on powers that can terrifyingly rip away our most cherished possessions. It rests on receptivity to that fact, and to the possibility of graceful, wondrous restoration of all we cherish. Faith (in *Fear and Trembling*) is a "double movement" of giving up (by our own strength) and getting back (through the power of "Another"). It is as if we were back with Abraham: Isaac is lost and is recovered. Or back with Job.[23] The terribly, wondrously "Unexpected" underlies our daily toils for self; it must be suffered, even by the just.

So far, I hope to have given sense to the freedom/ necessity contrast by locating it in the grounding power that founds a self—power that potentiates a self along these vectors. This couplet is complemented by the eternal /temporal and infinite/finite couplets.[24] Each of these contrasting vector-pairs can be specified as follows: a) as psychological factors within a self; b) as they might be modeled by a musical ensemble; or c) as they resonate at the level of divine grounding power. An eternal, infinite power is pulled toward, in struggle with, a worldly, temporal other. Here I can only note such theological modeling; it's the musical rendering of self we have been pursuing. Nevertheless, this rendering allows, seems even to require, an orbit vaster than the already expanded stage that ensemble performance encircles. This natural openness to ever wider spheres of interpretation, to my mind, speaks for the richness of Kierkegaard's formulations. We seem to work not just from "within" ensemble to its "grounding power," but also from "without"—from grounding power to the self-relations of ensemble. The vectors of self are infused, activated, empowered, from without.

UNIVERSAL AND PARTICULAR

Renderings of the infinite/finite, and eternal/temporal couplets are possible on analogy with the freedom/necessity pair. But I want to explore another contrastive pair—the familiar Hegelian-Kierkegaardian couplet "universal/particular." As Johannes de silentio (in *Fear and Trembling*) traces the emergence of specifically religious consciousness, he contrasts general, universal moral and religious injunctions ("Love thy kin and son") with more particular injunctions or demands. In the Abraham story the particular divine injunction is God's demand for Isaac. This "particular" demand clashes terribly with the familiar "universal" claims of social ethics and religion—the later *also* rooted in the sacred, but less strikingly so.[25] There is a musical analogue to this clash of universal and particular, of "passable," unexceptional patterns of social-religious behavior and the profound and often profoundly dissonant inward fields of spirit, where particular and universal can clash or seem in strange or wondrous opposition.

It is not uncommon in great music to hear unifying, universal patterns, familiar rhythms and tonalities that give us a solid, shared, accustomed sense of place. Yet it is also not uncommon to hear simultaneously the hint of something unexpected, something special to this performance. A "particular" aspect may in fact rise up in some moment of terror, surprise, or surpassing gentleness. We jump, snap alert, or melt. These moments—always lurking, then blindingly present—put the "universal" or habitually expected at risk, often through defiance or alteration or twist of some rhythmic or tonal expectation. There is such a moment in Richard Stoltzman's cadenza in Mozart's Clarinet Concerto: a soft descending passage slowly closes out in such extended silence that we're sure he's left the stage forever—only to have a tone unimaginably low and tender inaudibly reenter.[26]

Abraham must surely love and nurture Isaac, which pleases both God and our local pastor, and places him solidly within the realm of ordinary moral expectations. But he must also render Isaac up to God, which pits God against God, particular against universal, silence against expected sounds, to the deep distress or wonder of us all.[27] So we might say that a profound piece of music can wed (in degrees of unison or disharmony) the universal and particular, whether the unexpected latter becomes manifest as Stoltzman's cadenza silence, the uncannily attentive phrasing care of Gidon Kremer, or the unnerving thick and crushing power of Leontyne Price in her singing prime.[28] In these consummatory moments the expected and exceptional join. At such times, fixed between freedoms and necessities, between the familiar and the wondrous or terribly strange, Art becomes "transparently grounded in the power that constitutes it." Perhaps in the Muse herself.

SELVES, LIFE-SPHERES, AND TRANSFORMATIONS

A self (sextet) is a network of relationships that makes up a (perhaps incomplete) whole that relates to itself. This whole, or self ensemble then relates to something outside itself, a power that grounds or founds it. How does a self fit within a Kierkegaardian sphere or stage upon life's way? We might think of such a sphere or stage as a field of relationships in which the self is immersed. Since self, as we've sketched it, is *itself* a complex multi-layered field of relationships (rather than an atom, spot, or thread *within* a field), self and life-sphere can be conceptually coordinated, placed in reciprocal, mutually defining relationship.

Self and sphere are, in some respects, the same field sketched from different vantages. Self can be sketched from the inside out, as it is in the formula of *Sickness Unto Death*. The relevant vocabulary is then psychological, and concerns the "inner" space of self or spirit. Life-stages, on the other hand, are typically sketched by Kierkegaardian pseudonyms from the outside in. The relevant vocabulary does not exclude the "psychological"; but it is also interpersonal and social—even political. Family life, public institutions, friendship and marriage fit into the characterization of various stages. It's my thesis here that the ensemble we've called self (following Anti-Climacus) and what Marx in a not so different context also called the self, "the ensemble of social relationships," can be seen, with sufficient imaginative elaboration, as two sides of a single coin.[29] If there's a membrane here between an active self and a mobile social world, it's more porous or transparent than Kierkegaardians have supposed.

This, then, is a *fourth* (and much neglected) level of relationship in a Kierkegaardian schema for self. The self is a relation related "downward" to itself, to the power that grounds it, and "outward" to its sphere of interpersonal activity.[30] We make sense of self (at any given stage of development) by specifying the relational, reflexive field it constitutes. This means sketching its connections to various persons, institutions, and projects; it means sketching values, ideals, points of aspiration that, in the nature of the case, a self will fail to live up to. So sketching a self or sphere will also mean sketching its forms of failure or despair. This is the fundamental and explicit project of *Sickness Unto Death*. But other pseudonymous works, as well, sketch not just stages of self but their internal fractures, points at which they will fail, thus plunging self into waters ripe for change, for movement into a new equilibrium or stage.

What is the nature of such stage-change? Perhaps the dialectic of failure and reconstitution is Hegelian. If so, insofar as it's an individual who must toil for spiritual or moral advance, the role of individual passion and engagement becomes prominent. For Kierkegaard, there is no awaiting a progressive historical inevitability. Such stress on the passionate, "subjective" individual—rather than on change at the level of cultural and institutional forms—has led many to speak of a Kierkegaardian self as choosing itself, its sphere, or its principle: making an existential "leap" at each moment of decision or change. In the two sections that follow, I'll raise skeptical doubts about this view. Then in the remainder of this exploration, I sketch an alterative picture of the links between self and stage, and the dynamics of sphere- or self-transformation. This will mean elaborating further the idea of self and life-sphere as mutually-defining authorities.

CONTRA CHOICE OF SELF OR SPHERE

In *Either/Or* Judge Wilhelm offers as a substitute for the Socratic "Know thyself," the formula "Choose thyself"—a radical banner Sartre will raise exactly a century later. Throughout the pseudonymous authorship, Kierkegaard mocks the hope that philosophical, scientific, or historical knowledge, unassisted by a knower's passion or commitment, can lead to worthy human progress, be it spiritual or moral. "Choosing oneself" is at least the antithesis of robotic data collecting—as if that activity could save a soul. Additionally, "choosing oneself" might be seen as adopting a leading principle or regulative idea that would have authority over the sphere one enters. Alastair MacIntyre (among others) has given wide currency to this quasi-Sartrean scheme in *After Virtue*.[31] In any given stage-shift, the self is pictured as facing an "either/or" between two incommensurate life-spheres. Only an arbitrary, nonrational choice can relieve this crisis. But apart from the intrinsically problematic idea of a "disembedded" or deracinated self magically elevating—or grounding—itself by self-choice, by arbitrary leaps, this scheme does not match *Kierkegaard*'s notion of stage-shift.

The pre-ethical or esthetic individual is characterized (at least by selves passed *out* of the esthetic) as not-yet-a-self. This individual "proto-self" is described as in perdition precisely because *no* principle or guiding light has been chosen. Not only is there no self, strictly speaking, to face an "either/or" between esthetic and ethical lives but the "choice" of the esthetic could not *be* a choice. What *constitutes* the esthetic is drifting by default. Thus there is as yet no self *empowered* to choose. But difficulties go even deeper. It's not clear, first, that the contrast between *choosing* a self and *discovering* or *receiving* a self is as radically distinct as many (including Judge Wilhelm and MacIntyre) make it out to be. (We've noted this issue in Chapter 2, and I'll return to it below.) Second, *Either/Or* depicts a "movement" that approximates a structure MacIntyre installs as the *general* form of any stage-shift. But Kierkegaardian stage-shifts do not share a single structure.

There are several substages within the esthetic sphere. Presumably individuals can move (or be carried) even in a somewhat progressive fashion through sub-forms of esthetic drift. The crowd, the sensuous, the poetic-reflective are existentially independent ways of being self-alienated.[32] Moves between these subspheres could not be based on choice, for individuals in these straits are non-choosers. Worse, the infamous "leap" from ethical to religious spheres is not exactly chosen either. The quasi-religious state of resignation (say, as sketched in *Fear and Trembling*, or as sketched in the *Postscript* as a Socratic "religiousness A") is forcefully distinguished from a more biblical faith.[33] And the contrast between biblical faith and resignation or Socratic faith rests precisely on the fact that faith cannot be attained by dint of one's own strength or effort.

Faith is characterized as a proffered gift. Divine initiative or grounding power—the third level in our earlier schema of the self—is not something that we can simply *choose* to grasp or to take hold of. We must have willingness, receptivity—and something offered *for* our willing acceptance. But none of this entails a classic existential exercise of will.[34] We don't just pick out faith for our possession. Neither do heroic achievements of the will guarantee its attainment. Isaac is *given back* to Abraham, not wrested violently from God's control. Of course, willingness, will in its receptive guise, is present in accepting, refusing, or disregarding a proffered gift. But gifts or faiths do not just lie there inert, awaiting our resolute or vacillating purchase. They can be offered, but also hidden, withheld or withdrawn. The striving or choosing characteristic of the ethical sphere is supplemented in faith by nonstriving, nonchoosing receptivity.

Choosing resignation does not simply *cause* a reciprocal grant of Isaac's return, or a return of worldly life and joys. Resignation does not cause *Fear and Trembling's* "second" movement of faith. Movement from the world of ethical engagement to a deeper embrace of "the absolute," the movement Johannes de silentio calls "dying to immediacy," may in fact be effected by the will. This first "movement" may involve knightly prowess, or a Socratic disengagement from the worldly. But the ultimate empowering, engendering relationship for selves, the relationship of faith, has power flowing *from* "the absolute" *to* the waiting self in resignation. Johannes de silentio himself is equivocal about the centrality of struggle and strength in faith. In the image of the shopkeeping knight, he at last gives prominence to the virtues of humility and receptivity, calling into question the virtue of heroic will-to-power that we might expect a jousting knight to exercise.

Attaining faith is *not* at last an act of choice. It is, as Anti-Climacus has it, being grounded in another.

CONTRA CHOICE OF PRINCIPLE

If there are problems with the idea that each "movement" into or out of a sphere is a deliberate sphere-adopting choice, then there are also problems with seeing the difference in spheres as difference in reigning principle. A practical moral principle is self-endorsed. It is something an agent respects, has reverence for, or consciously adopts as a guide. Morally, one acts *from* such principles—not merely thoughtlessly or accidentally in *accord* with them.

Of course, to speak of "principles" of the esthetic sphere may help to characterize typical patterns of behavior. In that sense, there may be "principles" describing inanimate motion, too—say, "principles" of lava flow or cloud drift. But agent-endorsed principles are quite different. Patterns of esthetic behavior are by definition not governed by self-endorsed practical or moral principles. If principles are said to govern here, they capture thoughtless drift. In any case, they surely are unchosen. Perhaps the ethical sphere, if any does, may be dominated by a chosen principle. Nevertheless, as we have seen, it remains unclear how something lacking self-powers, for instance the preethical individual, acquires powers sufficient to endorse or choose a self-constituting principle. And what of the religious sphere? Is it governed by chosen principle?

Think of Abraham in *Fear and Trembling*. Two principles bear inexorably upon him. One seems ethical-religious, in any case "universal": *Love thy son, protect him!* The other seems religious only, or in any case "particular": *Deliver up Isaac, as I demand!* These principles or injunctions certainly demand acknowledgment. But it hardly seems that Abraham is positioned either to make a sensible choice *between* them, or (strangely) to *choose both*. Both might be affirmed, acknowledged, or honored—inwardly, if impossibly in action. But there is no space between these injunctions and the willingness to honor them, on the one hand, and on the other, the very fabric of his being, his identity. Hence there is no gap for a leap or choice to bridge. *Per impossibile*, to choose but *one* of these self-defining principles (and reciprocal commitments) would be to lose half of his identity.[35] The Abraham subsequent to an exclusive choice of religious principle or sphere (a choice rejecting ethics) or the Abraham subsequent to an exclusive choice of ethical principle (a choice rejecting the divine) would not be *Abraham*—not the Abraham Kierkegaard wishes to preserve in *Fear and Trembling*. If he is to survive as the moral-spiritual exemplar he is, then neither an "ethical" nor a "religious" principle can be abruptly chosen, concocted by deliberate decision to override or suppress the other. Abraham's love of Isaac is not simply set side or suppressed. Faith can't be a choice that defeats or blots out a competing moral line. For ethics to be in "teleological suspension," it cannot be forgotten or abolished.[36]

I don't intend to rehearse again the tangle of issues such suspension raises. My broad aim in the last few sections has been to raise questions about a standard account of Kierkegaardian self development through stages. Thinking about the suspension of ethics is just one way to raise doubts about the view that a person moves along the stags of life's way by *choice* of stage or principle.

TONALITY, AUTHORITY, AND CHANGE

Let me now spell out an alternative picture of movement through the Kierkegaardian spheres. A look at musical tonal structure and its alteration can give us clues for constructing a model to replace the more standard account. This will make it easier to shake the grip of the quasi-Sartrean "liberal" view of Kierkegaardian self-choice. In brief, my thesis will be that self is like the tonal center that defines a musical key, that the authority of a self is something like the authority of tonality within a musical piece, and that change of self can be modeled on change of musical key.

We might think of a musical key as setting a tonal center of gravity. We can think (within the frame of classical harmony) of various pitches and chords occurring within a tonal sphere. That sphere takes time to be established, however. An opening C major chord can sometimes immediately establish tonality. But we can easily be surprised. If Bach is the composer, such opening will mean one thing; if Charles Ives is the composer, it may mean nothing at all with regard to tonal centering. Music can become so fractured and disjointed that no sense of authoritative center, no sense of sustained tonality, is present. There can be notes, beautifully or roughly clustered, yet no tunes or key. A shift between musical keys can be radical, as critical for our musical understanding as a shift in theme, motif, or color. The change might emerge from previous material. It might or might not mark a radical joint, rupture, or break. And after change, the previous key may remain auditorially present, even as the new takes hold. Relations of authority, though not exactly of principle, are altered. What in the old key was a fundamental pitch may in the new key become a passing tone, relatively unimportant or subordinate. A return to original key will be a return to something both the same and altered—altered just in virtue of its momentary loss, or more sustained suspension.

Getting closer to Kierkegaardian terrain, we might say that key emerges with a sense of some tonality. Of course, established keys can be rocked, or only slightly altered. There can be modulations, suspensions, conflicts between tonal centers. Yet in the simpler cases, chords "want" to move toward or away from a tonal center; their distance from that center can be measured. In the language of our formula for relational self, these pitches, tunes, and chords want to be in this relational field (say, of notes within a chord) relating to itself (say, as a chord within a tonal field). If notes or chords move too radically in disrespect of center, then it seems the relation fails to want to be itself. The key may disappear, either replaced by a new center of gravity, or by utter loss of tonality itself.

What is the theoretical status of such an authoritative tonal center—or of the authoritative center we call self? The way the self lays out or shapes the field of interactions, the way it exerts authority, is often pictured in legal or political terms. We imagine a ruling, autonomous self on the model of a king or constitution structuring peopled realms, such authority backed up by will, power, and coercion. But as we've seen, a Kierkegaardian self is not a "little king" or ruler within a body, or within a sphere of projects and activities, feelings and beliefs. It is instead just the field of its relationships, relating to itself, and to a grounding power. No one element in this field dominates, or is even easily separated out from the others, for each element is defined in terms of its polar opposite, and in terms of its "downward" connection to itself and a grounding power. There *is* no single element to rule. Yet the idea of the self as center dies hard. Can we keep the idea (from *Sickness Unto Death*) of self as a relational ensemble—*and* the idea (from *Either/Or* and elsewhere) of the self as center?

Daniel Dennett suggests that the self is a *narrative center of gravity*.[37] This sounds close to our idea that musical key is a tonal center of gravity. Perhaps thinking about the theoretical status of a material object's center of gravity will clarify the respect in which self can be conceived as a narrative center, and simultaneously, as a complex field of relationships—an ensemble. The idea of a physical object's center of gravity (a chair's, say) is a precise and useful concept. It is also theoretical and heuristic. Although it is (sometimes) useful to locate an object's center of gravity, to know this location is not to have identified a separate physical object *within* the physical body in question. Knowing something about this chair, I can locate its center of gravity at the cross hairs of some physical variables having to do with size, weight, design, materials of composition, etc. Although observing the chair's properties can locate this center, logically it never could be an observable feature on a par with its size, weight, and so forth. Its postulation—its very *existence*—is an inference to the best explanation of a chair's capacity to be balanced like *this*, but not like *that*.

A chair's center of gravity can be more or less stable depending on a set of relationships—whether the seat or legs wiggle rather than hold firm, whether a weight is affixed under the arm, or the length of the legs is changed. Its center of gravity, we might say, is the authoritative center of its stability and ability to function. In a sense, its stability will "flow from" and be determined by that center. This is a relatively simple example. Now think of the complex, fluid, moving center of gravity of a skier flying down the slopes; consider its importance for a skilled performance. Could persons, especially in transition, have such complex, fluid, psychological centers of gravity—centers whose misplacement could spell disaster for the self?

Self is a *narrative* center of gravity. It is something of utmost importance for stability and function, unmistakably present, yet tantalizingly difficult to isolate. As Hume discovered, looking within for its impression, we find nothing. It is more or less stable, and more or less determined by a field of relationships. For some feature or some change of my person to be identified as belonging to my life, there must be a field of narrative connections into which it will fit. Just as an addition of 100 pounds of weight to a chair may or may not alter its center of gravity, so a new feature in my life or a change of heart may or may not alter my narrative center of gravity. My self might undergo drastic change, conversion, or merely become more complex. Or it might "fall apart," lose itself, its center. So a chair on which I'm sitting may have its field of relationships so disrupted that the idea of its practical center of gravity becomes all but useless—say as the chair and I are falling backwards off the porch. In any case, a person's center, especially in times of growth, will typically be fluid, changing like the plummeting skier's center, rather than static, like a firmly planted pew.

AUTHORITY OF SELF AND SPHERE

The self is an *authoritative* center in the way musical keys or centers of gravity can be authoritative. The structure and orientation of a self determine, lay out or "author" the meaning, weight and import of elements in a field. The elements of the self's field can be described abstractly, as Anti-Climacus does, by naming polar vectors in philosophical terminology. But we have less technical ways of describing this field, as well. The self is a network of interrelated movements, projects, impulses, utterances, decisions, promises, leaps, deferrals, travels, relationships. This possibility of description starting either from the self or from the interpersonal sphere to which it belongs raises again the issue of the interdefinability of Kierkegaardian selves and life-spheres.

From one angle of description, the self is surely authoritative, a center (abstract, or heuristic) from which a steady or conflicting pattern of beliefs, actions, feelings, seem to flow. But we could as well describe the self's authority or dominance from another angle. Perhaps a pattern of promises, acts, movements, thoughts, and sufferings will itself create or shape the authoritative seat we call the self. It would then be like the intersection of our varied cares, a self created *by* its field, by its sphere of social and interpersonal relationships.

We are tempted to think that one description must be fundamental, the other derivative. Is selfhood shaped *by* the field or does it instead *shape* the field? But I see no need to take these as competing alternatives. Consider a musical or sport analogy. So far as baseball fields are concerned, we can say, for convenience, that home plate is the authoritative spot from which baselines and pitching mound are aligned. Its placement can spell out the remainder of the field. But it's also true that the centrality of "home" is governed by the structure of the environing field. If we alter the placement of the pitching mound, third and seconnd base, that in turn will be authoritative for determining the placement of home. Similarly, we can say either that the key of C *makes* B-natural a leading tone and E a third; or equally, that by virtue of B leading into C, and E being a third, the key of C is "authored" (or *made* authoritative).

There is no deep paradox, then, in holding a) that self is the authoritative narrative "center" of a complex life—and, simultaneously, b) that a self is determined by the multileveled field of relationships in which it finds itself, including its relations to itself, its relations to its grounding power, its interpersonal relationships, and the relationships that constitute a Kierkegaardian life-sphere. Self as center, self ensemble, and existential life-sphere are mutually dependent aspects of a single complex phenomenon.

ETHICS AND STABILITY

Kierkegaard sees the esthetic sphere of existence as lacking any dominant center of gravity. The world of the esthete is like a piece wandering to find its key, never quite establishing any orienting tonality. It plays this possibility, then that, never establishing a stable harmony, authority, or self. However interesting or fun such homeless, absent wandering may temporarily be, Kierkegaard assumes it will ultimately fail, fall apart—not just in discord, but in death, despair, or passive suicide. From the standpoint of such aimless wandering, becoming a self will be like finding a home, a key, or a narrative center of gravity.

A piece of tonal music will establish, or have established in it, a "grounding" key which defines the fundamental grid around which all other pitches and chords are oriented, a kind of "home base." This tonal center lays out meaning and related lines, pitches, chords; it establishes what's fair and foul, what's in and out of key. Similarly, a moral self establishes a grid around which the actions, passions, beliefs, moods, and relationships of the individual take shape. In *Either/Or*, Judge Wilhelm will say we must *choose* the self we are and will become. But as I mentioned earlier, the finding/choosing contrast may not be as radical as one might suppose. The Judge will also say that the "more correct" formulation for self-acquisition is that we must recognize and *receive* the self we are and will become.

Imagine we are wandering in the fogged-up infield of a baseball diamond. We can *find* home plate (the placement of a few other landmarks in the field will confirm its proper placement). Or imagine an alternative. We have sky-blue days and approach a vacant lot, bases and yardstick in hand. We then can *choose* a placement for home base (thereby *giving* spots to other landmarks in the field). The Kierkegaardian task of *getting* selfhood oscillates between these conceptual poles— a pattern of giving and receiving shape, of active wrestling which can then imperceptibly shift toward relaxed and open receptivity. The individual is both creating and created, spins out verse and is spun out as verse.[38] When a pattern of activity jells as the activity of my *self* (say especially in passing from esthetic to ethical spheres), it will seem that I have both embraced and found my home, chosen and discovered myself, acknowledged something already there, and also brought something new to birth. In the idioms of Judge Wilhelm, the self receives *and* chooses itself.

If the onset of an ethical life resembles inhabiting a stable home, moving from tonal wandering to the security of an authoritative key, then what of the subsequent move from ethical to religious life? Are we cast again into homeless wandering? Is the uncertainty and suffering of the religious life a loss of ethical security?

SUFFERING AND SERENITY

The ethical sphere as characterized by Judge Wilhelm is not distinguished by great struggle, suffering, or conflict. As he describes it, the ethical life will be one of harmony and fulfilling tasks.[39] Moral patterns of respectable conduct and the claims of reason and passion will largely coincide. But the move from the ethical to the religious seems marked by conflict, disharmony, and crisis, especially if we take our cue from *Fear and Trembling*. The ethical self seems utterly shattered by the challenge God presents in claiming Isaac. Nevertheless, it would be a mistake to see the disruption Abraham undergoes as a return to the fragmentation of esthetic existence—although it is a return to direct, unmediated experience, a "second immediacy" and partially parallels the "first immediacy" of esthetic life.[40] The movement from esthetic to ethical is a movement from a collection of self-strands not yet crystallized to a crystallization that is a particular self, both found and "chosen." The movement from ethical to religious selfhood, however, is marked by crisis in an otherwise rich and functioning self, a crisis followed by a subsequent religious modulation or tempering of that moral self.

Abraham is solidly Abraham before his crisis—and solidly an ethical self. And Abraham is solidly himself after his ordeal is done—still solidly an ethical self. This continuity cannot be ascribed to the preethical esthete. He *becomes* a self, whereas Abraham *sustains* himself. The onset of the religious is marked by disharmony and dissonance. But these are identifiable as such only because the firm self of ethical life is—and remains—established.

The religious life, at least initially, raises a challenge to the authority of the ethical. But whatever its uncertainty and dissonance, the religious sphere cannot be a scattered field awaiting the patterning we call self. The suffering of Abraham is the suffering *of* a moral self. He is challenged by God, by the demands of a new and dissonant tonality. But the religious sphere is not vying to overtake or succeed the moral self. If a new, competing key is being introduced, the outcome cannot be the mere *replacement* of one center (the moral center) by another (a competing religious center). True, Johannes makes it tempting to construe Abraham as shattering the ethical. But the ethical cannot just be dropped. Every moment, Isaac is the object of his father's (moral) love. The religious sphere does not have a radical independence from the moral. Whatever crisis Abraham undergoes, the ethical sphere is only suspended, not abolished or replaced by something new.[41] It is finally preserved-while-transcended, an instance of an Hegelian *Aufhebung*.[42]

If the onset of religious dissonances—say, a terrifying command from God—is not prelude to an outright takeover, then given the resources of our musical analogies, how can we understand this challenge to the moral? We seem to have dissonance terrible enough to disrupt harmony and confidence of key, but apparently not inserted as a potential successor key, or as a destroyer of tonality itself.

Beethoven's late quartets, to my ear, at least, periodically insert persistent not just passing dissonance that nevertheless does not devastate the sense of key completely.[43] Instead, such suffering disharmony wonderfully—terribly—complicates, tests and stretches our notion of what strange and beautiful abuse a key can take. There's no predicting how these strains and stresses will occur, what they will demand of our ear, or what they portend for the survival or unity of the melodic self a quartet presents. Similarly, a God demanding Isaac puts Abraham to the test. But the point is not to replace one principle by another, to switch ethical for religious life. The startling, dissonant insertion of divinity complicates and stretches our sense of the ethical. The moral is in contest with some challenging particulars. But these dissonant particulars get their sweet bite from the assurance that tonality, selfhood, is not, cannot be, utterly lost—even as they seem bent on wreaking havoc with an established sense of home or place.

There can be serenity in dissonance, just as their can be happiness, peace, throughout the religious suffering of the moral self. The moral self is complicated, enriched through struggle with its strangely lifting adversities. From the vantage of a religiously tempered self, the life of an ethical Judge Wilhelm is all too complacent, all too certain, lacking passion, fear and trembling. But does this sense of insecurity, dissonance, or pain, abate? If a religious passion is desirable, are we not permitted to expect some resolution to the crisis faith foretells? In the Genesis story, Isaac is returned; ethics is sustained; the final word is reconciliation. A similar pattern unfolds in Job. He finds his life restored. But in the midst of moral-religious crisis, things are not so clear.

Once again, consider Beethoven's late work. If we were to ask if suffering is finally overcome, then the candid answer must be Yes and No. He penned above the opening bars of the final movement of his last quartet "The Difficult Resolution"—"The Hard-won Decision." (*Der schwer gefasste Entschluss.*) Yet to many listeners, it will seem that that quartet haunts as much by what it leaves unresolved as by what it resolves. Moving into the sphere of these late quartets raises as many new issues, new questions, as it answers in the making. And whatever serenities they can evoke, they hardly leave essential suffering aside. He also penned above this last quartet the question and answer *"Muss es sein?" "Es muss sein!"*—"Must it be?" "It must be!"—referring, I believe, to the dissonance and difficulty of his quartet. Yet it refers also to the inescapable suffering of a liberating death.[44] This acknowledgment of a paradoxically freeing yet necessary suffering as the way of human life links the composer and Kierkegaard in ways unfathomed. What deep serenities each provide lie in liquid pools sustaining unremitting struggle with threatening and self-saving power.

Notes

Preface

1. Kafka wrote his "Abraham Parable" two years after reading *Fear and Trembling*. In it, Kafka produces a God who is a kind of schoolmasterly jokester, and an Abraham who is a foolish student. In *Fear and Trembling*, Kierkegaard experimented with various retellings, in parable-form, of the story of Abraham bringing Isaac as a sacrifice to God. See Franz Kafka, *Parables and Paradoxes*, trans. Clement Greenberger (New York: Schocken Books, 1958), pp. 43–45. Abraham's ordeal is a background presence in Kafka's novels *The Trial* and *The Castle*. For connections between Kafka, Unamumo, and Kierkegaard, and more generally, on Kierkegaard's modeling of his quixotic knight of faith on Cervantes's *Don Quixote*, see Eric Ziolkowski, *The Sanctification of Don Quixote* (University Park: Penn State University Press, 1991). For a book-length treatment of Kafka and Kierkegaard see Claus Hebell, *Rechtstheoretische und Geistesgeschichtliche Voraussetzungen für Das Werk Franz Kafkas Analysiert an Seinem Roman "Der Prozess"* (New York: Peter Lang, 1993). The character Brand in Ibsen's play of that title is often taken to be modeled on Kierkegaard. Heidegger's unacknowledged debt to Kierkegaard is partially documented in Dreyfus and Rubin, "How Not to Get Something for Nothing: Kierkegaard and Heidegger on Nihilism," *Inquiry* (30) 1987, and in John D. Caputo, "Kierkegaard, Heidegger, and the Foundering of Metaphysics," in *International Kierkegaard Commentary, Fear and Trembling and Repetition*, ed. Robert L. Perkins (Macon: Mercer University Press, 1994), pp. 201–24. For Wittgenstein's debt, see *Wittgenstein's Vienna*, Alan Janik and Stephen Toulmin (New York: Simon and Schuster, 1973). The parallel is developed by James Conant, "Kierkegaard, Wittgenstein, and Nonsense," in *Pursuits of Reason: Essays in Honor of Stanley Cavell*, eds. Cohen, Guyer, and Putnam (Lubbock: Texas Tech University Press, 1993). Wittgenstein's Kierkegaardian comments in *Culture and Value* are explored in Alastair Hannay, "Refuge and Religion," in *Faith, Knowledge, and Action: Essays to Niles Thulstrup*, ed. George Stengren (Copenhagen: Reitzels Forlag, 1984).

2. See Martin J. Matustik, "Habermas's Reading of Kierkegaard," *Philosophy and Social Criticism*, 17 (4) pp. 313–323, 1991, included in his *Post-National Identity in Habermas, Kierkegaard, and Havel* (New York: Guilford Press, 1993). For a suggestion of the Ricoeur connection, see Jonathan Rée, "Narrative and Philosophical Experience," *On Paul Ricoeur*, ed. David Wood (London: Routledge, 1991), pp. 82–3. Putnam discusses Kierkegaard and Wittgenstein in his Gifford Lectures, published as *Renewing Philosophy* (Cambridge: Harvard University press, 1992); see also Stanley Cavell, "Kierkegaard on Authority and Revelation" in *Must We Mean What We Say* (Cambridge: Cambridge University Press, 1976), chap. 6, and his extended contrast of Wittgenstein's *Philosophical Investigations* and Kierkegaard's *Concluding Unscientific Postscript* in "Existentialism and Analytical Philosophy," *Daedalus*, The Journal of the American Academy of Arts and Sciences, 93, 3, (p. 46–74) 1964, reprinted in Cavell, *Themes Out of School* (San Francisco: North Point Press, 1984), chap. 11. A series, "Kierkegaard and Postmodernism," is issued by Florida University Press. See also, Michael Weston, *Kierkegaard and Contemporary Continental Philosophy* (New York:

Routledge, 1994), which contains chapters placing Derrida, Levinas, Nietzsche, and Heidegger in dialogue with Kierkegaard. Kierkegaard is read as a "literary deconstructionist" by Roger Poole, in *Kierkegaard, The Indirect Communication* (Charlottesberg: University of Virginia Press, 1993). Christopher Norris also provides a "deconstructionist" approach in *The Deconstructive Turn* (London: Methuen, 1983), chap. 4.

3. For a sampling of the thought and defense of the category of "postanalytic philosophy," see *Post-Analytic Philosophy*, eds. John Rajchman and Cornel West (New York: Columbia University Press, 1985), and Giovanna Borradori, *The American Philosopher: Conversations with Quine, Davidson, Putnam, Nozick, Danto, Rorty, Cavell, MacIntyre, and Kuhn* (Chicago: University of Chicago Press, 1994).

4. Stanley Cavell, *This New Yet Unapproachable America: Lectures after Emerson after Wittgenstein* (Albuquerque, New Mexico: Living Batch Press, 1989), p. 82.

5. Stephen Mulhall, *Stanley Cavell: Philosophy's Recounting of the Ordinary* (Oxford: Oxford University Press, 1994), p. 295.

Chapter 1

1. Stanley Cavell, quoted in *The American Philosopher*, Giovanna Borradori (Chicago: University of Chicago Press, 1994), p. 126.

2. M. Jamie Ferriera, *Transforming Vision: Imagination and Will in Kierkegaardian Faith* (Oxford: Oxford University Press, 1991), p. 159.

3. *Critique of Pure Reason*, trans. Norman Kemp Smith, "The Ground of the Distinction of all Objects in General into Phenomena and Noumena," (London: Macmillan, 1950) A 235–36, B 294–5.

4. In fact, the passage quoted above continues: "Before we venture on this sea, to explore it in all directions…." Thus the hazards do not deter him.

5. *Critique of Judgment*, trans. J. H. Bernard (New York: Macmillan, 1951), p. 171. The quote continues: "[Poetry] plays with illusion, […] but without deceiving by it; for it declares its exercise to be mere play, which however can be purposely used by the understanding.'

6. For the work of regulative ideals as a unifying focus in Kant's philosophy, see Susan Neiman, *The Unity of Reason: Rereading Kant* (Oxford: Oxford University Press, 1994). Kierkegaard has his heartsick esthete evoke the drama of poetic life "beyond the breakers" in *Repetition* as follows: "…long live the dance in the vortex of the infinite, long live the cresting waves that hide me in the abyss, long live the cresting waves that fling me above the stars!" *Fear and Trembling* and *Repetition*, eds. trans. Howard V. Hong and Edna H. Hong (Princeton: Princeton University Press, 1983), p. 222 (translation emended). Kant's imagery becomes sober when contrasted to this wild effusion. No doubt Kierkegaard himself is mocking the poetry's excess in this case.

7. *Critique of Judgment*, p. 160; the emendation "soul" for "*Geist*" in this context is suggested in J. M. Bernstein's comments on Kant: "works of genius must have soul (*Geist*)" He continues: "Soul, as the animating principle of the mind, is [in Kant's phrase] 'nothing else than the faculty of presenting esthetic ideas.'" Bernstein, *The Fate of Art: Aesthetic Alienation from Kant to Derrida and Adorno* (University Park: The Pennsylvania State University Press, 1992), p. 95.

8. Deleuze puts the matter darkly: "At the end, Kant discovers discord which pro-

duces accord" and raises a further question: "Could this be a Shakespearean side of Kant?" See Gilles Deleuze, *Kant's Critical Philosophy*, trans. Hugh Tomlinson and Barbara Habberjam (Minneapolis: University of Minnesota Press, 1993), p. xiii.

9. *The Concept of Irony, with Constant Reference to Socrates*, trans. Lee M. Capel (London: Collins, 1966). Kierkegaard successfully defended the dissertation for the *Magister* degree in September, 1841. Irony has been advocated as a way of life (the only possible postmodern way, it seems) in Richard Rorty, *Contingency, Irony, and Solidarity* (Cambridge: Cambridge University Press, 1989). See also David Wisdo, *The Life of Irony and the Ethics of Belief* (Albany: State University of New York Press, 1993).

10. *Repetition*, p. 154; see the discussion by George Pattison, *Kierkegaard: The Aesthetic and the Religious* (New York: St. Martin's Press, 1992), pp. 111–124.

11. The matter is not quite as simple as this implies. For good discussions, see Thomas Gould, *The Ancient Quarrel between Poetry and Philosophy* (Princeton: Princeton University press, 1990), and Stanley Rosen, *The Quarrel between Philosophy and Poetry* (New York: Routledge, 1993).

12. Plato, *Phaedo* (60e), trans. Raymond Larson (Arlington Heights: Harlan Davidson, 1980).

13. Two 18th-century examples of a literary-historical (rather than a mathematical or "physical-chemical") model directing philosophical pursuit are Giambattista Vico's *Scienza nuova* and Johann Herder's work. Hume presents a more complex case.

14. For a survey of German esthetics after Kant, see Andrew Bowie, *Aesthetics and Subjectivity, from Kant to Nietzsche* (Manchester: Manchester University Press, 1990), and Bernstein, *The Fate of Art*.

15. *Critique of Judgment*, p. 161 (B 181, 2 A 179; sect. 49).

16. *Ibid.*, p. 171.

17. *Ibid.*, p. 160.

18. See Kant's discussion of Job and Zoroaster as "archetypes" of faith and wisdom in *Opus Posthumum* (21, 4, 156), discussed in James Collins, *The Emergence of Philosophy of Religion* (New Haven: Yale University Press, 1967), pp. 205, f. See also Chapter Five, below.

19. With regard to Kant's complex relationship to German romanticism, consider his claim, in *The Critique of Judgment*, that esthetic ideas—his examples include love, death, envy, fame, and vice—can be explored by productive imagination, though reason cannot provide an exhaustive or determinate concept for them. See the discussion in Bernstein, *The Fate of Art*, pp. 96, f., and Rudolf A. Makkreel, *Imagination and Interpretation in Kant: The Hermeneutical Import of the Critique of Judgment* (Chicago: University of Chicago Press, 1990), pp. 118, f. For a masterful account of the milieu of idealism and romanticism affecting and affected by Kant, see Frederick C. Beiser, *The Fate of Reason: German Philosophy from Kant to Fichte* (Cambridge: Harvard University press, 1987).

20. See Ronald M. Green, *Kierkegaard and Kant: The Hidden Debt* (Albany: State University of New York Press, 1992) and R. Z. Friedman, "Kierkegaard: Last Kantian or First Existentialist?" *Religious Studies* 18 Spring 1982 (159–170).

21. Mikhail Bakhtin, *Problems of Dostoyevsky's Poetics*, ed. and trans. Caryl Emerson (Minneapolis: University of Minnesota Press, 1984).

22. *Ibid.*, p. 97.

23. The contrast between "living poetically" as a feature of the esthetic sphere exclu-

sively, and a sort of "poetical living" that can be a feature of predominantly religious and ethical living is spelled out in Sylvia Walsh, *Living Poetically: Kierkegaard's Existential Aesthetics* (University Park: The Pennsylvania State University Press, 1994).

24. "Attunement" is Hannay's translation of the Danish *Stemning*, which the Hongs's translation of *Fear and Trembling* renders "Exordium." See *Fear and Trembling*, ed. and trans. Alastair Hannay (Harmondsworth: Penguin Books, 1985), and *Fear and Trembling and Repetition*, ed. and trans. Howard V. Hong and Edna H. Hong (Princeton: Princeton University Press, 1983). For Heidegger's appropriation and deployment of "attunement" (*Stimmung*) and other Kierkegaardian concepts, see John D. Caputo, "Kierkegaard, Heidegger, and the Foundering of Metaphysics," *International Kierkegaard Commentary, Fear and Trembling and Repetition*, ed. Robert L. Perkins (Macon: Mercer University Press, 1993), pp. 201–224; Hubert Dreyfus and Jane Rubin, "You Can't Get Something for Nothing: Kierkegaard and Heidegger on How Not to Overcome Nihilism," *Inquiry*, 30, 1987, and Patricia J. Huntington, "Heidegger's Reading of Kierkegaard Revisited: From Ontological Abstraction to Ethical Concretion," in *Kierkegaard in Post/Modernity*, eds. Martin J. Matustik and Merold Westphal (Bloomington: Indiana University Press, 1995), Chap. 3.

25. "Preamble from the Heart" is Hannay's translation of the section that the Hongs translate "Preliminary Expectoration."

26. From an enormous literature on the integration of poetry and philosophy in Nietzsche, see Joan Stambaugh, *The Other Nietzsche* (Albany: State University of New York Press, 1993), *Nietzsche's New Seas: Explorations in Philosophy, Aesthetics, and Politics*, eds. Michael Allen GIllespie and Tracy B. Strong (Chicago: University of Chicago Pres, 1988), and Alan White, *Within Nietzsche's Labyrinth* (New York: Routledge, 1990). From an enormous literature on Heidegger, art, and philosophy, see Michael Haar, *The Song of the Earth: Heidegger and the Grounds of the History of Being*, trans. Reginald Lilly (Bloomington: Indiana University press, 1993), David A. White, *Heidegger and the Language of Poetry* (Lincoln: The University of Nebraska Press, 1978), and several essays in *The Cambridge Companion to Heidegger*, ed. Charles B. Guignon (Cambridge: Cambridge University press, 1993).

27. Friedrich Nietzsche *Thus Spoke Zarathustra*, Part Three, *The Portable Nietzsche*, ed. and trans. Walter Kaufmann (New York: Viking Press, 1954), pp. 331, f.

28. For an excellent discussion of Heidegger's "fourfold" in its connection with the full sweep of Heidegger's thought, see Frederick A. Olafson, "The Unity of Heidegger's Thought," *The Cambridge Companion to Heidegger*, chap. 3.

29. Dreyfus and Rubin argue that Heidegger's *Being and Time* is an articulation of Kierkegaard's "Religiousness A" in "You Can't Get Something for Nothing: Kierkegaard and Heidegger on How Not to Overcome Nihilism."

30. See Walsh, *Living Poetically*, for an comprehensive treatment.

31. *Sickness Unto Death*, trans. Alastair Hannay (Harmondsworth: Penguin Books, 1989), p. 109; *Repetition*, p. 228.

32. For the role of Hölderlin and Rilke in Heidegger's articulation of the sacred, see Michael Haar, *The Song of the Earth*.

33. On the breakdown of disciplines, and Heidegger's attempt to realign and unify them, see Hubert L. Dreyfus, "Heidegger on the Connection Between Nihilism, Art, Technology, and Politics," *The Cambridge Companion to Heidegger*, chap. 11, and Bernstein, *The Fate of Art*.

34. I favor Hannay's "on the strength of the absurd" to the Hongs's "by virtue of the absurd."

35. Charles Taylor, *The Sources of the Self* (Cambridge: Harvard University Press, 1989), pp. 57, f. Taylor does not connect his picture of practical reason, or his interest in transitions, with Kierkegaard's use of pseudonyms and Kierkegaard's focus on transitions between life-stages.

36. Stephen Mulhall, "*The Sources of the Self*'s Sense of Itself," paper delivered Feb. 2, 1995, at The Claremont Graduate School, [ms. pp. 37–8], forthcoming in *Can Religion Be Explained Away?* ed. D. Z. Phillips (London: Methuen).

37. *Concluding Unscientific Postscript*, trans. Howard V. Hong and Edna H. Hong (Princeton: Princeton University Press, 1992), p. 260; *Postscript*, trans. David F. Swenson and Walter Lowrie (Princeton University Press, 1941), pp. 232, ff. Resignation, as giving up a self-aggrandizing will vis à vis another, is a condition of respect for the other. Hence my bracketed insertion.

38. Kierkegaard at least *appears* to disavow responsibility for the views of the *Postscript*, and of the pseudonymous production generally, in *Postscript*, "A First and Last Declaration," Hongs trans. 624 ff., Swenson and Lowrie trans., 550 f.

39. See Charles Taylor, *The Ethics of Authenticity* (Cambridge: Harvard University Press, 1993) for a similar argument, and J. M. Bernstein, *Recovering the Ethical Life: Habermas and the Future of Critical Theory* (London: Routledge, 1995).

40. For a clarification of the label "postanalytical" see the opening paragraphs of Chap. 6, below.

41. Martha C. Nussbaum, "Aristotle on Human Nature and the Foundations of Ethics," *World, Mind and Ethics: Essays on the Ethical Philosophy of Bernard Williams*, eds. J. E. J. Altham and Ross Harrison (Cambridge: Cambridge University Press, 1995), p. 124.

42. The interconnections of choice, imagination, and vision in the constitution of the self are pursued at length in M. Jamie Ferreira, *Transforming Vision: Imagination and Will in Kierkegaardian Faith* (Oxford: Oxford University Press, 1991).

44. Of course poetic articulations of such indispensable meaning sources, in Kierkegaard's view, will remain approximations, provisional, leading us toward but not securely *delivering* the truth (say, the essential truth of Christianity). Nevertheless, we trust poetic depictions to unveil truths along the way, truths that can orient our pursuits if not deliver the goods. See especially Chap. 3 and the last sections of Chap. 5, below.

Chapter 2

1. *Either/Or: A Fragment of Life*, abridg., ed., and trans. Alastair Hannay (Harmondsworth: Penguin Books, 1992), first epigraph, p. 491; second p. 487. Henceforth, page references to quotes from *Either/Or* will cite the Hannay translation first. The second citation, in parenthesis, is to the Hongs's translation: *Either/Or, Vol. II*, trans. Howard V. Hong and Edna H. Hong (Princeton: Princeton University Press, 1987), first epigraph, (177); second epigraph, (169).

2. For the use of pseudonyms as a philosophical strategy, see my *Knights of Faith and Resignation: Reading Kierkegaard's Fear and Trembling* (Albany: State University of New York Press, 1991), Chapter One, and Roger Poole, *Kierkegaard: The Indirect Communication* (Charlottesville: University of Virginia Press, 1993).

3. p. 549 (258).

4. Kantian moral character might be presented in terms of frames of cognitive-affec-
tive perception, understanding, and judgment. See Robert Louden, *Morality and
Moral Theory* (Oxford: Oxford University Press, 1992), and Barbara Herman, *The
Practice of Moral Judgment* (Berkeley: University of California Press, 1993). For a thor-
ough discussion of the Kant-Kierkegaard connection generally, see Ronald M.
Green, *Kierkegaard and Kant: The Hidden Debt* (Albany: State University of New York
Press, 1992).

5. p. 487 (169).

6. p. 486 (169), hyphenation added, "good-and-evil."

7. p. 549 (258)

8. p. 550 (259), my emphasis.

9. See note 4, above.

10. p. 509, 517 (211, 214).

11. p. 518 (216).

12. p. 553 (261).

13. p. 552 (262).

14. p. 559 (271).

15. See my discussion of Kierkegaard's "Job Discourse," Chap. 3, below, and my essay
"Getting the World Back: *Repetition*" Chap. 6 in *Cambridge Companion to Kierkegaard*, eds.,
Alastair Hannay and Gordon Marino (Cambridge: Cambridge University Press,
1996).

16. See Robert Perkins, "Giving the Parson His Due" in Robert L. Perkins, ed.,
International Kierkegaard Commentary, Either/Or (Macon: Mercer University Press, 1995).
For an excellent discussion of Judge Wilhelm's religious standpoint, see George B.
Connell, "Judge William's Theonomous Ethics," in George B. Connell and C.
Stephen Evans, *The Foundations of Kierkegaard's Vision of Community* (Atlantic Highlands:
Humanities Press, 1991).

17. This is part of what makes stage-shift not an utterly arbitrary affair.

18. MacIntyre's misleading but widely cited view of *Either/Or* is found in *After Virtue*
(Notre Dame: University of Notre Dame Press, 1981). It is repeated in Charles
Taylor, *Sources of the Self* (Cambridge: Cambridge University Press, 1989), pp. 449–50.

19. p. 518 (217).

20. p. 4911 (177.)

21. p. 551 (260).

22. *Ibid.*

23. p. 525f. (225).

24. p. 491 (177).

25. *Contingency, Irony, Solidarity*, Richard Rorty (Cambridge: Cambridge University Press,
1989), p. xiv. See also Chap. 4. J. M. Bernstein argues, correctly, in my view, that
this sharp division "...leaves the private futile and the public empty.... As if we
knew and were content with our private self creations.... As if I can be...sensible
above all to me, apart from questions of suffering and justice." J. M. Bernstein, *The
Fate of Art: Aesthetic Alienation from Kant to Derrida and Adorno* (University Park: The
Pennsylvania State University Press, 1992), p. 286 n. 8.

26. p. 518 (216).

27. p. 539 (246).

28. p. 540 (247).
29. p. 559 (272).
30. p. 559 (271). The Hongs translate this passage: "[the choice] claims for the self the same as it claims for everyone else's self—no more, no less."
31. Rorty, *Contingency, Irony and Solidarity*, p. 43.
32. *Ibid.*
33. *Ibid.*, my emphasis. I return to the discussion of moral responsibility and community in the sections "Self Responsibility: The Case of Socrates," and "Responsibility for History and Milieu."
34. p. 491 (177).
35. See M. Jamie Ferreira's discussion of imagination and otherness in "Repetition, Concreteness, and Imagination," *International Journal for Philosophy of Religion*, vol. 25, 1989, and Chap. 3, below.
36. p. 491 (177) my emphasis.
37. The Hongs render the Danish, "The I chooses itself—or more correctly, receives itself." (177)
38. p. 487 (169).
39. See Robert Solomon, *The Passions* (New York: Doubleday, 1976).
40. Iris Murdoch, *The Sovereignty of Good* (New York: Schocken Books, 1971). Of course Murdoch believes that this widespread picture, once sketched out, will be impossible to believe.
41. Cf. Ross Poole, "Living with Reason," *Inquiry*, June 1991, and Meir Dan-Cohen, "Conceptions of Choice and Conceptions of Autonomy," *Ethics*, January 1992, for parallel discussions of the limits of the "choice-as-selection" model of moral agency.
42. This "meaning source" could be characterized as a power latent and awaiting acknowledgment which, in self-reception, becomes an object of transforming recognition. See M. Jamie Ferreira, *Transforming Vision*, and Ferreira, "Seeing (Just) is Believing," *Faith and Philosophy*, April 1992.
43. p. 419 (217).
44. When Wilhelm has the esthete choose, or more correctly receive itself from "the eternal power" (177), choice and reception are likewise joined (or conflated).
45. On varied "moral images of the self," see, among others, Murdoch, *The Sovereignty of Good*, Owen Flanagan, *The Varieties of Moral Personality* (Cambridge: Harvard University Press, 1991), Lawrence A. Blum, *Moral Perception and Particularity* (Cambridge: Cambridge University Press, 1994), Chap. 4, and Hilary Putnam, *The Many Faces of Realism* (Lasalle: Open Court Publishing, 1987). On narrative and dramatic forms of self-articulation, see, among others, Charles Taylor, *The Ethics of Authenticity* (Cambridge: Harvard University Press, 1992), and *The Sources of the Self: The Making of Modern Identity* (Cambridge: Harvard University press, 1989), and Martha Nussbaum, *Love's Knowledge* (Oxford: Oxford University Press, 1990).
46. See Charles Taylor's ground-breaking article, "Responsibility for Self," first printed in *The Identities of Persons*, ed. Amelie Oksenberg Rorty (Berkeley: University of California Press, 176), and later printed as "What is Human Agency" in Taylor's *Human Agency and Language* (Cambridge: Cambridge University Press, 1985).
47. This shift in idiom also raises the question whether, given an anthropocentric or naturalistic modern perspective, there can be any metaphysical argument for the

existence of such "independent" values, or of a "power" conferring them. The ontological or theological question of the origin and metaphysical status of values and moral selves, and of "the eternal power" conferring them is fundamental, but I'll not address it here.

48. p. 543 (251), my emphasis.

49. Of course, these arguments that I call "shallow or contrived" are presented by Socrates himself. But I think he does not believe them to be as significant as his argument that the traditions, the "laws," of Athens bring him up, give birth to him. And I think Plato takes the latter argument as the central one, as well.

50. For a detailed discussion of a broadened sense of responsibility among those who sheltered Jews in Nazi Europe, see Lawrence A. Blum, *Moral Perception and Particularity* (Cambridge: Cambridge University Press, 1994), "Altruism, and the Moral Value of Rescue: Resisting Persecution, Racism, and Genocide," Chap. 6.

51. See William Carlos Williams, *Six American Poets*, ed. Joel Conarroe (New York: Random House, 1991) p. 146. Consider also Henry Bugbee's remarks on philosophy as "a meditation of the place," *The Inward Morning* (New York: Harper and Row, 1976), p. 138.

52. p. 542 (251).

53. The account I give of self-responsibility is meant to illuminate the Judge's conception in *Either/Or*. In later works, Kierkegaard will cast doubt on our ability to become transparent enough to ourselves to take sufficient responsibility for who we are. The ground for a relatively virtuous self then becomes not just *taking* responsibility for oneself but also realizing a radical dependence on "the eternal power" that *confers* virtue, security, and selfhood, and which lifts the burden of fault. See Chap. 4, below.

54. For an account of the social context of self-construction, see *Foundations of Kierkegaard's Vision of Community, Religion, Ethics, and Politics in Kierkegaard*, in particular Chap. 5.

55. I elaborate the idea of self as a crystallized particular in Chap. 3, below.

56. See Ferreira, *Transforming Vision.*

57. See Chap. 8, below.

58. p. 518 (216).

59. p. 518 (216).

60. See Bas C. von Frassen, "The Peculiar Effects of Love and Desire," *Perspectives on Self-Deception*, eds. Brian P. McLaughlin and Amelie O. Rorty (Berkeley: University of California Press, 1988), and my *Knights of Faith and Resignation*, Chap. 9.

61. p. 509 (206).

Chapter 3

1. Bernard Harrison, *Inconvenient Fictions: Literature and the Limits of Theory* (New Haven: Yale University Press, 1991), p. 69f. Chap. 6 takes up the *Book of Job*, which might be called an inconvenient scripture; Kierkegaard is certainly an inconvenient author.

2. Søren Kierkegaard, *Fear and Trembling* and *Repetition*, ed. and trans. Howard V. Hong and Edna H. Hong (Princeton: Princeton University Press, 1983).

3. Søren Kierkegaard, *Eighteen Upbuilding Discourses*, trans. and ed. Howard V. Hong and Edna H. Hong (Princeton: Princeton University Press, 1990) [Hereafter, *Discourses*].

What I'll call "The Job Discourse," pp. 109–24, has as its title the three-part verse beginning "The Lord gives…": Job (1:21).

4. For a discussion of loss and repossession in the Abraham-Isaac case, see my *Knights of Faith and Resignation: Reading Kierkegaard's Fear and Trembling* (Albany: State University of New York Press, 1991), especially Chaps. 7 and 8.

5. *Repetition*, p. 294.

6. *Fear and Trembling*, trans. and ed. Alastair Hannay (Harmondsworth: Penguin Books, 1985), p. 70.

7. Sylvia Walsh traces the idea of esthetic experience, and of living poetically, as both are dimensions not only of the esthetic life-view but of the ethical and religious life spheres, as well. See Walsh, *Living Poetically, Kierkegaard's Existential Aesthetics* (University Park: Penn State University Press, 1994).

8. Kierkegaard distinguishes ethical repetition from a deeper religious repetition in his papers, quoted in the Hongs, *Fear and Trembling and Repetition*, supplementary materials, p. 301 f. [Pap. IV B 117.] For the profound religious, moral, and existential dimensions of ceremony developed in quite another context, see Herbert Fingarette, *Confucius: The Secular as Sacred* (New York: Harper and Row, 1972).

9. In *Repetition* and *Postscript*, Kierkegaard will contrast "repetition" with Platonic "recollection." Their parallel role in meaning—(or knowledge)—acquisition is suggested in the following, from the *Symposium*: "Forgetting is loss of knowledge, and studying preserves knowledge by creating memory afresh in us, to replace what is lost. Hence we have the illusion of continuing a knowledge." Plato, *Symposium* [208a] trans. Tom Griffith (Berkeley: University of California Press, 1989). Kierkegaard (or *Repetition*'s Constantine Constantius) makes it clear that "recollection" is a "pagan" or Greek notion, not a "modern" notion. Johannes Climacus claims it is incompatible with *Postscript*'s "Religiousness B" or Christianity. See my discussion "Repetition: Getting the World Back" in *The Cambridge Companion to Kierkegaard*, eds. Alastair Hannay and Gordon Marino (Cambridge: Cambridge University Press, 1996).

10. See note 22, below, for Charles Taylor's contrast between "relations of subsumption" and "relations of renewal."

11. Søren Kierkegaard, *Either/Or*, Vol. II, trans. and ed. by Howard V. Hong and Edna H. Hong (Princeton: Princeton University Press, 1989), p. 142. Constantine Constantius speaks of "consciousness raised to the second power," *Repetition*, p. 295. This phrase provides a bridge to Harry Frankfurt's concept of "second-order care" in *The Importance of What We Care About* (Cambridge: Cambridge University Press, 1988) discussed in Chap. 6, below.

12. Quoted in Alastair Hannay, *Kierkegaard, The Arguments of the Philosophers* (London: Routledge & Kegan Paul, 1982), p. 67.

13. I discuss frame-shifts at greater length, and expand the musical analogy, in Chap. 8, below.

14. For characterization of God as freedom-granting, consider the claim that God "…communicates in creating, so as by creating to give independence over against himself," *Concluding Unscientific Postscript* trans. David F. Swenson and Walter Lowrie (Princeton: Princeton University Press, 1941), p. 232; *Concluding Unscientific Postscript*, trans. Howard V. Hong and Edna H. Hong (Princeton: Princeton University Press, 1992), p. 260. This is also a theme in *Fear and Trembling*: consider the opening quartet

of failed Abrahams, where Johannes de silentio likens Abraham's ordeal to the ordeal of a mother weaning (and hence conferring independence on) her child. I discuss this in *Knights of Faith and Resignation*, p. 30, f.

15. *Discourses*, p. 109.

16. See Harrison, especially Chap. 1, section V, for the contrast between referential and constitutive use of language in narrative accounts. Job's specific words, "acting in asserting them," constitute who he is, just as the larger tale is constituted by the poet of the *Book of Job* through "acting in asserting."

17. On this matter, again, see Harrison's account.

18. The Job Discourse neglects this protest phase of the narrative, letting the quoted verse stand alone. In contrast, complaint, bewilderment, some rebellion at undeserved suffering show through in the unsigned "Job letters" in *Repetition*.

19. *Discourses*, p. 122.

20. I thank M. Jamie Ferreira for directly raising this question for me.

21. The idea that philosophy raises far more questions than it has resources to answer—without this being a defect—is a persistent theme in Thomas Nagel's *The View From Nowhere* (Oxford: Oxford University Press, 1986), discussed in Chap. 7, below.

22. See Taylor's provocative remarks on this contrast between relations of renewal and relations of subsumption in *On Paul Ricoeur: Narrative and Interpretation*, ed. David Wood (London: Routledge, 1991), p. 178. This idea also appears in Taylor's *Sources of the Self* (Cambridge: Harvard University Press, 1989), pp. 72 f. I return to this contrast in Chap. 4.

23. Narrowly construed, poetry has only what Kierkegaard calls "first immediacy." The poetry of *Job*, say of the Whirlwind's Voice, at least for ears properly attuned, is a "second immediacy."

24. M. Jamie Ferreira takes imagination as a vehicle for grasping ways in which reality can transform a world, and alter the demands it makes upon us, in "Repetition, Concreteness, and Imagination," *International Journal for Philosophy of Religion*, vol. 25, 1989, pp. 13–34. This essay generally has helped me to focus the role of repetition in Kierkegaard's work, and its link with imagination, which I pursue at greater length below. Ferreira provides a more extensive treatment of imagination's role throughout the Kierkegaardian corpus in *Transforming Vision: Imagination and Will in Kierkegaardian Faith* (Oxford: Oxford University Press, 1991).

25. A slightly amended version of Herder's translation of Job 38:12–15, found in Nahum N. Glatzner, *The Dimensions of Job* (New York: Schocken Books, 1969), p. 149.

26. *Inconvenient Fictions*, p. 171.

27. Kant, "On the Failure of All Attempted Philosophical Theodicies" in Michel Despland, *Kant on History and Religion* (Montreal: McGill University Press, 1973). Kant's essay, and its relevance to Kierkegaard, is discussed in *Kierkegaard and Kant: The Hidden Debt*, Ronald M. Green (Albany: State University of New York Press, 1992), pp. 22–24.

28. *Discourses*, pp. 113–15, and 120.

29. *Repetition*, p. 305.

30. Ferreira, p. 31 (*my emphasis*). Kierkegaard speaks of the contrast between "circumnavigating the self" and finding its "Archimedean point" in *Repetition*, p. 186.

31. Ferreira contrasts imagination's *demands* with its *possibilities*, p. 30. I take the refer-

ence to vision as a "doing" (in the last sentence of the quoted passage) to be linked to my idea of vision furnishing demands which require active response. (I'm not sure if Ferreira would accept this way of putting the contrast between "live-options" and "demands," or the active element in vision. My interpretation of "otherness as such," although prompted by her discussion, clearly diverges from her construal, as I note in the text.)

32. *Ibid.*

33. Ferreira, p. 29.

34. *Discourses*, p. 120.

35. For several alternative translations of Job's "recantation" that differ from the Revised Standard Version's "despise myself and repent," I've drawn freely from Terrence Tilley, *The Evils of Theodicy* (Washington D.C.: Georgetown University Press, 1991), p. 96.

36. Herbert Fingarette suggests "melts away," as the best translation of the Hebrew, and gives an extended rationale for this rendering in "The Meaning of the Law in *The Book of Job,"* *Revisions*, eds. Stanley Hauerwas and Alastair MacIntyre (Notre Dame: University of Notre Dame Press, 1981). I owe much throughout to Fingarette's detailed and penetrating study of *Job*.

Chapter 4

1. Immanuel Kant, *Religion Within the Limits of Reason Alone*, trans. Theodore M. Greene and Hoyt H. Hudson (New York: Harper and Row, 1960), p. 62. (The quoted biblical saying is from *Phillipians* II, 12.)

2. At least one writer claims that the Professor Levy of Woody Allen's film is modeled on Martin S. Bergmann, author of *In the Shadow of Moloch: The Sacrifice of Children and Its Impact on Western Religions* (New York: Columbia University Press, 1993). See the review of this book, "Why God Changed His Mind About Isaac" by Wendy Doniger, *The New York Times Book Review*, August 1, 1993. In a Kierkegaardian vein, we can wonder if Bergmann the author has perhaps modeled himself on "Professor Levy" of the film, the creation of Woody Allen—or if instead Woody Allen documents an individual who in real, noncinematic life, is an author of books. Kierkegaard would appreciate this conundrum, but he would reject the Bergmann claim that the point of the Abraham story is to bring a halt to child sacrifice, and the Levy claim that God is an imaginative construct. An alternative model for Allen's Professor Levy would be the Italian writer and Holocaust survivor Primo Levi, who might have asked how the God of Abraham could have so utterly abandoned his children. (I thank David Averbuck for alerting me to the Doniger review, and Theo Bruinsma for reconnecting me with *Crimes and Misdemeanors.*)

3. This essay began as a reply to four responses to my book *Knights of Faith and Resignation: Reading Kierkegaard's Fear and Trembling* (Albany: State University of New York Press, 1991), presented at the March 1992 American Philosophical Association meetings in Portland, Oregon. I thank David Wisdo, Ronald Green, John Donnelly, and Alastair Hannay for their helpful critiques and discussions.

4. I thank Andrew Cross for this way of putting it in a paper, "Two Dilemmas in *Fear and Trembling*" delivered to the Kierkegaard Society, 1991.

5. Johannes calls himself not a philosopher but a "freelancer" in the Preface, *Fear and*

Trembling, trans. Alastair Hannay (Harmondsworth: Penguin Books, 1985), p. 43. The Hongs's translation has "supplementary clerk" in place of Hannay's "free-lancer." *Fear and Trembling and Repetition*, ed. and trans. Howard V. Hong and Edna H. Hong (Princeton: Princeton University Press, 1987), p. 7.

6. Taylor contrasts relations of subsumption with relations of renewal in his contribution to *On Paul Ricoeur: Narrative and Interpretation*, ed. David Wood (London: Routledge, 1991), p. 178. His view of practical reason as embedded in dialogue between exemplars (rather than suspended as a "view from nowhere") is elaborated in his *Sources of the Self* (Cambridge: Harvard University Press, 1989), Part One. Unfortunately, Taylor fails to see the exemplification of his view in Kierkegaard's creation of a pseudonymous authorship.

7. See my discussion of a view of practical reason as implicit in the use of pseudonyms in Chap. 1, above.

8. Stephen Mulhall, "*Sources of the Self*'s Sense of Itself," paper read at Claremont Graduate School of Theology, February 3, 1994, unpublished ms., p. 36, forthcoming in *Can Religion Be Explained Away?* ed. D. Z. Phillips (London: Methuen).

9. Charles Taylor, *The Ethics of Authenticity* (Cambridge: Harvard University Press, 1992), discussed in Chap. 1, above.

10. Mulhall, p. 103.

11. *Fear and Trembling*, p. 103.

12. *Concluding Unscientific Postscript*, trans. Edna V. Hong and Howard H. Hong (Princeton: Princeton University Press, 1992), p. 550n. (*Concluding Unscientific Postscript*, trans. Swenson and Lowrie (Princeton: Princeton University press, 1968), p. 447n.).

13. *Fear and Trembling*, trans. Hannay, p. 68.

14. *Postscript*, trans. Hongs, p. 262 (Swenson and Lowrie trans., p. 234).

15. Immanuel Kant, *Conflict of the Faculties*, trans. Mary J. Gregor (New York: Abaris Books, 1979), p. 115n.

16. See George Connell, "Judge William's Theonomous Ethics," *Foundations of Kierkegaard's Vision of Community*, ed. George B. Connell and C. Stephen Evans (Atlantic Highlands, NJ: Humanities Press, 1992).

17. For an excellent account of transitions between scientific frameworks and between moral viewpoints that is directly pertinent to Kierkegaardian stage-shifts, see Charles Taylor's "Explanation and Practical Reason," *The Quality of Life*, ed. Martha Nussbaum and Amartya Sen (Oxford: Oxford University Press, 1993).

18. *Either/Or*, abridg., trans. and ed. by Alastair Hannay (Harmondsworth: Penguin Books, 1992), p. 555; (*Either/Or*, Vol. II, trans. Edna H. Hong and Howard V. Hong, [Princeton: Princeton University Press, 1987], p. 265.)

19. *Fear and Trembling*, pp. 44–48.

20. These three examples are from *Fear and Trembling*, pp. 52, 80, and 143. For a full list of instances of Abraham's unfaithful obedience, see my *Knights of Faith and Resignation*, p. 28. Note also the example of unfaithful disobedience, where Abraham thrusts the knife into his own breast, p. 54.

21. See *Knights of Faith and Resignation*, Chap. 5.

22. *Fear and Trembling*, p. 54.

23. For an earlier discussion of Maharba, a refusing Abraham, and of the Teleological Suspension, see my "Abraham and Dilemma: Kierkegaard's Teleological Suspension Revisited," *International Journal for Philosophy of Religion*, 1986, pp. 23–41, and

Knights of Faith and Resignation, throughout.

24. John Donnelly frames Abraham's dilemma this way: God clearly demands Isaac's life; yet just as clearly Abraham knows that God expects him to love Isaac unreservedly. So Abraham will do something wrong whichever option he picks. This unhappy circumstance prompts Donnelly to propose that there is a third option so far overlooked. Abraham should have refused the two obvious alternatives— obedience and disobedience—and embraced abstention. Abraham could then avoid the onus of harming Isaac and the onus of disobeying God. He'd place himself outside the bounds of ethical conflict—just refuse to get on the moral playing field. But can we be persuaded that a stay-at-home, abstaining Abraham is other than a procrastinating or hesitant or refusing Abraham? Second, where does this "permission-to-abstain" get its validation? If the permission is religious, then we have religious sponsorship of conflicting demands on Abraham, and also religious sponsorship of permission to abstain from such demands. So the conflict gets relocated, rather than solved; and it stays within the ethical-religious domain. If the permission-to-abstain is not religious, what sponsors it? If the sponsor is moral, self-interested, or expedient, these options too would only redescribe rather than remove a conflict. See John Donnelly, "Mooney's Maharba: The Teleological Suspension of the Religious?", *Søren Kierkegaard Newsletter*, March 1992, published by the Howard and Edna Hong Kierkegaard Library, St. Olaf College, Northfield, Minnesota, pp. 9–14.

25. A more contemporary dialectical poet might display the Kantian shift by having God appear to Abraham in a professorial explanatory mood:

Look, Abe, it's ok to act in *accord* with duty. But I want you to act *from* duty, as well. Acknowledging the good that underwrites all duty is not itself a simple duty transparent to reason. So I set you a practical antinomy—a task that would force you to drop deeper than convention. I put you through the mill. You had to be loyal to Isaac and to me. If you went toward the mountain, you'd seem a killer; if you refused, in your heart you'd seem a blasphemer. I wouldn't have asked this of most mortals. I don't tempt professors or serving maids or shopkeepers with these rough alternatives. But you're a special case, the father of faith—after all, I'd tested you before. I had faith you'd hold your own. Of course there was no simple command to murder. You knew that and kept your loves alive even as they tore your soul in two.

Have the heavens close. (Could an operatic phantom *really* speak God's aims?)

26. An early version of some of the following remarks were read to the Kierkegaard Society meeting APA, Portland, Oregon, March 27, 1992, in response to an essay by Andrew Cross on the two dilemmas prominent in *Fear and Trembling*.

27. Andrew Cross, *ibid*.

28. See the following two chapters for an elaboration of this phrase, which is introduced by Thomas Nagel in *The View from Nowhere* (Oxford: Oxford University Press, 1986).

29. Which of these verbs, "express," "form," or "discover," best capture the moral-religious phenomena is, of course, a question that threads through all these chapters. In the present case, Abraham is in something like the position of the esthete admonished by Judge Wilhelm—similar not because he leads an esthetic existence, but because he must discover, rediscover, or "receive" himself anew in the process

of coming to terms with God's demand for Isaac. So the idioms of "self-choice" and "self-reception" have some bearing here. For a discussion of the constitutive-expressive theory of language and its role in self-expression, see Charles Taylor, "Heidegger, Language, and Ecology" in *Heidegger: A Critical Reader*, eds. Hubert L. Dreyfus and Harrison Hall (Cambridge: Blackwell Publishers, 1992), Chap. 13.

Chapter 5

1. Ludwig Wittgenstein, *Culture and Value*, trans. Peter Winch (Chicago: University of Chicago Press, 1980), p. 26.
2. See Chap. 4, note 3, above.
3. Of course, the sketches in this present text stand equally ready for revision. I take it as characteristic of lyrical dialectical philosophy (if not of all philosophy) that such continual refinement of rendition will as a matter of course be ongoing.
4. Ronald M. Green, "Deciphering Fear and Trembling's Secret Message," *Religious Studies* 22, 1987; see also *Kierkegaard and Kant: the Hidden Debt* (Albany: State University of New York Press, 1992), Chap. 5.
5. Immanuel Kant, *Religion Within the Bounds of Reason Alone*, trans. John Silber (New York: Harper and Row, 1960), p. 28f. For an excellent account of Kant's sense of evil, of the antinomy it creates, and of the human needs that lead to a postulation of God, see Gordon E. Michaelson, Jr., *Fallen Freedom: Kant on Radical Evil and Moral Regeneration* (Cambridge: Cambridge University Press, 1990), and Susan Neiman, *The Unity of Reason: Rereading Kant* (Oxford: Oxford University Press, 1992), Chap. 4.
6. Ronald Green, *Kierkegaard and Kant*, p. 196, and *Concluding Unscientific Postscript*, trans. Howard V. Hong and Edna H. Hong (Princeton: Princeton University Press, 1992), p. 266 (Swenson and Lowrie trans. p. 238.)
7. Climacus does *not* suggest that *Fear and Trembling*'s hidden message centers on sin and forgiveness. He says rather that a *new* account of the teleological suspension must be given. This challenges Ronald Green's view that sin and forgiveness is *Fear and Trembling*'s secret subtext. Climacus fails to exploit this clear opportunity to reveal this secret here, and instead suggests we try a *new* attempt at understanding ethics and its suspension.
8. Alastair Hannay uses this phrase in "Reading *Knights of Faith and Resignation*," an unpublished response to my earlier book on *Fear and Trembling*. Johannes de silentio describes Abraham's encounter in *Fear and Trembling*, trans. and ed. Alastair Hannay (Harmondsworth: Penguin Books, 1985), p. 124. (*Fear and Trembling and Repetition*, trans. Howard V. Hong and Edna H. Hong [Princeton: Princeton University Press, 1983], p. 99.) In a version of a "pseudo-Abraham" not included in the published version of *Fear and Trembling* Kierkegaard has Abraham consider the possibility of forgiveness for the crime of killing Isaac. Yet he immediately adds that this thought would disqualify him as the father of faith. See Hongs, Supplement, p. 269.
9. Hannay, "Reading *Knights of Faith and Resignation*." Hannay stresses the unintelligibility of God as "absolute Other." Can an unintelligible source provide unambiguous guidance? Phil Clayton reminds me of that an unambiguous verdict arrives from a most unintelligible source in Kafka's *Trial*.
10. *Ibid.*
11. Charles Taylor, "Interpretation and the Sciences of Man," *Philosophy and the Human*

Sciences: Philosophical Papers, Vol. 2 (Cambridge: Cambridge University Press, 1985), p. 50; and *Sources of the Self* (Cambridge: Harvard University Press, 1989), Part One. Bernard Williams, "Persons, Character, and Morality," *Moral Luck* (Cambridge: Cambridge University Pres, 1981).

12. *Fear and Trembling*, p. 84 f. (Hongs, 56).

13. M. Jamie Ferriera has pointed out that the general absence in Kierkegaard of a worked-out conception of practical reason forces him into anti-theoretical polemics. (Private correspondence.) For a sustained argument that reason, for Kant, is oriented practically toward freedom rather than exclusively and theoretically toward knowledge, see Neiman, *The United of Reason.*

14. Kant, *Religion Within the Limits*, pp. 54–72, Kant, *The Critique of Practical Reason*, trans. Lewis White Beck (New York: Bobbs-Merrill, 1956), p. 110, and the constructive discussion by Gordon E. Michaelson, Jr., *Fallen Freedom*, pp. 20–29.

15. Susan Neiman writes: "Rather than viewing Kant as positing a necessary proportionality between happiness and virtue, we might see him more immediately as responding to a complaint about their disproportionality that is a least as old as the *Book of Job....* [B]oth indignation and despair presuppose a need of reason to find, or create, a necessary connection between happiness and virtue" in order to sustain "moral resolution over the course of a lifetime." Neiman, *The Unity of Reason*, p. 174–76.

16. *Postscript*, p. 179n.

17. Hannay speaks of the "repair" of antinomies in "Reading *Knights of Faith and Resignation.*"

18. See Kant's *Prolegomena to Any Future Metaphysics*, Carus trans., intro. Lewis White Beck, Bobbs-Merrill, 1950, p. 106.

19. Kant's essay "On the Failure of All Attempted Philosophical Theodicies" is discussed by Green, *Kierkegaard and Kant*, p. 23, and by Michael Despland, *Kant on History and Religion* (Montreal: McGill University Press, 1973), p. 285.

20. Kant speaks of a chasm between a (subjective) schema and objective fact which, when disregarded, leads one to the "death leap" (*salto mortale*) of literal-minded anthropomorphism in attempted descriptions of God. *Religion within the Bounds*, p. 59. Cf. the discussion of Ronald Green, *Kierkegaard and Kant*, p. 140–46. A *symbolical* anthropomorphism is permitted, provided we keep uppermost the uncertainty of our conjectures. In *Religion within the Bounds* Kant also speaks of an *archetype* of moral perfection found as a regulative ideal within reason, p. 54. And God occurs famously in the second *Critique* as a necessary postulate of practical reason. Perhaps Abraham is in defiance of Kantian reason in *each* of these guises. But if so, this should be shown. If something like an antinomy of reason is at work here, then the object of our striving both does and doesn't lie beyond intelligibility: or better, the structure of the antinomy is intelligible, but its "repair" is unintelligible—at least given the functions of non-practical, knowledge-aimed reason alone.

Susan Neiman writes that the real threat of the "antinomy of pure practical reason" is not the difficulty of theoretically understanding how the unity of virtue and happiness is possible, but the threat the antinomy presents to morale, to moral psychology. The threat of this antinomy is "disillusioned idealism, cynicism, despair and indifference." Faith is trust that our moral efforts are not in vain, will not be undermined by this threat. Neiman, *The Unity of Reason*, p. 176.

21. Hannay, "Reading *Knights of Faith and Resignation*."

22. The *Postscript* contrasts the stages as "enjoyment-perdition, action-victory, and suffering," Hongs trans., p. 294 (Swenson and Lowrie trans. p. 261).

23. Hannay, "Reading *Knights of Faith and Resignation*."

Chapter 6

1. Bernard Williams, *Ethics and the Limits of Philosophy* (Cambridge: Harvard University Press, 1985), p. 200.

2. See Cornel West and John Rachjman, eds., *Post-Analytical Philosophy* (New York: Columbia University Press, 1985), which includes, among others, essays by Nagel, Kuhn, Rorty, Putnam, and Cavell; and Giovanna Borradori, *The American Philosopher: Conversations with Quine, Davidson, Putnam, Nozick, Danto, Rorty, Cavell, MacIntyre, and Kuhn* (Chicago: University of Chicago Press, 1994). Note that Borradori classifies even Quine and Davidson as "postanalytic."

3. Bernard Williams discusses the moral psychology underlying Greek tragedy in *Shame and Necessity* (Berkeley: University of California Press, 1993). See Stanley Cavell, *Disowning Knowledge: In Six Plays of Shakespeare* (Cambridge: Cambridge University Press, 1987), and his book on Thoreau, *The Senses of Walden* (San Francisco: North Point Press, 1972). Charles Taylor provides a lengthy discussion of modern poetry and its relevance to moral psychology in *Sources of the Self* (Cambridge: Harvard University Press, 1989). Richard Rorty writes on Dickens (among others) and the breakdown of the philosophy-literature distinction in *Essays on Heidegger and Others* (Cambridge: Cambridge University Press, 1991). See also Martha C. Nussbaum, *The Fragility of Goodness, Luck and Ethics in Greek Tragedy and Philosophy* (Cambridge: Cambridge University Press, 1986) and *Love's Knowledge: Essays on Philosophy and Literature* (Oxford: Oxford University Press, 1990).

4. Stanley Cavell, "Kierkegaard on Authority and Revelation," in *Must We Mean What We Say* (Cambridge: Cambridge University Press, 1976), Chap. 6, and his extended contrast of Wittgenstein's *Philosophical Investigations* and Kierkegaard's *Concluding Unscientific Postscript* in "Existentialism and Analytical Philosophy," *Deadalus, The Journal of the American Academy of Arts and Sciences*, 93, 3 (pp. 46–74), 1964, reprinted in Cavell, *Themes Out of School* (San Francisco: North Point Press, 1984), Chap. 11. Note also his repeated citation of *Fear and Trembling*'s knight, who "finds the sublime in the ordinary," for example in the Borradori interview, *The American Philosopher*, p. 136.

5. Hilary Putnam, *Renewing Philosophy* (Cambridge: Harvard University Press, 1992).

6. For a representative sample, see Alastair Hannay, *Kierkegaard* (London: Routledge, 1982), the contributors to *The Cambridge Companion to Kierkegaard* ed. Alastair Hannay and Gordon Marino (Cambridge: Cambridge University Press, 1996). Robert C. Adams, *The Virtue of Faith* (Oxford: Oxford University Press, 1987), Chap. 2 and 3; C. Stephen Evans, *Kierkegaard's Fragments and Postscript* (Atlantic Highlands, NJ: Humanities Press, 1983), James Conant, "Kierkegaard, Wittgenstein, and Nonsense," *Pursuits of Reason, Essays for Stanley Cavell*, Cohen, Guyer, Putnam eds. (Lubbock: Texas Tech University Press, 1993), and M. Jamie Ferriera, "The Point Outside the World: Kierkegaard and Wittgenstein on Nonsense, Paradox, and Religion," *Religious Studies* 30, pp. 29–44, 1994.

7. Charles Altieri's *Subjective Agency* (Cambridge: Blackwell Publishers, 1994) has excel-

lent critical discussions of Taylor and Cavell, but, quite typically, no discussion of Kierkegaard.

8. The centrality of subjectivity becomes qualified, or revoked, when Climacus writes that subjectivity is not the last word—in fact, it becomes "untruth." *Postscript*, p. 185 (Hongs, 207). In addition, in a postscript to the *Postscript*, the book's "final declaration," Kierkegaard at least *says* that he revokes all that he has written hitherto. This revocation can be read in different ways. One point may be that neither Climacus nor Kierkegaard have a *doctrine* of subjectivity. See Ferreira, "The Point Outside the World," and Conant, "Kierkegaard, Wittgenstein, and Nonsense."

9. Harry Frankfurt, "Freedom of the Will and the Concept of a Person," *Journal of Philosophy*, Jan. 1971, and "The Importance of What We Care About," *Syntheses* 1982. Cf. Gary Watson's response to Frankfurt, "Free Agency," *Journal of Philosophy*, Apr. 1975, and Watson's useful anthology, *Free Will* (Oxford: Oxford University Press, 1982), which contains a number of articles cited here, including Charles Taylor, "Responsibility for Self," pp. 111–26.

10. "Ground project" is Williams's term. See "Persons, Character, and Morality," *Moral Luck* (Cambridge: Cambridge University Press, 1981). The central character in Camus's *The Stranger* is depicted as largely devoid of higher-order care—not caring which way his movements carry him, not comprehending the sorts of commitments that might override momentary whim or desire. He lacks any cares or desire or values that might supervene to unify, organize, or direct the transitory flow of impulse and impression. See my "Care, Guilt, and Responsibility: Notes on *The Stranger*," *Humanities*, May 1973.

11. *Concluding Unscientific Postscript*, trans. Swenson and Lowrie (Princeton: Princeton University Press, 1941) and *Concluding Unscientific Postscript*, Howard V. Hong and Edna H. Hong, trans. (Princeton: Princeton University Press, 1992). Those familiar with these basic *Postscript* themes and concepts will recognize that some are too pervasive for useful page citation. "Becoming Subjective," for example, is the title of an entire chapter, pp. 115–67 (Hongs trans. 129–88).

12. *Postscript*, pp. 67–74, (Hongs trans. pp. 72–80). For an interesting discussion of Hume's notion of "double reflexion," of a sentiment corrected or refined by a second-level reflection *on* that sentiment, see Annette C. Baier, "Hume, the Woman's Moral Theorist?" in *Women and Moral Theory*, Eva Feder Kittay and Diana T. Meyers, ed. (Totowa, NJ: Rowman & Littlefield, 1987), espec. p. 53, and Baier, *A Progress of Sentiments* (Cambridge: Harvard University Press, 1991).

13. See the discussion of "acting in asserting," Chap. 3, above.

14. *Postscript*, p. 181 (Hongs, 202).

15. *Postscript*, pp. 67–74 (Hongs, 72–80), and J. Kellenberger, "Indirect Communication," *The International Journal for the Philosophy of Religion*, Vol. 16, 1984, pp. 153–60. I give an expanded account in "Exemplars, Inwardness and Belief: Kierkegaard on Indirect Communication," in *International Kierkegaard Commentary: Concluding Unscientific Postscript*, ed. Robert L. Perkins (Macon, GA: Mercer University Press, 1996).

16. See the *Postscript* passage where Climacus writes that "God communicates so as to convey independence over against himself." *Postscript*, p. 232 (Hongs, 260).

17. See Ferreira's helpful discussion in "The Point Outside the World."

18. *Postscript*, pp. 169–224 (Hongs, 189–251). (For helpful treatments of Kierkegaardian subjectivity from a more or less analytical standpoint, see citations in notes 4, 5,

and 6, above.)

19. *Postscript*, p. 181 (Hongs, 202).

20. *Postscript*, p. 219 (Hongs, 245). For ways in which the range of proper objects of religious are limited, see my *Knights of Faith and Resignation: Reading Kierkegaard's Fear and Trembling* (Albany: State University of New York Press, 1991), p. 82f.

21. John Austin's work is presented in *How To Do Things With Words* (Oxford: Oxford University Press, 1962). My application of Austin to issues of self- and community creation is inspired by Herbert Fingarette's *Confucius, The Secular as Sacred* (New York: Harper and Row, 1972), and *Self-Deception* (London: Routledge and Kegan Paul, 1969). See also Robert Solomon, "Kierkegaard and 'Subjective Truth,'" in *Philosophy Today*, Fall 1977, pp. 202–15. Solomon shows how truth need not be restricted to faithful representations. He does not take the further step of showing how the model of performatives can suggest world- and self-production. Cavell pursues the connection between Austin, Derrida, and self-expression in *A Pitch of Philosophy: Autobiographical Exercises* (Cambridge: Harvard University Pres, 1994), Chap. 2.

22. *Postscript*, p. 178 (Hongs, 199).

23. *Postscript*, p. 182 (Hongs, 203).

24. *Moral Luck*, p. 81.

25. *Moral Luck*, p. 18.

26. Thomas Nagel, *Mortal Questions* (Cambridge: Cambridge University press, 1979), Chap. 2, "The Absurd," and *The View from Nowhere* (Oxford: Oxford University Press, 1986). See also Chap. 7, below.

27. Taylor, "Responsibility for Self."

28. Stephen Mulhall, "*The Sources of the Self*'s Sense of Itself," paper delivered at Claremont Graduate School of Theology, February 3, 1995, ms., p. 38, to appear in D. Z. Phillips, ed., *Can Religion Be Explained Away?* (London: Methuen, 1997).

Chapter 7

1. Thomas Nagel, *The View from Nowhere* (Oxford: Oxford University Press, 1986), p. 27.

2. *The View from Nowhere*, p. 3. Henceforth pages numbers lacking other citation will be to this book.

3. p. 27.

4. Williams, *Ethics and the Limits of Philosophy* (Cambridge: Harvard University Press, 1985), p. 200.

5. p. 112.

6. *Concluding Unscientific Postscript*, ed. and trans. Howard V. Hong and Edna H. Hong (Princeton: Princeton University Press, 1992), pp. 165–70; (Lowrie and Swenson, pp. 149–53).

7. p. 227.

8. In *Fear and Trembling*, Johannes de silentio writes, "It all rests on temporality," a concept later appropriated by Heidegger. *Fear and Trembling*, trans. Alastair Hannay (Harmondsworth: Penguin Books, 1985), p. 78.

9. pp. 7–8.

10. Even Nagel's earlier *The Possibility of Altruism* (Cambridge: Cambridge University press, 1970), required that objective reasons in ethics be always dominant.

11. Nagel doesn't claim that objectivity is *only* internally powered: but he doesn't dis-

cuss external factors, either.

12. p. 222.

13. *Ibid.*

14. See Chap. 2, above, for a discussion of Judge Wilhelm's "repentance back into the race."

15. Dostoyevsky, *The Brothers Karamazov*, trans. David Margarshack (Harmondsworth: Penguin Books, 1958), Vol. 1, Book Five.

16. Ivan's remark to Alyosha occurs just before his "Grand Inquisitor" poem. Dostoyevsky, *The Brothers Karamazov*, p. 275. How can Ivan *judge* others, blame them, find them wicked, from a position of "objective detachment"? Why doesn't his detachment undermine his moral conviction that the world is evil? One possibility is that Ivan deceives himself. He is attached, but not necessarily to the good. He might embody a cynical pose falsely parading as concern for human suffering. If the root of his disenchantment and apparent indignation is a deep contempt for humankind, even a sadistic hatred of others, then his nihilism is not based on a detached indifference, and not simply the outcome of the modern, enlightenment drive toward objectivity. It is based on an attachment to evil that is rationalized as a compassion disappointed by the world. Do we have here an instance of Kierkegaard's "Demonic," described in *Fear and Trembling* and in *Sickness Unto Death*?

17. Larry Blum writes as follows: "…particularity as a dimension of *morality* and of a moral consciousness…is neither impersonal nor personal [in Nagel's terms], neither subjective nor objective. It is a dimension of moral life that is "theorized away" by an exhaustive division of reasons for action into these two types." *Moral Perception and Particularity* (Cambridge: Cambridge University Press, 1994), Chap. 2 "Iris Murdoch and the domain of the moral," p. 16. (In an earlier version of this essay, he had written, against Nagel's view, that "Personal conduct is not simply a struggle between an impersonal rightness and a personal good, between impersonal principles and personal desires." *Philosophical Studies*, Vol. 50, No. 3 (1896), p. 359.)

18. pp. 186–87.

19. Immanuel Kant, *The Critique of Judgment*, trans. James Creed Meredith (Oxford: Clarendon Press, 1928), p. 157. Kant continues, "[W]e have reason for presuming the presence of at least the germ of a good moral disposition in the case of a man to whom the beauty of nature is a matter of immediate interest." *Ibid.*, p. 160. (I owe these references to Richard Eldridge's paper, "Is Animism Alive and Well?", to appear in *Can Religion Be Explained Away?* ed. D. Z. Phillips [London: Methuen].)

20. *Critique of Judgement*, sect. 59, p. 354; quoted in Bernstein, *The Fate of Art*, p. 29.

21. Sylvia Walsh, *Living Poetically: Kierkegaard's Existential Aesthetics* (University Park: Penn State University Press, 1994).

22. Larry Blum, "Iris Murdoch and the domain of the moral," *Philosophical Studies*, Vol. 50, No. 3 (1986) [?], p. 359. See Iris Murdoch, *The Sovereignty of Good* (New York: Schocken, 1971) for a discussion of the connection between aesthetic and moral attention.

23. Martha C. Nussbaum, "Finally Aware and Richly Responsible: Literature and the Moral Imagination," *Love's Knowledge* (Oxford: Oxford University Press, 1990), Chap. 5. Exploration of the excellence of such finely honed moral attention to particular persons has been, until quite recently, absent in ethical discussion. This pattern became set and reinforced by the allegiance of Plato, Kant, and Mill to something

like the objective/subjective polarity, interpreted in a way detrimental to attention to particular selves. Detachment from special concern for those close to you can lead to the sort of "impartial survey of the scene" characteristic of utilitarianism, or to the sort of impartial identification with reason characteristic of Kantians. But a concerned and focused attention on a singular other, in her particularity and for her own sake, also presupposes a sort of detached "disinterested interest." For an extended argument that an absolute contrast between esthetic and practical or cognitive attention is distorting and self-alienating, see J. M. Bernstein, *The Fate of Art: Aesthetic Alienation in Kant, Heidegger, and Adorno* (University Park: Penn State University Press, 1993).

24. Alastair Hannay, "Nietzsche and Naturalism," unpublished ms., 1994, p. 2. The phrase "yes and no of the palate" is from Habermas's critique of Nietzsche in *The Philosophical Discourse of Modernity*, trans. F. Lawrence (Oxford: Polity Press, 1987), p. 96f.

25. Ronald de Sousa distinguishes at least five distinct meanings of subjectivity, which he labels phenomenology, projection, relativity, perspective, and agency. See Ronald de Sousa, *The Rationality of Emotion* (Cambridge: MIT Press, 1987), pp. 145–48, and note 2, p. 312.

26. I thank Alastair Hannay for reminding me of this latter Kierkegaardian point.

27. p. 39

28. p. 88. Consider also: "When we ask ourselves how to live, the complexity of what we are makes a unified answer difficult. I believe the human duality of perspectives is too deep for us reasonably to hope to overcome it." (p. 185)

29. See Martha C. Nussbaum, *The Fragility of Goodness* (Cambridge: Cambridge University Press, 1986).

30. *Postscript*, p. 308, Hongs trans. (*Postscript*, p. 273, Swenson and Lowrie trans.)

31. *Postscript*, p. 199, Hongs trans. (*Postscript*, p. 178, Swenson and Lowrie trans.)

Chapter 8

1. Stephen Crites, "The Self in Sickness Unto Death: a Social Interpretation," in *Foundations of Kierkegaard's Vision of Community*, eds. George B. Connell and C. Stephen Evans (Atlantic Highlands, NJ: Humanities press, 1991).

2. George Eliot, *The Mill on the Floss* (New York: Bantam Books, 1987), p. 374. Cf. Rilke: *Ich bin die Ruhe zwischen szeien Tonen, / die sich nur schlecht aneinander gewohnen: / denn der Ton Tod will sich erhöhn—/ Aber im dunklen Intervall versöhnen / sich beide zitternd. / Und das Lied bleibt schön.* [I am the rest between two notes, / which are somehow always in discord / because Death's note wants to climb over—but in the dark interval, reconciled, / they stay there trembling. / And the song goes on, beautiful.], from *Das Stundenbuch, Selected Poems of Rainer Maria Rilke*, trans. Robert Bly (New York: Harper, 1981), p. 30f.

3. Recent literature linking philosophy and music includes Eva T. H. Brann's "The Music of the Republic," in *Four Essays on Plato's Republic*, St. John's Review, Vol. XXXIX, 1984; "Nietzsche's Musical Politics," Michael Allen Gillespie, in *Nietzsche's New Seas*, eds. Michael Allen Gillespie and Tracy B. Strong (Chicago: University of Chicago Press, 1988); Kathleen Marie Higgins, *Nietzsche's Zarathustra* (Philadelphia: Temple University Press, 1987), 1991; Stephen Crites, "The Narrative Quality of Experience," in *Why Narrative?, Readings in Narrative Theology*, eds. Hauerwas and Jones

(Grand Rapids, MI: Wm. Eerdmans Publishing, 1989), Michael Tanner, "Metaphysics and Music," in *The Impulse to Philosophize*, ed. A. Phillips Griffiths (Cambridge: Cambridge University Press, 1992); Joan Stambaugh, *The Other Nietzsche* (Albany: State University of New York Press, 1994); and Stanley Cavell, *A Pitch of Philosophy: Autobiographical Essays* (Cambridge: Harvard University Press, 1994). Ronald L. Hall considers music, and more narrowly, Kierkegaard's discussion of Don Giovanni, as a paradigm of the esthetic sphere. My sights are on musical performance as providing a more general model in terms of which selfhood—not just esthetic "proto-selfhood," can be understood. See Hall, *Word and Spirit: A Kierkegaardian Critique of the Modern Age* (Bloomington: Indiana University Press, 1993).

4. Søren Kierkegaard, *Either/Or*, ed., trans., and intro., Alastair Hannay (Harmondsworth: Penguin Books, 1992), pp. 58–135.

5. Kierkegaard, *Fear and Trembling*, trans. and Intro. Alastair Hannay (New York: Penguin Books, 1985).

6. See my *Knights of Faith and Resignation: Reading Kierkegaard's Fear and Trembling* (Albany: State University of New York Press, 1991), Chap. 2 and index references to "music," "song," "refrain," and "lyric."

7. This is Hannay's daring and apt departure on the standard renderings. Lowrie translates the Danish *stemning* as "Prelude." *Fear and Trembling*, trans. Walter Lowrie (Princeton: Princeton University Press, 1968); the Hongs translate it "Exordium." *Fear and Trembling*, trans. Howard V. and Edna H. Hong (Princeton: Princeton University Press, 1983).

8. For *stemning*, my Danish dictionary gives "mood; atmosphere; feeling; tuning." The German *Stimmung* is translated as "attunement" in the following passage from Kant's *Critique of Judgement*: "...nature must give the rule to art in the subject (and through the attunement [*Stimmung*] of the subject's capacities...." (B 181, 2 A 179), quoted in Andrew Bowie, *Aesthetics and Subjectivity from Kant to Nietzsche* (Manchester: Manchester University Press, 1990). The musical resonances of "attunement" might throw light on Kant's view of art, imagination, the interplay between perception and objective rules and the role of esthetic genius. *Stimmung*, attunement, later becomes a central term of art in Heidegger's *Being and Time*, where delineating one's attunement to the world becomes a paramount concern.

9. "Preamble from the Heart" is Hannay's improvement on the standard "Preliminary Expectoration," found in both the Lowrie and the Hongs' translations.

10. See *Knights of Faith and Resignation*, Chap. 2. Nietzsche imagines a music-playing Socrates in *The Birth of Tragedy from the Spirit of Music*.

11. *The Sickness Unto Death*, trans. with introduction by Alastair Hannay (New York: Penguin Books, 1989), p. 43.

12. Stephen Crites, "Sickness Unto Death: A Social Interpretation," in *Foundations of Kierkegaard's Vision of Community*. In this essay Crites also provides an illuminating discussion of Kierkegaard's choice of Anti-Climacus as author of *Sickness Unto Death*.

13. Alastair MacIntyre, *After Virtue* (Notre Dame: University of Notre Dame press, 1984).

14. *Sickness Unto Death*, p. 43.

15. *Ibid*.

16. In conversation, Alastair Hannay suggested considering specific instrumentation.

I have no idea if he'd approve of these particular choices.

17. See Harry Frankfurt on first- and second-order cares: *The Importance of What We Care About* (Cambridge: Cambridge University Press, 1988), and Chap. 6, above. As early as *Either/Or*, Kierkegaard has Judge Wilhelm aver that a self "modulates, proportions, evaluates" the various "factors" or "needs" to which the esthetic "proto-self" is subject. In this way, an emerging self expresses in judgment or action, a balance or unity *among* competing self-factors. *Either/Or*, Vol. II, trans. Walter Lowrie and D. F. Swenson (Princeton: Princeton University Press, 1971), pp. 266 f.

18. See *Sickness Unto Death*, p. 43, for the contrast between "positive" and "negative" unity.

19. Anti-Climacus also mentions the pair soul and body. For commentary on Kierkegaard's sketch of the "factors" of selfhood and their relation to despair, see *International Kierkegaard Commentary: Sickness Unto Death*, Robert L. Perkins, ed. (Macon, GA: Mercer University Press, 1987). The terminology for the *relata* is Aristotelian, but also Hegelian, even Kantian. See Ronald M. Green: *Kierkegaard and Kant: The Hidden Debt* (Albany: State University of New York Press, 1992).

20. *Sickness Unto Death*, p. 43. I have interpolated two phrases here, for clarity's sake.

21. *Ibid.*, p. 44.

22. *Ibid.*, p. 70; also, *Fear and Trembling*, p. 75.

23. See Mark Lloyd Taylor, "Ordeal and Repetition in Kierkegaard's Treatment of Abraham and Job," in *Foundations of Kierkegaard's Vision of Community*.

24. See Alastair Hannay, "Spirit and the Idea of the Self as a Reflexive Relation," *International Kierkegaard Commentary: Sickness Unto Death*. Philip Clayton reminds me that Bergson discusses the respect in which musical perception involves a "factor" of eternity and a contrasting "factor" of temporality. See *Matter and Memory*, trans. Nancy Margaret (New York: Zone Books, 1988).

25. See George B. Connell, "The Theonomous Ethics of Judge Wilhelm," *Foundations of Kierkegaard's Vision of Community*.

26. I have in mind Stolzman's RCA Victor recording of Mozart's *Clarinet Concerto* K. 622, second movement, performed with the English Chamber Orchestra.

27. In *Fear and Trembling* at least, God underwrites not just the religious sphere, but the sphere of ethics, as well. Thus the challenge to "the universal" sets up not just a conflict between normal ethics and God, but between two apparently contrary demands of God. Abraham's crisis is played out *within* the ethico-religious sphere. See Chap. 5, above.

28. I have in mind especially Kremer's CBS Records recording of the Mozart *Divertimento*, K. 563, with Kim Kashkashian and Yo-Yo Ma. Price's RCA Victor's "Verdi Heroines" is an accessible collection.

29. Marx defines the self as "the ensemble of social relationships" in *Theses on Feuerbach*, Thesis VI, *The Portable Marx*, ed. Eugene Kamenka (New York: Viking Penguin, 1983).

30. Habermas, for example, while realizing the force of Kierkegaard's critique of the loss of individuality within state institutions, fails to see the extent to which individual development, for Kierkegaard, requires a relationship to social others. See Jürgen Habermas, *The New Conservatism: Cultural Criticism and the Historians' Debate*, ed. and trans. Shierry Weber Nicholsen (Cambridge MA: MIT Press, 1989), and Martin Matustik, *Post-National Identity in Habermas, Kierkegaard, and Havel* (New York: Guilford Press, 1993).

31. *After Virtue*, pp. 40–43. I challenge this view throughout *Knights of Faith and Resignation*, espec. Chaps. 1, 4, and 5.

32. For an excellent discussion of the subtle differences between the dozen or so "stages on life's way," see Richard Schacht, "Kierkegaard's Phenomenology of Existence," in *Hegel and After* (Pittsburgh: Pittsburgh University Press, 1975).

33. *Concluding Unscientific Postscript*, trans. David F. Swenson and Walter Lowrie (Princeton: Princeton University Press, 1941).

34. Alastair McKinnon shows by computer-generated analysis that no Danish equivalent of the phrase "leap of faith" appears *even once* in the Kierkegaardian corpus. We have the *Postscript* allusions to Lessing's ditch (over which one must leap), the image of the faithful dancer's leap (in *Fear and Trembling*), and the same book's notion of death being "a remarkable leap." Nevertheless, getting faith, or being in faith, can't be merely a matter of a leap—or arbitrary choice.

35. See *Knights of Faith and Resignation*, especially Chaps. 4 and 5.

36. For an extended attempt to domesticate the tangles around "a teleological suspension of ethics," see Chaps. 3 and 4 above, *Knights of Faith and Resignation*, Chaps. 5, 6, and 8, and Merold Westphal, "The Teleological Suspension of Religiousness B," *Foundations of Kierkegaard's Vision of Community*.

37. Daniel Dennett, "Why We are All Novelists," *Times Literary Supplement* (September 16, 1988).

38. See *Either/Or*, Vol. II (Princeton: Princeton University Press, 1971), p. 137. An "activity-passivity" reciprocity is present within each life-sphere—its meaning changing relative to a sphere. So, for example, in *Fear and Trembling* there is a reciprocity in faith between "giving (Isaac) up and getting (Isaac) back."

39. The *Postscript* characterizes "the ethical" in more strenuous, less placid terms. Ethics does not grant peace or absence of conflict because we are constantly striving for a goal beyond our grasp.

40. In the *Postscript*, Kierkegaard calls religious existence a "second immediacy." Although the first immediacy of the esthetic is distinct from the second immediacy of the religious, the distinction does not rest on a difference in descriptive terms. For example, there is a place in the religious sphere for joy and sorrow— though these terms take on a different color and import for the soul when modulated downward to the esthetic. As a consequence, the project of this study, using musical models to illuminate the religious sphere, can't be blocked at the start because music is an esthetic phenomenon. The religious soul will hear the musical with different ears. For an account of the persistence of esthetic themes in the religious life, see Sylvia Walsh, *Living Poetically: Kierkegaard's Existential Aesthetics* (University Park: Penn State University Press, 1994).

41. Kierkegaard (or Johannes de silentio) claims this directly. Additionally, the return of Isaac is the return of the Universal. The religious and ethical Abraham never ceases loving Isaac, never ceases to be confident in his return, and is unhalting in welcome of Isaac's return. Abraham's embrace of the ethical is (paradoxically) sustained throughout his ordeal.

42. The best discussion of Kierkegaardian stage-shifts as Hegelian *Aufhebung* is found in Merold Westphal's "The Teleological Suspension of Religiousness B," in *Foundations of Kierkegaard's Vision of Community*.

43. Recordings of these late quartets, Op. 129–132, are numerous.

44. Some scholars pass off these words as jest, glimpsing only an aspect of the occasion of their writing: apparently Beethoven's cleaning lady was hounding him for payment as he wrote *"Muss en sein?"*

Bibliography

SELECTED WORKS BY KIERKEGAARD

Concluding Unscientific Postscript, trans. David F. Swenson and Walter Lowrie (Princeton: Princeton University Press, 1941).

Concluding Unscientific Postscript, trans. Howard V. Hong and Edna H. Hong (Princeton: Princeton University Press, 1992).

Eighteen Upbuilding Discourses, trans. and ed. Howard V. Hong and Edna H. Hong (Princeton: Princeton University Press, 1990).

Either/Or, Vol. II, trans. Howard V. Hong and Edna H. Hong (Princeton: Princeton University Press, 1987).

Either/Or: A Fragment of Life, abridg., ed., and trans. Alastair Hannay (Harmondsworth: Penguin Books, 1992).

Fear and Trembling and Repetition, ed. and trans. Howard V. Hong and Edna H. Hong (Princeton: Princeton University Press, 1993).

Fear and Trembling, ed. and trans. Alastair Hannay (Harmondsworth: Penguin Books, 1985).

Sickness Unto Death, trans. Alastair Hannay (Harmondsworth: Penguin Books, 1989).

The Concept of Irony, with Constant Reference to Socrates, trans. Lee M. Capel (London: Collins, 1966).

OTHER WORKS CITED

Adams, Robert C. *The Virtue of Faith* (Oxford: Oxford University Press, 1987).

Altieri, Charles. *Subjective Agency* (Cambridge: Cambridge University Press, 1994).

Austin, John. *How To Do Things With Words* (Oxford: Oxford University Press, 1962).

Baier, Annette C. "Hume, the Woman's Moral Theorist?", *Women and Moral Theory*, eds. Eva Feder Kittay and Diana T. Meyers (Totowa, NJ: Rowman-Littlefield, 1987).

———. *A Progress of Sentiments* (Cambridge: Harvard University Press, 1991).

Bakhtin, Mikhael. *Problems of Dostoyevsky's Poetics*, ed. and trans. Caryl Emerson (Minneapolis: University of Minnesota Press, 1984).

Bergson, Henri. *Matter and Memory*, trans. Nancy Margaret (New York: Zone Books, 1988).

Bernstein, J. M. *The Fate of Art: Aesthetic Alienation from Kant to Derrida and Adorno* (University Park: Penn State Press, 1992).

Blum, Lawrence. "Iris Murdoch and the domain of the moral" *Philosophical Studies*, Vol. 50, No. 3, 1986.

———. *Moral Perception and Particularity* (Cambridge: Cambridge University Press, 1994).

Borradori, Giovanna. *The American Philosopher: Conversations with Quine, Davidson, Putnam, Nozick, Danto, Rorty, Cavell, MacIntyre, and Kuhn* (Chicago: University of Chicago Press, 1994).

Bowie, Andrew. *Aesthetics and Subjectivity from Kant to Nietzsche* (Manchester: Manchester University Press, 1990).

Brann, Eva T. H. "The Music of the Republic," *Four Essays on Plato's Republic*, St. John's Review, Vol. XXXIX, 1984.

Bugbee, Henry. *The Inward Morning* (New York: Harper Torch, 1976).

Caputo, John D. "Kierkegaard, Heidegger, and the Foundering of Metaphysics," *International Kierkegaard Commentary, Fear and Trembling and Repetition*, ed. Robert L. Perkins (Macon, GA: Mercer University Press, 1994).

Cavell, Stanley. *The Senses of Walden* (San Francisco: North Point Press, 1981).

_____. "Kierkegaard's 'On Authority and Revelation,'" in *Must We Mean What We Say* (Cambridge: Cambridge University Press, 1976).

_____. "Existentialist and Analytical Philosophy," in *Themes Out of School* (San Francisco: North Point Press, 1984).

_____. *Disowning Knowledge: In Six Plays of Shakespeare* (Cambridge: Cambridge University Press, 1987).

_____. *A Pitch of Philosophy: Autobiographical Exercises* (Cambridge, MA: Harvard University Press, 1994).

Cohen, Guyer, and Putnam, eds. *Pursuits of Reason: Essays in Honor of Stanley Cavell* (Lubbock, Texas: Texas Tech University Press, 1993).

Collins James. *The Emergence of Philosophy of Religion* (New Haven: Yale University Press, 1967).

Connell, George. "Judge William's Theonomous Ethics," *Foundations of Kierkegaard's Vision of Community*, eds. George B. Connell and C. Stephen Evans (Atlantic Highlands, NJ: Humanities Press, 1991).

_____ and Evans, C. Stephen. *The Foundations of Kierkegaard's Vision of Community* (Atlantic Highlands, NJ: Humanities Press, 1991).

Creegan, Charles. *Wittgenstein and Kierkegaard* (London: Routledge, 1989).

Crites, Steven. "The Self in *Sickness Unto Death*: a Social Interpretation," in *Foundations of Kierkegaard's Vision of Community*, eds. George B. Connell and C. Stephen Evans (Atlantic Highlands, NJ: Humanities Press, 1991).

_____ . "The Narrative Quality of Experience," in *Why Narrative?, Readings in Narrative Theology*, eds. Hauerwas and Jones (Grand Rapids, MI: Eerdmans Publishers, 1989).

Cross, Andrew (1991). "Two Dilemmas in *Fear and Trembling*," paper delivered to the Kierkegaard Society, Portland, OR, 1991.

Dan-Cohen, Meir (1992). "Conceptions of Choice and Conceptions of Autonomy," *Ethics*, January, 1992.

de Sousa, Ronald. *The Rationality of Emotion* (Cambridge, MA: MIT Press, 1987).

Deleuze, Gilles. *Kant's Critical Philosophy*, trans. Hugh Tomlinson and Barbara Habberjam (Minneapolis: University of Minnesota Press, 1993).

Dennett, Daniel. "Why We Are All Novelists," *Times Literary Supplement*, September 1, 1988.

Despland, Michael. *Kant on History and Religion* (Montreal: McGill University Press, 1993).

Dostoyevsky, Fyodor. *The Brothers Karamazov*, trans. David Magarshack (Harmondsworth: Penguin Books, 1958).

Dreyfus, Hubert and Rubin, Jane. "How Not to Get Something for Nothing: Kierkegaard and Heidegger on Nihilism," *Inquiry* (30), 1987.

Dreyfus, Hubert L. "Heidegger on the connection between Nihilism, Art,

Technology, and Politics," *The Cambridge Companion to Heidegger,* ed. Charles Guignon (Cambridge: Cambridge University Press, 1993).

Eldridge, Richard. "Is Animism Alive and Well?" paper delivered at Claremont Graduate School, 1995, to appear in *Can Religion Be Explained Away?* ed. D. Z. Phillips (London: Methuen).

Eliot, George. *The Mill on the Floss* (New York: Bantam Books, 1987).

Evans, Stephen C. *Kierkegaard's Fragments and Postscript: The Religious Philosophy of Johannes Climacus.* (Atlantic Highlands, NJ: Humanities Press, 1983).

Ferreira, M. Jamie. "Repetition, Concreteness, and Imagination," *International Journal for Philosophy of Religion,* vol. 25, 1989.

_____. *Transforming Vision: Imagination and Will in Kierkegaardian Faith* (Oxford: Oxford University Press, 1991).

_____. "Seeing (Just) is Believing," *Faith and Philosophy,* April, 1992.

_____. "The Point Outside the World: Kierkegaard and Wittgenstein on Nonsense, Paradox, and Religion," *Religious Studies* 30, 1994.

Fingarette, Herbert. *Self-Deception* (New York: Humanities Press, 1969).

_____. *Confucius, the Secular as Sacred* (New York: Harper Torch, 1972).

_____. "The Meaning of the Law in *The Book of Job*," *Revisions,* ed. Stanley Hauerwas and Alastair MacIntyre (Notre Dame; University of Notre Dame Press, 1981).

Flanagan, Owen. *The Varieties of Moral Personality* (Cambridge: Harvard University Press, 1991).

Frankfurt, Harry. "Freedom of the Will and the Concept of a Person," *Journal of Philosophy,* January 1971.

_____. *The Importance of What We Care About* (Cambridge: Cambridge University Press, 1988).

Friedman, R. Z. "Kierkegaard: Last Kantian or First Existentialist?" *Religious Studies,* no. 18 (Spring), 1982.

Gillespie, Michael Allan, and Strong, Tracy B., eds. *Nietzsche's New Seas: Explorations in Philosophy, Aesthetics, and Politics* (Chicago: University of Chicago Press, 1988).

_____. "Nietzsche's Musical Politics," in *Nietzsche's New Seas,* ed. Michael Allen Gillespie and Tracy B. Strong (Chicago: University of Chicago Press, 1988).

Glatzner, Nahum N. *The Dimensions of Job* (New York: Schocken Books, 1969).

Gould, Thomas. *The Ancient Quarrel between Poetry and Philosophy* (Princeton: Princeton University Press, 1990).

Green, Ronald M. *Kierkegaard and Kant: The Hidden Debt* (Albany: State University of New York Press, 1992).

Guignon, Charles B., ed., *The Cambridge Companion to Heidegger* (Cambridge: Cambridge University Press, 1993).

Haar, Michael. *The Song of the Earth: Heidegger and the Grounds of History of Being,* trans. Reginald Lily (Bloomington: Indiana University Press, 1993).

Habermas, Jürgen. *The New Conservatism: Cultural Criticism and the Historians' Debate,* ed. and trans. Shierry Weber Nicholsen (Cambridge: MIT Press, 1989).

Hall, Ronald L.. *Word and Spirit: A Kierkegaardian Critique of the Modern Age* (Bloomington: Indiana University Press, 1993).

Hannay, Alastair. *Kierkegaard* (London: Routledge, 1982).

_____, and Gordon Marino. *The Cambridge Companion to Kierkegaard* (Cambridge: Cambridge University Press, 1996).

_____. "Refuge and Religion," *Faith, Knowledge, and Action: Essays to Niles Thulstrup*, ed. George Stengren (Copenhagen: Reitzels Forlag, 1984).

_____. "Spirit and the Idea of the Self as a Reflexive Relation," *International Kierkegaard Commentary: Sickness Unto Death*, ed. Robert L. Perkins (Macon, GA: Mercer University Press, 1987).

Harrison, Bernard. *Inconvenient Fictions, Literature and the Limits of Theory* (New Haven: Yale University Press, 1991).

Hebell, Claus. *Rechtstheoretische und Geistegeschichtliche Voraussetzungen für Das Werk Franz Kafkas Analysiert an Seinem Roman "Der Prozess"* (New York: Peter Lang, 1993).

Herman, Barbara. *The Practice of Moral Judgment* (Berkeley: University of California Press, 1993).

Higgins, Kathleen Marie. *Nietzsche's Zarathustra* (Philadelphia: Temple University Press, 1987).

_____. *The Music of our Lives* (Philadelphia: Temple University Press, 1991).

Huntington, Patricia J. "Heidegger's Reading of Kierkegaard Revisited" in Martin J. Matustik and Merold Westphal, eds., *Kierkegaard in Post-Modernity* (Bloomington: Indiana University Press, 1995).

Janik, Allan and Toulmin, Stephen. *Wittgenstein's Vienna* (New York: Simon & Schuster, 1973).

Kafka, Franz. *Parables and Paradoxes*, trans. Clement Greenberger (New York: Schocken Books, 1958).

Kant, Immanuel. *Critique of Pure Reason*, trans. Norman Kemp Smith (London: Macmillan, 1950).

_____. *Prolegomena to Any Future Metaphysics*, Carus trans., intro. Lewis White Beck (New York: Bobbs Merrill, 1950).

_____. *Critique of Judgment*, trans. J. H. Bernard (New York: Macmillan, 1951).

_____. *Religion Within the Limits of Reason Alone*, trans. Theodore M. Greene and Hoyt H. Hudson (New York: Harper and Row, 1960).

_____. "On the Failure of All Attempted Philosophical Theodicies," in Michel Despland, *Kant on History and Religion* (Montreal: McGill University Press, 1973).

_____. *Conflict of the Faculties*, trans. Mary J. Gregor (New York, Abaris Books, 1979).

Kellenberger, John. "Indirect Communication," *The International Journal for the Philosophy of Religion* (16), 1984.

Kremer, Gidon. CBS Records recording of the Mozart *Divertimento*, K. 563, with Kim Kashkashian and Yo-Yo Ma.

Louden, Robert. *Morality and Moral Theory* (Oxford: Oxford University Press, 1993).

MacIntyre, Alastair. *After Virtue* (Notre Dame: University of Notre Dame Press, 1984).

Marx, Karl. *Theses on Feuerbach*, Thesis VI, *The Portable Marx*, ed. Eugene Kamenka (New York: Viking Books, 1983).

Marino, Gordon, and Alastair Hannay, eds. *The Cambridge Companion to Kierkegaard* (Cambridge: Cambridge University Press, 1995).

Matustik, Martin J. "Habermas's reading of Kierkegaard," *Philosophy and Social Criticism* 17(4), pp. 313–23, 1991.

_____. *Post-National Identity in Habermas, Kierkegaard, and Havel* (New York: Guilford Press, 1993).

_____. and Merold Westphal, eds., *Kierkegaard in Post-Modernity* (Bloomington:

Indiana University Press, 1995).

Mooney, Edward F. "Care, Guilt, and Responsibility: Notes on *The Stranger*," *Humanities* (May), 1973.

_____. "Abraham and Dilemma: Kierkegaard's Teleological Suspension Revisited, *International Journal for Philosophy of Religion*, 1986.

_____. *Knights of Faith and Resignation: Reading Kierkegaard's Fear and Trembling* (Albany: State University of New York Press, 1991).

————. "Exemplars, Inwardness and Belief: Kierkegaard on Indirect Communication," in *International Kierkegaard Commentary: Concluding Unscientific Postscript*, ed. Robert L. Perkins (Macon, GA: Mercer University Press, 1996).

_____. "Repetition: Getting the World Back," in *The Cambridge Companion to Kierkegaard*, eds. Alastair Hannay and Gordon Marino (Cambridge: Cambridge University Press, 1996).

Mulhall, Stephen. "*Sources of the Self*'s Sense of Itself," paper delivered at the Claremont Graduate School, February 3, 1995, to appear in *Can Religion Be Explained Away?* ed. D. Z. Phillips (London: Methuen).

Murdoch, Iris. *The Sovereignty of Good* (New York: Schocken Books, 1971).

Nagel, Thomas. *The Possibility of Altruism* (Cambridge: Cambridge University Press, 1978).

_____. *Mortal Questions* (Cambridge: Cambridge University Press, 1979).

_____. *The View from Nowhere* (Oxford: Oxford University Press, 1986).

Neiman, Susan. *The Unity of Reason: Rereading Kant* (Oxford: Oxford University Press, 1994).

Nietzsche, Friedrich. *The Birth of Tragedy from the Spirit of Music*, trans. Francis Golffing (New York: Doubleday, 1956).

_____. *Thus Spoke Zarathustra, The Portable Nietzsche*, ed. and trans. Walter Kaufmann (New York: Viking Books, 1954).

Norris, Christopher. *The Deconstructive Turn* (London: Methuen, 1983).

Nussbaum, Martha C. *The Fragility of Goodness, Luck and Ethics in Greek Tragedy and Philosophy* (Cambridge: Cambridge University Press, 1986).

_____. *Love's Knowledge, Essays on Philosophy and Literature* (Oxford: Oxford University Press, 1990).

Olafson, Frederick A. "The Unity of Heidegger's Thought," *The Cambridge Companion to Heidegger*, ed. Charles Guignon (Cambridge: Cambridge University Press, 1993).

Pattison, George. *Kierkegaard: The Aesthetic and the Religious* (New York: St. Martin's Press, 1992).

Perkins, Robert L. "Giving the Parson His Due," in Robert L. Perkins, ed., *International Kierkegaard Commentary, Either/Or* (Macon, GA: Mercer University Press, 1995).

_____, ed. *International Kierkegaard Commentary, Sickness Unto Death* (Macon, GA: Mercer University Press, 1987).

_____, ed. *International Kierkegaard Commentary, Fear and Trembling and Repetition* (Macon, GA: Mercer University Press, 1994).

_____, ed. *International Kierkegaard Commentary: Concluding Unscientific Postscript* (Macon, GA: Mercer University Press, 1996).

Poole, Roger. *Kierkegaard, The Indirect Communication* (Charlottesberg, VA: University of Virginia Press, 1993).

Poole, Ross. "Living with Reason," *Inquiry*, June, 1991.

Price, Leontyne. "Verdi Heroines," RCA Victor recording.

Putnam, Hilary. *The Many Faces of Realism* (Lasalle, IL: Open Court, 1987).

_____. *Renewing Philosophy* (Cambridge: Harvard University Press, 1992).

Rajchman, John and Cornel West, eds. *Post-Analytic Philosophy* (New York: Columbia University Press, 1985).

Rée, Jonathan. "Narrative and Philosophical Experience," *On Paul Ricoeur*, ed. David Wood (London: Routledge, 1991).

Rilke, Rainer Maria. *Das Stundenbuch: Selected Poems of Rainer Maria Rilke*, trans. Robert Bly (New York: Harper Torch, 1981).

Rorty, Richard. *Contingency, Irony, and Solidarity* (Cambridge: Cambridge University Press, 1989).

_____. *Essays on Heidegger and Others* (Cambridge: Cambridge University Press, 1991).

Rosen, Stanley. *The Quarrel Between Philosophy and Poetry* (New York: Routledge, 1993).

Schacht, Richard. "Kierkegaard's Phenomenology of Existence," *Hegel and After* (Pittsburgh: University of Pittsburgh Press, 1975). ·

Solomon, Robert. *The Passions* (New York: Doubleday, 1976).

_____. "Kierkegaard and 'Subjective Truth,'" *Philosophy Today*, (Fall, 1977), pp. 202–15.

Stambaugh, Joan. *The Other Nietzsche* (Albany: State University of New York Press, 1993).

Stengren, George, ed. *Faith, Knowledge, and Action: Essays to Niles Thulstrup* (Copenhagen: Reitzels Forlag, 1984).

Stoltzman, Richard. RCA Victor recording, Mozart's *Clarinet Concerto*, K. 622, second movement, with the English Chamber Orchestra.

Tanner, Michael. "Metaphysics and Music," *The Impulse to Philosophize*, ed. A. Phillips Griffiths (Cambridge: Cambridge University Press, 1992).

Taylor, Charles. "Responsibility for Self," *The Identities of Persons*, ed. Amelie Oksenberg Rorty (Berkeley: University of California Press, 1976).

_____. *Sources of the Self* (Cambridge: Harvard University Press, 1985).

_____. "Heidegger, Language, and Ecology," in *Heidegger: A Critical Reader*, eds. Hubert L. Dreyfus and Harrison Hall (Cambridge: Cambridge University Press, 1992).

_____. "Interpretation and the Sciences of Man," *Philosophy and the Human Sciences: Philosophical Papers*, Vol. 2 (Cambridge: Cambridge University Press, 1985).

_____. "Explanation and Practical Reason," *The Quality of Life*, eds. Martha Nussbaum and Amartya Sen (Oxford: Oxford University Press, 1993).

_____. *The Ethics of Authenticity* (Cambridge: Harvard University Press, 1993).

Taylor, Mark Lloyd. "Ordeal and Repetition in Kierkegaard's Treatment of Abraham and Job," in *Foundations of Kierkegaard's Vision of Community*, George B. Connell and C. Steven Evans, eds. (Atlantic Highlands, NJ: Humanities Press, 1991).

Tilley, Terrence. *The Evils of Theodicy* (Washington, D.C.: Georgetown University Press, 1991).

von Frassen, Bas C. "The Peculiar Effects of Love and Desire," *Perspectives on Self-Deception*, eds. Brian P. McLaughlin and Amelie O. Rorty (Berkeley: University of California Press, 1988).

Walsh, Sylvia. *Living Poetically, Kierkegaard's Existential Aesthetics* (University Park, PA: Penn State University Press, 1994).

Weston, Michael. *Kierkegaard and Contemporary Continental Philosophy* (New York: Routledge, 1994).

Index